ERRORS and FOULS

Related Titles from Potomac Books

*Baseball's Most Wanted™: The Top 10 Book of the National Pastime's
Outrageous Offenders, Lucky Bounces, and Other Oddities*
—Floyd Conner

Pull Up a Chair: The Vin Scully Story
—Curt Smith

*A Tale of Three Cities: The 1962 Baseball Season in New York,
Los Angeles, and San Francisco*
—Steven Travers

ERRORS and FOULS

Inside Baseball's Ninety-Nine Most Popular Myths

PETER HANDRINOS

Potomac Books
Washington, D.C.

Library of Congress Cataloging-in-Publication Data
Handrinos, Peter.
    Errors and fouls : inside baseball's ninety-nine most popular myths / Peter Handrinos.
        pages cm
    Includes bibliographical references and index.
    ISBN 978-1-61234-560-4 (hardcover : alk. paper)
    ISBN 978-1-61234-561-1 (electronic)
1. Baseball—Miscellanea. I. Title.
    GV873.H264 2013
    796.357—dc23

                                                                      2012047590

Printed in the United States of America on acid-free paper that meets the American
National Standards Institute Z39-48 Standard.

Potomac Books
22841 Quicksilver Drive
Dulles, Virginia 20166

First Edition

10 9 8 7 6 5 4 3 2 1

When the legend becomes fact, print the legend.
—The Man Who Shot Liberty Valance

No thanks.
—Anon.

Contents

STATE OF PLAY

THE NUMBERS

CLUTCHED

IN THE MARKETS

TAKE YOUR TICKETS

MINOR CONSIDERATIONS

MAJOR SALARIES

AGENCY

PAYROLL

MONEY FOR NOTHING

THROUGH THE PARKS

IN BALANCE

PLAYING MONOPOLY

THE OFFICE

LABORING

AND IN CONCLUSION

EXTRAS

EXTRA EXTRAS

The Fans

MYTH #1

"Football Is the New National Pastime"

Baseball likes to think of itself—indeed bills itself—as the national pastime but that time is long gone, a distant memory.

—JIM DONALDSON, "Football, Not Baseball, Is the True National Pastime," *Providence Journal*, November 3, 2009

For at least 20 years football has had unquestioned supremacy among America's major spectator sports.

—ANDREW O'HEHIR, "Football's Death Spiral," Salon.com, February 3, 2013

One of the most mystifying myths in sports has football surpassing baseball as America's favorite pro team sport.

It's not hard to find claims about the "new" national pastime. *Sports Illustrated, ESPN The Magazine*, and the *Washington Post* have described how baseball has been displaced from the top spot. The *Atlanta Journal-Constitution* has mourned the game's slippage. The *Boston Herald* has bought into the hype. So has the *Texas Monthly*. As has the *Christian Science Monitor* along with the *San Diego Union-Tribune* and the *Denver Post*. Almost every publication this side of *Ladies' Home Journal* has jumped aboard the bandwagon.

Football's edge over baseball is apparently so obvious that it requires little in the way of supporting evidence. That's a curious omission but, as it turns out, a necessary one, because the more you contemplate the pro-football view, the more it fades away.

Sports fans vote by turnstile, and the National Football League's boosters certainly cannot point to unsurpassed attendance feats. In a typical year like 2011, NFL teams combine for an annual gate of about 16.6 million, while Major League Baseball clubs combine to welcome more than 73.5 million spectators; if popularity is to be measured in the time and energy devoted to live sporting events, baseball is more than four times more popular than football.

At this point NFL teams are routinely outdrawn by MLB teams within markets shared by both sports, and the contrast filters down to the Minor Leagues as well. Pro football attendance was less than half of overall Minors attendance in 2011, when the latter drew 48.1 million spectators, and no less than ten Minor League clubs outdrew NFL franchises from coast to coast, including those located in shared metro areas like Indianapolis and Buffalo.

Fans who vote with their feet have rendered landslide victories for baseball, but some commentators look away from the salient facts. Some say that baseball's popularity as a live draw can be explained away by relatively low prices and high levels of content.

The average MLB ticket is an estimated one-third the price of a typical NFL ticket and the former's regular season encompasses nearly ten times as many games, but affordable prices and vast seating inventories are virtues rather than vices, and only one sport is uniquely capable of translating them into colossal popularity. After all, it's conceivable that soccer, lacrosse, or the Hunger Games could draw tens of millions of annual spectators. Assuming a 162-game NFL season didn't lead to the incredibly violent death of every single athlete involved, pro football could elevate its attendance totals several times over. Such notions are ridiculous, of course, because only the authentic pastime has both the beloved status and accommodating structure needed to draw so many people to so many contests.

Football partisans tend to ignore the one-sided attendance metrics, instead asserting that that the gridiron is the greatest draw among in on-air sports. The NFL does typically post 10.0 national ratings that blow away the pastime's 2.6 average on Fox Sports, which would be impressive but for two qualifiers.

First, most baseball fans feel no urgent need to view national broadcasts that can feature clubs based hundreds of miles away. Rather, they usually take rooting interests in local teams, first and foremost. (The national pastime is a very *local* phenomenon in that way.) To measure the baseball's popularity in terms of national broadcasts is to measure it in largely irrelevant terms.

Second, focusing on individual, one-game-per-week ratings misreads the basis of the pastime's appeal. Even as they march on from March into October, ball clubs can attract an unmatched interest in the day to day, week to week, and month to month. Broadcasts for teams like the Red Sox, Mariners, and Cardinals have been viewed by more than 100,000 households per game for over 100 broadcasts per year.

All of these audiences count, too, and they can accumulate a viewership of hundreds of millions per year, a total far greater than that of the NFL. Baseball's edge explains why the new millennium has seen television revenue records not only for the Majors as a whole but also for pastime teams located in supposedly football-first markets like Dallas and smaller baseball towns like San Diego.

Now that everything's been cleared up . . .

What was that?

A greater than four-to-one attendance advantage isn't impressive enough?

A huge advantage in overall TV views isn't a big deal? All right, fine. In the interests of balance, it should be said that some popularity measures do favor the NFL.

The NFL's annual revenues can outpace MLB dollars by a billion dollars or more, for instance, mostly because the football owners act as a cartel in licensing tchotchkes like coffee mugs, towels, and miniature helmet-phones. This is important to those who love tchotchkes. The NFL also draws far more gambling money than baseball; this is relevant to those who care about big bets. The NFL also leads in video game sales; among dedicated gamers, this means that football has surpassed baseball and that, maybe, Sonic the Hedgehog has replaced the eagle as our national emblem.

The NFL is undoubtedly the most popular *sports business* in the United States, but there's a different perspective for those interested in more than money. Among the faithful, America's favorite sport is defined by unmatched holds on our country's crowds and communications, and they might invite those seeking a new national pastime to look for a new nation.

"The Super Bowl Is Bigger than the World Series"

The NFL has been head and shoulders above everyone else when it comes to popularity, especially when it comes to its grand stage, the Super Bowl.

**—JOE AIELLO, "MLB Is Primed to Make a Comeback,"
ESPN.com, March 6, 2011**

The Super Bowl is the greatest sporting event of them all.

**—MIKE CELIZIC, "How Did the Super Bowl Get to Be Like This?," MSNBC.com,
February 5, 2010**

Imagine you're a show producer.

Like any other showman, you must attract the largest possible audience, but in our hypothetical, you have a choice in how to go about the task: you can aim to attract a single blowout crowd or you can try for smaller-but-still-substantial numbers over several nights.

Most would probably see this as a six of one, half dozen of the other choice. Accumulating viewers over either one night or multiple nights is irrelevant to reaching the final totals. Keep that in mind whenever you hear comparisons between the ratings for the Super Bowl and the World Series.

The Super Bowl is your prototypical one-shot extravaganza. From 2004 to 2006, for example, its television ratings averaged about 41.4 points, numbers that topped all American programs for those years. Baseball's championship showcase, in contrast, had a smaller-but-still-substantial thing going. For example, the World Series games of the 2004 to 2006 period averaged a 12.3 rating, good enough to be among the highest-rated prime-time network programs in their time slots, and the several strong showings added up to overall viewership levels that outdid the Super Bowl. (An average of 103 million total viewers per annum to football's 88.9 million.)

It so happened that 2004 to 2006 saw the smallest number of World Series games of any three-year period in history, and in addition, only three of the six participating teams (Chicago, Houston, and Boston) were based in top ten markets.

If not for those pieces of bad luck, the contests may have garnered the viewers to surpass the Super Bowl's totals in an even more convincing fashion.

If there has been a relatively narrow but noticeable gap between the Series and the Super Bowl in terms of overall popularity, there has been a greater gap in the intrinsic appeal of the two events. This is because the Super Bowl's draw has little to do with its actual sport and much to do with an array of highly artificial, if effective, marketing gimmicks.

The Super Bowl is scheduled for the dead of winter, when baseball is still in hibernation, the television season is in reruns, and Hollywood is burning off the B-list movies that weren't good enough for a Christmas season release. The game is played on a predetermined date and on a weekend night, so a great many prospective viewers can find ways to set aside leisure time. It's the final payday of the season so there's every incentive for losing gamblers to place bets big enough to square up with their bookies. Finally, the Super Bowl is set up by two weeks featuring little more than extended promotional shows. Within the telecast itself there are bombastic halftime shows plus dozens of corporately mandated commercials for sugar water, junk food, beer, sneakers, this or that dot-com, pickup trucks, and whatever company convinced Danica Patrick to transition from race car driver to bikini model.

I oppose neither beer nor bikini models, but a question does come to mind: how many Super Bowl viewers actually focus on King Hut to the exclusion of the filler, point spreads, puff pieces, variety shows, and adverts? Only God and, possibly, A. C. Nielsen know for certain, but the pileup tends to indicate that actual football doesn't matter nearly as much as the filler.

In contrast, the World Series is popular largely because baseball is popular.

World Series contests, arriving in October, must compete against the best new shows and films of the autumn season. There are no predetermined dates for the broadcasts, so several games may air during weekday nights, and their opening games are set off from preceding playoff competitions by, at most, a couple of days. Most gamblers don't look at the event as a big payday (bookmakers generally don't take an interest in the pastime). The event's pregame shows are also measured in hours rather than days and the telecasts don't routinely veer off into kitsch extravaganzas.

The World Series doesn't peddle fluff. It sells a straight-up sport, and that's still more than enough for it to surpass the Super Bowl.

MYTH #3

"The All-Star Game Ratings Are Signs of Serious Trouble"

Years ago, Americans breathed baseball. Teachers turned on televisions during the All Star Game and World Series. Plays were rehashed at water coolers, coffee shops—practically everywhere. The way football is now.

—TIM WOODWARD, "Vern Law's 'Golden Days of Baseball,'" *Idaho Statesman*, January 16, 2011

In summertime the living isn't always easy. Picnics can attract their share of ants, firework displays might include a few duds, and lemonades sometimes capture stray bugs.

Sadly, the game of baseball is hardly immune from the negativity. Every July media pundits fret that the All-Star Game is declining in popularity and they do have a point, insofar as its raw Nielsen television ratings have gone from 1990's 16.2 points down to 2010's 7.5.

For all the gloom in the TV ratings, however, the event's real forecast is sunnier. According to its most important measures, the All-Star Game is doing just fine.

To see how that's so, it's important to remember that ratings for the mid-summer classic have always been driven by supply and demand, more specifically by the supply of TV broadcasts available to match fan demand for the sport's best, most popular stars.

Up until relatively recently, the game's track record on that front was pretty dismal. In the mid-1950s, no teams were based outside a relatively small region composed mostly of New England and the upper Midwest (it was a quadrangle representing less than one-seventh the landmass of the continental United States). Television broadcast ranges were limited and even those fans within the TV ranges could rarely take in more than a few dozen telecasts per year. (Dodgers fans, for example, could only avail themselves of 26 annual broadcasts.) Even as the broadcast media expanded its reach during the 1960s, game accounts usually reached at-home fans through abbreviated newspaper accounts, crackling radio stations, and a few minutes at the end of the local news.

And bad as the media outreach may have been, the outlook was even worse for fans interested in viewing teams outside their local markets. For them, the main option was the one-size-fits-all *Game of the Week* (a.k.a. *The Yankees vs. Everybody Else Show*).

Old-time fans always had the choice to forgo airwaves in favor of the grandstands, of course, but they still had few options in that direction. With an immutable separation between American Leaguers and National Leaguers, fans living outside two-team markets like New York or Chicago rarely saw half of the game's star players. This meant that Cleveland's AL fans had no chance to watch career NL stars like Bob Gibson and that a National League town like Cincinnati never saw live games featuring American Leaguers like Al Kaline.

With so much artificially pent-up fan demand, of course All-Star Game ratings went through the roof. The law of supply and demand—as irrefutable as the law of gravity—called for no other result.

Then free agency dawned and changed everything.

When intensive bidding on player contracts caused star player salaries to skyrocket in the 1970s, team owners were forced to cover costs with more wide-ranging, complete broadcast operations. Fledgling outfits like Turner Communications and ESPN introduced their own media presence, thereby igniting a movement that would, in time, bring satellite broadcasting and streaming Internet video within reach of almost every fan. By the time the new millennium rolled around, we had *Baseball Tonight* most every night.

When so many new spectators could finally check out so many All-Star players in games that actually counted in the standings, they weren't forced to wait for all the stars to finally align in July. The All-Star Game always had a special loosey-goosey feel and tradition all its own, but the exhibition's former popularity was built around an era that was gone for good.

With all that in mind, there's no need for carping about low All-Star Game ratings. It still delivers strong ratings in comparison to rival summertime programming and its Nielsen drop-off, while regrettable, has been a by-product of progress rather than regress. There are better measuring sticks for the All-Star Game of the new millennium. If the event is still strong, one would expect strong showings in fan balloting and attendance. Guess what? Check and check.

Today's fans register tens of millions of All-Star votes in four languages, in seven countries, on paper and online, and in ballparks and retail stores alike. All-Star candidates usually garner more than 32 million votes per annum, a total greater than the combined population of 27 American states.

Simultaneous with the record ballot levels are record attendance levels. Despite ticket prices that can climb upward of $1,000 and seating capacities of 40,000 or more, All-Star Games are perennial sellouts, with an additional 110,000 or more fans typically joining through neighboring "Fan Fests." What were once one-shot exhibitions have become bustling, multiday affairs encompassing street displays, memorabilia shows, autograph sessions, concerts, and aligned funnery.

It's important to keep all of it in mind. Consider how many passionate fans watch star performances throughout the season, fill up the ballot boxes, and wade through the crowds. The All-Star Game is in fine shape. Stellar shape, really.

MYTH #4

"Once Upon a Time, Baseball Was More Popular"

"Everything I'm reading says that baseball's popularity is diminishing,"
said David Hester, the [Pittsford (NY) Little League's] president.

—MARK HYMAN, "On Sandlot Day, Children Call Their Own Shots,"
New York Times, March 28, 2010

Baseball is declining in popularity in the U.S.

—DAVID GOLDBLATT, "The Decline of Baseball," *Prospect*, August 25, 2010

Baseball isn't poised for a renaissance—it's in the middle of one right now. The contemporary game has blossomed, according to multiple indicators.

Today's Majors, as supplemented by additional expansion teams, has more than doubled its live attendance since the mid-1970s, tripled its numbers since the mid-1960s, and quadrupled its counts since the 1950s. Despite a ubiquitous on-air presence, the annual growth of its live attendance has far outstripped the annual growth rate of the national population in the years since 1960 (about 3.7 percent to 1.7 percent). In an important way "America's game" has become more than twice as American.

The rising tide has translated to startling changes in its specifics. Teams like the Yankees and Red Sox are now capable of selling out spring training exhibitions with numbers that surpass the pennant race games of the 1960s, and a middling, nothing-special game in the new millennium draws virtually the same attendance that made Mark Fidrych a people's hero in a previous generation. (A regular season contest now averages about 30,200 spectators while the 1976 Tigers averaged about 31,000 home attendance for "The Bird" starts.)

The sport's attendance boom has quietly spread to Minor League franchises in 42 states. More than 200 organizations have set attendance records in the new millennium with the Minors as a whole more than doubling its turnstile count since 1990 (the total is usually 49 million or so).

No matter the location, it's much the same success story. In Williamsport, Pennsylvania, record crowds greet the Little League World Series. In Omaha, Nebraska, record gates view the College World Series. In Dyersville, Iowa, unprecedented numbers visit the *Field of Dreams* site.

The game has seen a record number of records, presumably, and the raw numbers are even more impressive when considering the incomparably more numerous entertainment options of the modern day. If historical eras are to be graded according to some kind of curve, the pastime has been far, far more visible than ever.

Those hardy few who would seek to deny baseball's historical popularity seem to base their thinking not on facts but perceptions. They note, correctly, that the pastime is no longer unchallenged among the big three team sports.

The National Football League hasn't reached Major League Baseball in either attendance or overall media viewership, but as recently as the 1960s the sport wasn't even in the same conversation. Pro basketball, similarly, can't hold a candle to MLB's current popularity, but in the 1970s it was widely perceived as "too urban" (read: "too black") to ever court mainstream acceptance.

The unstated supposition is that the ascent of football and basketball required the descent of the pastime—that their gains could only come at the expense of baseball's retreat.

The evidence tells us that contemporary baseball has been more than equal to the challenges, though. On balance, the rival sports have probably served to *enhance* baseball's popularity, if only because they've reminded fans why the pastime is such a welcome alternative. On the diamond, the strutting and chest-thumping are nonexistent. The trash talk is blissfully rare. The cheap theatrics are missing. As befitting a timeless sport, the clock-watching is absent.

Far from becoming obsolete, baseball's contrast has made the game all the more refreshing and, yes, more popular.

The Youth Movement

MYTH #5

"The Fans Are Too Old"

Baseball has the lowest level of interest among its youngest fans and the highest level of interest among fans 65 and older.

—GARY GILLETTE, ESPN.com, August 4, 2006

The game's fan base is aging and baseball is doing little to attract a younger following.

—"New Book Examines the Troubled Business of Major League Baseball," *Brookings Institution*, 2003

There are those who believe that the pastime has passed its time.

According to a recent ESPN/Chilton sports poll, just 12 percent of Major League fans are between the ages of 12 and 17. Different polls vary in their exact numbers, but the average baseball fan seems to be anywhere from 38 to 45 years old, an average significantly older than that attached to either football or basketball.

Graying poll numbers sound pretty negative but are, to say the least, shaky.

First, baseball never seems to poll very well, even in the best of times. Even as the game bounced back from the 1994–1995 strike with record attendance, ratings, and revenues, it still dragged around dire poll numbers. No one seems to know why there has always been a disconnect between the fan appreciation as expressed in the polls versus the expressions in the real world; an interest in baseball seems to increase in later life, many surveys seem to be flawed in their methodologies and deeply negative media portrayals may have contributed to outlooks. The timing of the polls may play a key role, also, with popular interest in the sport rising and falling depending on how it coincides with particular moments in its regular season or playoffs.

The polls are incomplete, too. Older fans do buy tickets—they're the ones with the jobs and the money—but we don't know how many of those tickets are later passed on to kids. It's apparently too expensive and/or complex to take that polling picture, and that's a crucial omission.

Even those who have attended dozens or hundreds of games can recall the details of their first look at a live contest. *My First Ball Game* is practically a literary genre in itself, complete with descriptions of an approach to a larger-than-life building, the bustle of tens of thousands of fans all around, the journey through dark passageways, and the explosive green-and-tan tones of a full-scale diamond. Such lingering memories tend to lead to many happy returns later in life.

Though live attendance is crucial, pollsters have never bothered to gauge it. Until they do, we cannot measure the differences between the polls and the realities.

MYTH #6

"Losing the Kids"

Millions of kids have probably grown up never having watched a complete World Series game. Little wonder that few of them grow up with a love of the game.

—DOUG NYE, "Poor TV Ratings Reflect MLB's Popularity Slide,"
South Carolina State, November 3, 2006

Commissioner Bud Selig doesn't seem to care that every World Series game ends past the bedtimes of his future paying customers.

—BILL SIMMONS, "Slicing Up the Red Sox's Boring Pie," ESPN.com, July 29, 2010

There's an oft-told baseball story.

It's said that, once upon a time, all World Series games were played in the daytime hours. These were the carefree days when grade-schoolers smuggled transistor radios into their classrooms to catch afternoon broadcasts, thereby forming some of the precious memories that won them over as lifelong fans. All was well under God's own sunshine.

Darkness fell upon the land, however, through evildoers known as broadcasting executives and team owners. Crazed by the pursuit of cash, these madmen scheduled nighttime broadcasts that pushed World Series endings past many youthful bedtimes. Slowly, ominously, the game began "losing the kids."

Such was the oft-told story, but the real story wasn't nearly as forlorn or fanciful. In actuality, nighttime scheduling was not fueled by greed and has not produced serious generational problems.

Separated from carefree memories of past generations, the daytime World Series games of the 1950s and 1960s represented fairly glaring outreach failures. Those who stole away a few daylight moments on old transistor radios made admirable efforts, to be sure, but what was the point in their taking such pains? Starting times shifted later in the 1970s simply because the potential viewing audience was far greater in the nighttime. (Some estimated that the audience is 25–50 percent greater after sundown.) The "night shift" was all about convenient viewer access, a feature that proved all the more valuable as kids found pre-sunset hours consumed by more schoolwork, extracurriculars, day jobs, and miscellaneous errands.

There's reason to believe that, as postseason games shifted to prime time, some kids nodded off before contest conclusions. There's also reason to believe that this has been a relatively small trade-off.

Current policy has many, though not all, of the World Series games ending on the East Coast by about 11:30 p.m., when the networks transition to lucrative programs like *The Tonight Show*. That 11:30 period might've been dark, forbidden territory for those who grew up 40 or 50 years ago, but it's standard operating procedure for a 'round-the-clock, on-the-go generation.

Other factors mitigate later ending times. Kids residing west of the Mississippi River see earlier conclusions within their time zones and at least a couple of World Series games are broadcast on Friday and Saturday nights, when kids needn't worry about wake-up times the following mornings. Only East Coast weekdays are potentially problematic.

Even for the relatively few kids who do doze off, there are alternative viewing options. It's 2012, not 1972, when World Series contests represented relatively rare opportunities for viewers to take in high-profile stars. No, today's kids can access a barrage of regular season baseball over more than six months, so it's safe to assume that they form allegiances well before the last innings of the last games of the year. If kids must absolutely confine themselves to World Series games alone, much of the action is still available through ESPN highlights, online recaps, or TiVo reruns. All the above may explain why the pastime has only retained its popularity in the four decades since it supposedly began imperiling its future.

As far as nighttime games go, it seems, the kids are all right. Those repeating a tired old storyline may be sleeping on the job.

A Matter of Time

MYTH #7

"The Games Are Too Slow"

The line at the post office is slow. Baseball is slower.

—NORMAN CHAD, "Time after Time, Yankees/Red Sox Game Drags On,"
Cleveland Plain Dealer, April 26, 2010

Q: What should Major League Baseball do to increase its TV audience?
A: Speeding up the game would be a good idea in general.

—BOB COSTAS, "Every NFL Playoff Game Is a 7th Game,"
USA Today, December 23, 2010

Baseball is America's most historic team sport, and conventional wisdom says that it's . . . just . . . too . . . slow. It's running behind the times.

For all the gripes, you might think that MLB ball games have dragged out over the years. This isn't the case.

Let us harken back to the golden days of 1960, back when the martinis were cold, the cigars were smooth, and the ties were skinny. The whole thing. *Surely* baseball was at its very best back then; surely it wasn't too slow. Well, back in 1960, games clocked in at an average of 150 minutes. That average game time has increased by about 20 minutes over more than 50 years.

Apart from the fact that the pastime's allegedly "slow" pace remains largely unchanged over the decades, there's another strange feature in its slow-poke nature: the typical baseball game is actually 15 minutes faster than the average pro football game. Some have been slow to notice.

MYTH #8

Action!

The runty little brother of "the games are too slow" myth is the notion that baseball doesn't have enough action.

If "action" is to be defined by 300-pounders colliding into each other at high velocities, football and sumo wrestling have, indeed, cornered the markets. If sports are to be measured by the number of plays and scoring chances per minute instead, then baseball easily outclasses the NFL.

The pastime's excitement comes through continuous scoring chances. They're called pitches and there are about 290 of them in a typical ball game. Pitchers must throw within the strike zone—if they can do nothing else, they must do that—and what do those hittable pitches allow? The potential for the hits necessary to set up scores and, in the case of a home run, the impacts needed to create instant scores. There's no possibility of "killing the clock," which helps explain why the average Major League contest has about 25 minutes of pure in-play time (when the ball is the process of being pitched, hit, or fielded). Even when they're not in motion, they're anticipating action through pickoffs, base-stealing leads, and defensive positioning.

The average NFL contest, in contrast, is relatively short on action but long on time. There are about 140 plays in a typical pro football game, most of them taking place in such distant field positions that teams don't have realistic chances to either set up scores or to actually score. "Killing the clock" is, very often, a preferable strategy and that's a significant reason why the average pro football contest only has about 12 minutes of in-play time (from the snaps that begin plays to the whistles that end them). Of course, when the gridiron athletes aren't actively knocking each other around they're doing little more than huddling, settling into formation, contemplating how the severely injured will soon be carted off to the nearest hospital, and then causing the severely injured to be carted off to the nearest hospital.

In sum, the NFL brings less than half the action of MLB. It's a chief reason why football viewers are subjected to continual replays, electronic pens, and rambling broadcasters even as the sport's live spectators are constantly pummeled with Jumbotron flashes, ear-shattering rock/rap, marching bands, and assorted marginalia; the impositions are necessary to distract audiences who would otherwise deal with tons of dead time.

A baseball has a lot of substance packed inside, but a football is mostly filled with hot air. This is true in more ways than one.

MYTH #9

"There Are Reasonable Ways to Speed Up the Games"

If he wants to help baseball, only one change is really necessary: speeding up the games. Numerous tweaks remain that are reasonable. . . .

—STAN McNEAL, "Memo to Selig's Special Committee: Speed Up the Game,"
The Sporting News, December 18, 2009

Two years before umpire Joe West deemed slow play to be "pathetic and embarrassing," . . . Major League Baseball had already made increasing the pace of game play a priority. New rules have been implemented. . . .

—JOE LEMIRE, "Amid Debate on Pace of the Game, One Group is
Unconcerned: Players," SportsIllustrated.com, May 7, 2010

Suppose that today's ball games are running long in either historical terms or in comparison to football. Let us further imagine that the fans don't enjoy the pacing enough to reward the pastime with all-time highs in attendance and viewership.

None of this is true, of course, but let us speak in hypothetical terms.

The primary cause of the game-time "problem" is, undoubtedly, rooted in pitcher specialization. As baseball moved into a hitter-friendly era in the 1990s, managers decided to maximize effective innings pitched through the use of relievers, be they matchup specialists or ninth-inning closers. Whereas the mid-1960s featured about one pitcher substitution per game, it's not unusual for a new millennium contest to see three or four changes, many of them necessitating mid-inning breaks.

We might seek to cut down on bullpen substitutions in order to hurry things up, but that wouldn't be possible without a radical reshaping of the game's rules. To play baseball without free pitching substitution is to play a very different sport.

Other time-saving measures would be equally impractical. New rules could limit throws to first base or pitcher-catcher conferences, for instance, but the handcuffing would only work to the advantage of offenses, thus leading to more runs scored and, through them, longer games. The "solutions" would be worse than the original "problem."

Another proposal would have teams cut down on the few minutes between innings, but this may be the most unreasonable suggestion of all. Pitching substitutions are a natural part of the game and can yield many millions of dollars in concession sales and commercial airtime. The day that team owners intentionally cut themselves off from that kind of money will be the day that sharks vote for vegetarianism.

With prominent time-cutting moves effectively left off the table, most would-be reformers are left to micromanage at the edges. More umpires are hectoring pitchers and batters to hurry up, for example, as if the game isn't difficult enough when conducted at a natural pace. Some have also suggested cutting intro songs like "Enter Sandman" and "Hell's Bells," as if we can gain entertainment while losing Metallica and AC/DC.

MYTH #10

"Instant Replay Gets It Right"

[James] Loney advocated wider use of replay review. "The more calls that happen, the more people will want the technology involved to get it right. Get it right, whatever it takes," he said.

—DYLAN HERNANDEZ, "Dodgers Lose to Brewers but Are about to Gain a Star: Matt Kemp," *Los Angeles Times*, May 28, 2012

If the goal is to get it right, and we have the technology, I don't care how much time it takes . . . let's get it right.

—THOMAS NEUMANN, "Q&A: Hall of Fame Shortstop Ozzie Smith," ESPN.com, May 10, 2012, quoting former player Ozzie Smith

Like many bad ideas, instant replay can look like a good idea.

Fans who care enough to watch ball games most often care enough to strongly disagree—all right, holler—when umpires make controversial calls, and such disagreements can come fairly often. With perhaps a dozen or more close plays in the typical ball game, there are many opportunities for reviews and replays.

In recent years there were well-publicized instances where instant replay technology coulda, shoulda, or woulda corrected wrong calls. In the 2005 American League Championship Series (ALCS), for instance, a catcher may have made a clean catch on a third strike, only to see the batter dash to first base and later score a winning run. In a 2007 season finale, the winning run was scored by a base runner who may not have touched home plate. In 2012 a perfect game may have been finished off by a check swing.

There have been other plays, too, all coming without umpires utilizing instant replay. Since all of us can use some help from upstairs now and again, it *seems* reasonable to give game officials some additional help, but what seems reasonable isn't always so.

The first strike against instant replay is in the logistical difficulty involved. Batted balls are tiny spheres (less than three inches in diameter) that can travel at initial speeds upward of 100 miles per hour and can land anywhere within thousands of square feet of turf and at virtually any angle (think of how fan interference might occur at virtually any place along the fences or the ways trap catches can be made by fielders diving in all directions). Such close calls are best made by relatively well-positioned umpires, and when there is indecision by the closest umpire, decisions can be confirmed through the views of backup umps.

Play calling is defined by very spontaneous movements and angles, and it's hard to see how instant replay cameras can match those elements. Cameras are always positioned far from game actions—sometimes hundreds of feet away—and unless the playing field is ringed by perhaps dozens of units, the machines will rely on less-than-direct views, too. It's highly implausible that the more distant, partially blocked reviews will provide great accuracy, especially when replay reviewers are cut off from real-time consultations. It's highly plausible that the reviewer's imperfect view and isolated perch will instead create new controversies and contentions.

The officiating process can always be improved, of course, but there's no need for robotics to set it right. More intensive training or more realistic work schedules might be introduced, for example, while umpire accountability can be enforced through stringent performance reviews. It may make sense to employ an additional arbiter on every crew.

Even if we make the unwarranted assumption that only instant replay would present a better-than-human improvement, there are other practical reasons why we shouldn't go to the videotape.

Instant replay has actually been used in the NFL for more than 25 years and has sometimes caused in-game delays of up to ten minutes per review. (This is a major reason why the average pro football game runs about 15 minutes longer than the average MLB contest.) Should baseball attempt to follow the gridiron's misguided example, not-so-instant replay would probably grind ball games to a halt. As anonymous officials puzzle over freeze frames, on-field personnel could do little more than dawdle about the diamond as live spectators watch the outfield grass grow.

What would be the ultimate results of replay-induced downtimes? Maybe inconclusive outcomes, maybe wrong calls. If a call is overturned in connection to a trapped ball or a home-plate collision, that would prompt further delays as on-field umpires attempt to predict how base runners would've advanced in light of the new ruling.

Finally, if ineffectiveness and the pacing poison aren't enough to banish the replay, there's the human element.

Umpiring mistakes are as old as the game itself but their frustrations centered not on unseen technologies but on visible, flesh-and-blood individuals. Umps know that anthologies could be filled with jokes at their expense* but they can play along because the public has learned to handle the imperfections of all Major Leaguers, be they men in uniform or men in blue.

That acceptance is so important and can produce moments beyond the reach of machines. Once, in 1960, Vin Scully's broadcast mentioned that umpire Frank Secory was celebrating a birthday, which prompted the home crowd to give the startled umpire a round of applause. Don Denkinger's miscall in the 1985 World Series prompted more than a little anger from the Cardinals dugout, but the chagrined Denkinger appeared at the club's 20th-year reunion in order to be presented with a gold wristwatch—written in Braille. On another occasion, Eric Gregg became notorious for his over-generous strike zone in the 1997 National League Championship Series, but that only supplemented Gregg's post-retirement appearances as a self-deprecating storyteller.

More recently, in 2010, when Jim Joyce blew the call that would've completed Armando Galarraga's perfect game, Joyce had the humility to later admit he was wrong and Galarraga had the grace to say, "Nobody's perfect." How human.

---

*My third-favorite umpire joke has President Harry Truman stating that he couldn't be a player due to bad eyesight, so he had to serve as an umpire instead. My second-favorite umpire joke: a frustrated manager waves his arms around, kicks the dirt, and says that the umpire is blind, only to have the ump point to the sky and say, "Well, the sun is far away and I can see that." My favorite joke involves a manager storming out of the dugout, yelling, "You called him out, but the 50,000 people here know he was safe!"

Into the Talent Pool

"There Are Fewer Black Players Nowadays"

*Over the last few decades black players have all but
disappeared from the national pastime.*

—ROB RUCK, "Where Have African American Baseball Players Gone?,"
Slate, March 5, 2011

With the number of black players in MLB at an all-time low . . .

— JAY SCOTT SMITH, "Is Quintin Berry Baseball's Next Great Black Hope?,"
TheGrio.com, July 25, 2012

One of the commonly accepted claims about today's pastime is the notion that it's falling behind in terms of black recruitment. In recent years high-profile pieces carrying titles like *Blackout* and *A Game Behind* have informed fans that Jackie Robinson's sport, the sport that once led the way in America's social integration, may now be turning away from racial inclusion.

This would be sad if true. Happily, it's false.

According to surveys from the Institute for Diversity and Ethics in Sport, in 2011 about 9 percent of all Major League players were U.S.-born African Americans, down from a 27 percent representation in the mid-1970s.

The diminished numbers were no cause for celebration, but neither did they represent a great crisis. Present-day African Americans represent roughly 12 percent of our nation's overall population, so their representation on today's rosters isn't far removed from their representation in the public at large. African

Americans went from being vastly overrepresented in relation to the overall population to lagging behind by a few percentage points.

More importantly, the poll numbers aren't reliable in tracking "black" representation. The numbers refer only to U.S.-born African Americans, but the United States hardly owns a monopoly on black populations. In fact, a great number of African descendants hail from nations like the Dominican Republic, Cuba, and Panama. Surely dark-skinned players like David Ortiz, Aroldis Chapman, and Mariano Rivera would've been barred in the days before Jackie Robinson, but surveys can lump such individuals into a catchall "Latino" category instead.

Foreign-born players deserve an accounting, an accounting that would belie the assertion that black athletes are uninterested in the game. In fact, a comprehensive survey of African-heritage players would move a slight "representation deficit" into something very different. Comparisons to the past are problematic because of a lack of data, but it's possible that the presence of foreign-born players makes today's rosters more racially diverse than ever. The involvement of so many foreign-born black players may indicate an even greater inclusiveness than the raw numbers would indicate, in the sense that player merits have trumped both racial and cultural/language barriers.

No doubt, baseball's composition has changed over the years, but no doubt, it's still diverse. We can only ask why so many sportswriters so often bemoan the "shortage" of blacks in baseball.

Well, some may not realize that black people can speak with a Spanish accent or live beyond our 50 states. Beyond that, some seem to operate through a racial stereotype.

Since U.S.-born African Americans make up about two-thirds of pro football and four-fifths of pro basketball, some seem to believe that it would be only natural for their racial group to dominate all sports, including baseball. The relatively close balance between African American representation on the pastime rosters and the general population does go against stereotype, but this means that the stereotype, rather than the pastime, should change.

MYTH #12

"Expansion Diluted the Talent Pool" (Pt. 1)

The expanding leagues have diluted the talent.

—RICK MAESE, "Since Talent Is Watered Down, Don't Blame Juice,"
Baltimore Sun, June 13, 2006

Too many teams diluting the talent pool, a problem stemming
from the addition of four new franchises from 1993 to 1998.

—ERIK SPANBERG, "In Arms Race, Young Pitchers Win Out,"
Christian Science Monitor, October 6, 2006

It still sticks like George Brett's pine tar or Gaylord Perry's Vaseline. Whenever someone wants to gripe about the national pastime's failings, it's a favorite weapon. It's the dreaded "talent dilution" myth.

As the lament goes, the quality of play in the Majors was diminished ("diluted") since the 1960s because baseball eventually added 14 expansion teams, thereby opening 350 or so new jobs to players who would otherwise be toiling in the Minors.

In reality, away from the grumbling, the "talent dilution" theory fixates on roster spots numbers in a misleading way. This must be emphasized: *the talent level of Major League rosters has nothing to do with the number of available jobs*. Rather, the overall talent level is a function of the number of players competing for each job.

To see how this is true, imagine a random group of 100 people competing to fill a job requiring elite skills. There's a certain likelihood that this group will have a star performer within it, but if the group suddenly expands to 1,000, the chance of finding a star increases tenfold. If the candidate pool expands to 10,000, the star search will be even more promising, and if a million job applicants are involved recruiters might find a one-in-a-million talent.

As an executive once observed, quantity *is* quality in the recruitment of talent, be it in sports or most any other field. As long as the number of would-be competitors increases at a faster rate than the number of available slots, the overall talent level should be fine.

Fortunately, astoundingly, this is what happened during baseball's modern popularity boom.

As the Majors moved away from the 16-team configuration of 1960 to the 30-team league of the late 1990s, the 88 percent roster increase was far behind the more than sevenfold increase in America's Little League teams (from about 27,400 clubs to about 200,000). There were probably more ad hoc youth teams 50 years ago, this is true, but the astonishing growth in organized teams makes it safe to assume that there are, in toto, far more kids now in line to eventually compete for Major League jobs.

Even more important than our nation's expanded talent pool has been an exploding interest in countries throughout the Caribbean, South America, and the Pacific Rim. In the 50 years after MLB nearly doubled the number of available jobs, the pastime's international representation actually tripled (from 9 percent to 27 percent). With an estimated 25 million to 30 million kids playing baseball beyond our borders, many of our greatest talents now emerge from San Pedro, Caracas, and Osaka, as well as Bakersfield, Memphis, and Stamford.

It'll always be fashionable for some to say that there still aren't "enough" quality Major Leaguers, but the metrics say that an increased quantity has yielded increased quality. Because many great young talents enjoy it, the pastime has grown both bigger and stronger. No myth.

MYTH #13

"Expansion Diluted the Talent Pool" (Pt. 2)

The quality of baseball was at an all-time high after World War II because there was such a concentration of talent on just 16 teams.

—RALPH KINER, *Baseball Forever*, 2004

The talent pool is thinner now.

—JOE MORGAN, "Chat with Joe Morgan," ESPN.com, June 27, 2006

With the new jobs provided by 1990s expansion teams, dozens of otherwise marginal players were suddenly given a shot to work on the Major League level. Did this lower the quality of play in the Majors? Kind of yes, but mostly no.

On the one hand, if we had fewer teams today, we would, indeed, concentrate better players among the surviving clubs. Decreasing the number of job openings at a certain fixed time *always* increases talent quality. Taking the concept to its logical extremes, today we would yield the greatest possible quality in a two-team league manned exclusively by All-Stars and the lowest possible quality in a 2,000-team league desperate enough to recruit The Last Guy Picked in Middle School Gym Class.

The talent dilution theory doesn't suppose that a 30-team league is contracted in one day, however. Instead, the theory compares the ratio of competitors to jobs in different historical eras and that ratio has only risen over the years.

Think of it this way: today's top players have already proved that they can succeed against competitors hailing from every corner of the United States, not to mention Venezuelan pitchers like Johan Santana or Japanese hitters like Ichiro Suzuki. Since they've already taken on the world, there's every reason to believe that they would've also succeeded against the smaller talent pools of the past.

If the Major Leaguers of previous generations somehow jumped forward to the present day, however, it would probably be a different story. The old-timers never had to prove themselves against a national and global talent pool. While stars on the order of Tom Seaver and Jim Palmer would distinguish themselves in any era, the more ordinary athletes of their generations would probably fall behind.

MYTH #14

"Baseball Is the Ninth-Toughest Sport"

We sized them up. We measured them from top to bottom. We've done our own tale of the tape and we've come to a surprising conclusion: pound for pound, the toughest sport in the world is boxing.

—**"Boxing's Knockout Punch," ESPN.com, 2004**

Have you heard? Baseball is only the ninth-toughest sport in the land. It's official. The experts have ruled.

Several years ago ESPN formed a panel that included academics and journalists, then charged the blue-ribbon group with measuring the overall athletics involved in the major American sports. They scored the various sports on criteria like agility and flexibility before setting out the results in a helpful little *Ultimate Degree of Difficulty Grid*.

Alas, poor baseball finished behind eight other major sports, its overall score (62.3) trailing far behind number one–ranked boxing (72.4). According to the ESPN panel, at least, pastime play is relatively easy. Easier, at least, than boxing.

And ice hockey.

And football.

And basketball.

And wrestling and the martial arts. Plus tennis.

Oh, and gymnastics, too.

This is pretty grim news, if you believe it. After all, sports are built on the desire to become better, to accomplish feats so remarkable that they might be remembered through the ages. Kids grow up dreaming about striking out cleanup batters or hammering ace pitchers and kids of all ages want "major league" to be synonymous with "best of the best." If athletes are to be measured by the company they keep, no true competitor would seek out a less than worthy opponent.

The ESPN finding seemed to tear at that idea, but it was nonsense. In reality, baseball is the toughest game in the land.

The ESPN ranking system began with the assumption that sports difficulties can be measured according to an objective standard, but making comparisons between inherently different sports is like comparing kangaroos to battleships.

Sports are challenging in such specialized ways that few athletes can excel at two or more of them as professionals. Someone with the size to dominate as a pro linebacker can look pretty foolish in playing shortstop, about as foolish as Michael Jordan looked in going after Minor League curve balls. Athletic bodies and skills are just too varied to fit into ESPN's arbitrary grid.

The best way to measure relative difficulties is more indirect—by counting the number of athletes vying for every available job. As discussed in a previous chapter, the number of athletes involved in a sport's talent pool largely determines the overall skill level within that sport. This is where baseball comes in first.

There is no disputing the fact that baseball is the best career option for young athletes in this country. The pastime brings the potential for significantly more wealth, for one thing, with the average Major Leaguer making $1 million per year more than the average NFL player. And if the financial angle isn't enough, there's the fact that pro football players are about eight times more likely to suffer debilitating injuries like brain damage and paralysis.

In baseball there's far more gain in exchange for far less pain, a well-known fact that has translated into easily read statistics. According to the *Wall Street Journal* the young ballplayers (age 18 or younger) of 2012 outnumbered the high school/college football players by more than three to one (about 3 million to 1.1 million). Even when allowing for the fact that football rosters are about twice as large as baseball rosters, the NFL lags far behind in the ratio of competitors to available jobs.

Baseball also thinks globally in terms of talent recruitment, but only 3 percent of all NFL players are foreign born. When taking into account both domestic and international athletes, the NFL's talent pool resembles a talent puddle.

Basketball, the third most popular team sport in this country, lags even further behind, with a recent *Statistical Abstract of the United States* estimating that about 500,000 young athletes are playing in school programs. While the NBA is growing in its appeal, estimates still have the sport's foreign-born representation lagging behind the pastime (about 10 percent to 27 percent).

All this indicates that, contrary to ESPN's publicity-stunt survey, baseball is the toughest game on the schedule.

State of Play

Fundamentalism

"They Don't Have the Fundamentals"

*I think the guys in my era knew how to play the game
more than the guys of today. They had more baseball instincts,
knew the fundamentals of the game.*

—FAY VINCENT, *It's What's Inside the Lines That Counts*, 2010,
quoting former player Willie McCovey

*I've never seen so much bad baseball. It's all about a lack of
fundamentals. There are no fundamentals at all in baseball today.*

—HAL BODLEY, "Teamwork, Fundamentals Dear to Rice," MLB.com,
July 24, 2009, quoting former player Jim Rice

If you want to know where pro baseball instruction is today, it helps to know where it came from.

The sad fact is that, throughout at least the 1970s, the overwhelming majority of up-and-coming prospects received little or no proper teaching in the finer points of hitting, pitching, and fielding. With little ready access to instructional manuals or training schools, the majority of amateurs had no detailed grasp of mechanics, plate discipline, situational adjustments, and such.

Some of the more fortunate kids learned from experienced fathers and older brothers and some of the more gifted youngsters found ways to teach themselves through trial and error, but many others became too discouraged or hurt to fulfill their full potential. Not many kids were similar to a young Brooks Robinson, who learned to protect himself from tricky hops by bouncing rubber balls off pockmarked stairways and dirt roads.

The situation was scarcely better for young players fortunate enough to sign pro contracts. Many managers weren't thrilled by their Minor League postings and, even if they relished their jobs, they had little time to teach the game to 25 or more raw recruits joining their team rosters on a continual basis. The managers' inattention was a big negative because very few farm clubs provided instruction through full-time hitting or pitching coaches, either. When nickels and dimes could've made a difference, the majority of teams pinched payroll pennies.

In older times many organizations did employ roving instructors, but it would've been more accurate to label them temporary instructors, since they typically stayed with a given team for only a few days at a time. Minor Leaguers were often left without outside perspectives, even when they were called to correct the raw mechanics that they may have utilized since they were little boys. Many players—no matter how physically talented—floundered well before they reached the Major League level. Whatever was broken was often left unfixed.

Old-time prospects were starved for effective coaching even at the Major League level. Until the 1950s most MLB teams didn't hire dedicated pitching and hitting coaches and the few coaches who were hired were distinguished mostly for their connections to the higher-ups. Individuals like Johnny Sain tutored a bevy of 20-game winners starting in the 1960s but was repeatedly fired because his bosses prized go-along cronyism over get-ahead coaching.

One might have hoped that established Major League players would provide the hands-on instruction but most Major Leaguers were, not to mince words, assholes. They had little incentive to mentor the prospects who were angling to take away the jobs of those on the preexisting rosters and in the absence of secure, team-oriented players like Whitey Ford or Sal Bando, many veterans actively excluded rookies from pregame batting practices. The worst of the hazing was imposed on the minorities and foreign-born players, who faced quite enough harassment in outside society.

That was the big picture for the old days. When a star said, "It's unbeliev-able how much you don't know about a game you've been playing all your life," what was often taken as an expression of humility or wonderment would have also worked as a truism regarding the training regimes of the 1950s and 1960s. It *was* hard to believe how much they didn't know.

With all that being said, in fairness, there were a couple of qualifiers.

First, there were some happy exceptions to the non-teaching rule, some oases in the desert. Organizations like the Yankees and the Dodgers did hire full-time coaches, adopt standardized practices, and thereby put prospects upon proven, step-by-step paths. As a result they often fielded the healthy and well-prepared rookies who allowed them to stay highly competitive in the long term, but unfortunately those organizations succeeded mostly because their competi-tors failed in their teaching programs.

Second, the young players who came up through the old learn-by-doing process weren't without certain advantages. Those who met organizational indif-ference were immune to *bad* instruction or overwork, at minimum. In addition, self-taught youngsters like Jim Bunning and Mel Ott could use trial and error to come up with quirky pitching motions or batting stances suited to their own timing. Other kids adopted instinctual approaches and this may have been what Yogi Berra had in mind when he said, "You can't think and hit at the same time."

Even so, the lack of old-era training was harmful. Peak athletic perform-ance is so often based on nuances best learned through careful, constant super-vision. Empowering students with proven tactics can always spare them years of frustration and in this way you'd want a well-coached young athlete just as much as you'd want a well-credentialed engineer or a highly trained architect.

Exceptional physicality is always helpful but pro baseball isn't something a workout warrior, a next-generation Ray Lewis or Dwight Howard, can readily dominate through bulging muscles or a towering body. Kids in football and bas-ketball don't need any tremendous sophistication in out-running or out-jumping others, but ballplayers have little choice but to work with coaches, especially when it comes to inherently tricky mechanics. Bruce Snyder of the Atlanta Braves has said that, after 40 years in Minor League development, he has *never* seen a player succeed primarily through physical talent rather than acquired skills.

Of course, the dark ages eventually made way for more enlightened times. After the game of baseball introduced big money rewards through the free agency system of the 1970s, it created the financial incentives for introductions through books, DVDs, and live seminars. Today, finally, kids have great opportunities to learn the fundamentals and see youthful potential mature into adult performance.

"Prospects Are Rushed"

The desire by teams to justify huge investments in young players is at the root of the problem. When a player is a high draft pick the organization might rush that kid to the Major Leagues ahead of his time because of what they paid him to sign.

—TIM KURKJIAN, "Mental Mistakes a Real Drag on the Game," *ESPN The Magazine*, April 30, 2010

They don't have the years of experience to learn some of the finer points that'd put them on top.

—IRA BERKOW, *The Corporal Was a Pitcher*, 2009, quoting former player Lou Brissie

Baseball is a game for the longest of long runs.

Today's stars are routinely lined up against numbers that may have been recorded several decades before. Fans notice when a hitter has one good season, but they may not bestow star status until the player excels through perhaps three years (1,800 or so at-bats). A player might not become an all-time great, a Hall of Famer, until he has stayed at the top of the game for maybe 15 or 20 years. It's a long time; the Beatles only stayed on top for about seven years.

The value placed on the long run may explain why so many get so worked up about the possibility that young players are being rushed up to the Majors. The thought is hard to understand, much less counter, mostly because few critics bother to explain why prospects are hurried.

If the "rushed" fear relates to economic incentives, it's plainly invalid; if anything, today's salaries may encourage Major League teams to grow overcautious in calling up ballplayers. Young stars can put up big numbers while working for salaries up to 40 times less than what veteran free agents earn, so franchises seeking to maximize their investments must ensure that prospects are mature enough to be effective by the time they reach the highest level.

The rules governing young players also encourage maturation. Teams retain exclusive rights over their draft picks, thereby forcing potential holdouts to either stay out of the sport, make a college commitment, or sign up for an independent league; any of those options can lead to an erosion of service time or full health, so the great majority of amateurs sign up almost immediately. Once in the Minors the new players are under organizational control for up to six years, and a lack of union protection means that they cannot receive anything but bare-bones salaries before their Major League debuts. At no point do eager youngsters have the leverage needed to demand a hurried promotion up to the Majors.

Business purposes and legal leverage both work against premature call-ups and another risk in reputational damage. If prospects are unduly rushed they would be more likely to flop, which would:

1)   hamper prospect morale (*this would be bad*) and
2)   tick off the fan base (*very bad*) and
3)   jeopardize front office jobs (*even worse*) and
4)   eat up the team's service control (*worst of all*).

Such negatives are even more likely among the struggling teams that might be otherwise tempted to seek quick fixes.

The critics might realize that organizations seek to bring prospects up at the right times but that they miscalculate just when the right times might roll around. The evidence tells us that new millennium rookies match previous generations in their pro experience, however.

The average age of first-year Major Leaguers has barely gone up or down for decades (most rookies are about 23 years old). A 2010s phenom like Bryce Harper can make a splash before his 20th birthday, of course, but a teenage call-up of the new millennium still stands out as a rarity, one no more exceptional than Robin Yount was in the 1970s and Bob Feller was back in the 1930s.

Developmental patience leads to long-term results, which, again, is driven by underlying dynamic. No one believes that the game has become any less challenging in either its game-time performances or off-time temptations, and there are few practical alternatives to the game-time preparation and real-world character tested through years of Minor League experience.

Scouts and executives have learned some pivotal valuable lessons of their own. They've seen how wunderkinds like Todd Van Poppel and Ben McDonald were derailed by stunted preparations while guys like Elijah Dukes and Rick Ankiel gave in to personal troubles. At the same time, evaluators have seen guys like Hanley Ramirez and Freddy Sanchez prove themselves through several pro seasons before blossoming as Major League rookies. No clubs want to endure the cautionary tales in the former examples; all organizations want to reap benefits from the latter examples.

Finally, it's worth mentioning that objective data is now playing a big role in proper, all-in-due-time player development. Very few Minor League evaluators are still impressed with batting-practice fireworks or an unpolished athleticism sometimes associated with "the good face." Instead, scouts and their supervisors now keep detailed logs of player productivity not only in traditional categories like slugging or earned run average (ERA) but in finely tuned stats like pitches per at bat, missed swings, and ground ball hits. Such Minor League stats are most reliable when there are enough data points for meaningful analysis, and those data points can only come when prospects are thoroughly vetted.

By the time the front offices have finished crunching all the numbers, analysts have more objective and complete profiles. These help ensure that young players aren't hurried up to the Majors.

Pitching

"Old-Time Pitchers Were Tougher"

There's no reason kids today can't pitch as many innings as people did in my era.

—ALBERT CHEN, "Nolan Ryan's Crusade," *Sports Illustrated,*
May 24, 2010, quoting former player Nolan Ryan

Former players attribute the lack of complete games to starting pitchers being coddled and managed to the point that they've lost the endurance of their predecessors.

—BENJAMIN HOFFMAN, "Complete Games Are Dwindling,"
New York Times, **April 9, 2006**

Old-timers say that the Greatest Generation was tougher than the Not-Greatest Generation, and very often, they're right.

There was a time when lean-and-hungry Americans had to conquer Nazi Germany with blood and iron. Their plump grandchildren play *Call of Duty* on Xbox.

There was a time we could only find skyline views by scaling mountain ranges with bare hands and pickaxes. Now we can download travel clips off the Internet.

Real men once took the time to hunt, gut, and roast wild animals. Now we unwrap breakfast burritos.

The trend toward contemporary comforts even seems to extend to pitching, or at least to innings pitched. In the 1950s and 1960s Major League starters were expected to be finishers in anywhere from 25 percent to 30 percent of Major League games, with a workhorse like Fergie Jenkins registering 20 or more complete games per season. It wasn't unusual for a hurler to put in 300 innings or more during the regular season. (The mark was reached more than 50 times in the 1950s and 1960s.)

In the 1990s and new millennium, by contrast, pitchers appear to have slacked off. Only about 5 percent of pitchers now finish what they start, so it can take a contemporary league leader like Livan Hernandez nearly a decade to surpass the complete game total that old-school Juan Marichal once put up in a single big year. League-leading starters are now expected to go about 240–260 innings. (No one has thrown 300 frames since 1980.)

With innings-pitched numbers melting like ice cream in July, it's easy to conclude that the new pitching generation isn't quite as tough. Whether due to a lack of training or a lack of character, our current hurlers seem to acquire all the glory while displaying half the guts.

The reality behind the perception is somewhat different. The fact that past generations of pitchers threw a lot more innings doesn't mean that their workloads had either the same quantity *or* the same quality as today's pitchers.

The first part of the story, the quantity, has to begin with the fact that "innings pitched" stats are unreliable for strict comparisons between the 1960s and the 2000s.

Let's start off with the proposition that a pitcher's effort isn't defined by *inning* totals but by *pitch* totals. Everyone knows this, but many wrongly assume that many more innings pitched can automatically correlate to more pitches thrown. To see how this isn't always the case, imagine that we have two equally effective pitchers being placed in two very different situations:

- Pitcher #1 is facing a swing-happy, impatient lineup that goes after a lot of first or second pitch offerings. He knows how to pitch, however, so he induces a lot of quick groundouts and weak pop-ups. Pitcher #1 ends up throwing about 11 pitches per inning and 99 pitches per nine innings.
- Pitcher #2 is facing a very patient lineup, one that consistently looks to take borderline pitches, foul off tough strikes, and coax walks. Pitcher #2 is as good as Pitcher #1, but if his savvy opponents can force him to toss an additional three pitches per inning, they can bring the hurler to the 99-pitch level after only seven innings.

In terms of both ability and effort, Pitcher #1 and Pitcher #2 are equals, but in our example, Pitcher #1 pitched two more innings in the game, a rate that would translate to about 60 additional innings in a full season. If you count the innings-pitched numbers and nothing else, one would conclude that Pitcher #1 was made of sterner stuff, but a look at the interior situation would show that Pitcher #2 was exerting himself just as much.

What is true in our hypothetical comparison is probably true in comparing a past era to our own. Prior generations of batters often acted like Pitcher #1's opposing lineup in that they allowed pitchers to rack up relatively high innings-pitched totals without forcing relatively high pitch counts.

We know that, as recently the 1960s, when Jenkins and his hardy cohorts were toiling away, batters were mostly judged by runs batted in and strikeouts, metrics that encouraged batters to put the ball in play with short, controlled swings. It was not uncommon for players to choke up on their bats, not unlike Little League lightweights. To be sure, Ron Santo, Jimmy Wynn, and others conscientiously worked the counts, but they were relatively rare. For the most part hitters went up looking to hammer their first hammer-able pitch.

In the new millennium, however, that all changed. In the decades after Ted Williams wrote the book on plate discipline, what was once the derided view of a lone genius has, over the decades, morphed into something like conventional wisdom. With a fuller appreciation of the advantages gained in forcing pitchers to show secondary pitches and back into fastball-first counts, batters were frequently evaluated according to the number of pitches they saw per at-bat.

We'll never know for sure—there were no comprehensive pitch counts before the 1980s—but the modern "war of attrition" strategy has forever changed the import of innings-pitched numbers. When a star like Justin Verlander can be forced into an average of 16 pitches per inning during a Cy Young year, it's likely that a league-average pitcher put the same energy into seven innings that an old-timer put into a full nine. Even as the innings-pitched totals have gone down, the underlying pitch counts may have remained even.

Now, even if today's pitchers actually tossed fewer pitches in the average game, that doesn't necessarily indicate lesser toughness. Beyond the quantity question is the quality issue, and that one *definitely* favors today's pitchers over their predecessors.

It's beyond dispute that hurlers now face the most marked offensive environment since the 1960s. The surroundings include shorter outfields, reduced foul territories, and more effective lighting. Opponents take up maple bats with hand-sculpted barrels and rock-hard surface coatings. Body armor was authorized. League offices mandate smaller strike zones. General managers pass over banjo hitters in favor of offense-first types. Coaches build vast video libraries revealing minute patterns of pitching deliveries and selections. If kitchen sinks were at hand, they would've been tossed in.

As all kinds of new pressure came down on pitchers, their countermeasures proved limited. Pitchers lost some energy when they protected themselves through intensive pregame routines. Novel injury threats visited those who put more movement on breaking balls and extra zip on fastballs. Batters still retained enough advantages that they need not fear those "pitching to contact." Brushback pitches were taken as suspension-worthy offenses, not just another aspect of hardball.

Today's pitchers may appear less impressive, but that's because they toil in hitter-friendly times. The earned run averages changed with the eras, but if hitting conditions ever get tougher the pitchers will look tougher, too.

MYTH #18

"Pitch Counts Make Them Soft"

"The pitch count has come into play," [Bert] Blyleven said. "The players today are bigger and stronger. Well, then, why can't a pitcher go nine innings?"

—SID HARTMAN, "Blyleven Thinks Little of Drugs, Pitch Counts," *Minneapolis Star Tribune,* January 28, 2011

"I can't deal with the philosophy now, the pitch counts, the limits put on pitchers," [John] Smoltz scoffed. "Today's pitchers have been brainwashed."

—MURRAY CHASS, "A Man of Many Means," MurrayChass.com, March 14, 2010

Old-timers and the old-at-heart constantly declare that the Major League pitchers of yore were more manly men because their top performers notched significantly more innings pitched. Unfortunately the innings-pitched statistic comparisons aren't very reliable and there's every reason to believe that their pitchers faced significantly less stressful game conditions.

So poor old grandpa probably didn't get to school by walking barefoot for five miles in the snow. No, he put on loafers. And took a stroll down the block. When it was sunny.

The "pitchers have it easier" storyline gets weaker still when you consider that old-time pitchers, as a group, weren't nearly as durable as they might have appeared at a glance.

It may be hard to believe from today's perspective, but for most of baseball's history, teams treated their pitchers as highly disposable commodities. The bosses simply worked pitchers without regard to how much arm damage was caused by athletes ringing up 100 or more pitches per game or hundreds of innings per season. Those who resisted that kind of madness had no power to stop it and, at any rate, players who attempted to resist were either blacklisted or told to take a "tougher" (read: "more oblivious") attitude.

Alas, macho attitudes proved to be an inadequate protection against severe muscle ruptures and cartilage tears. A huge number of promising pitchers suffered career-ending injuries before they even reached the Major Leagues. We'll never know the exact number—their organizations were too blasé to keep track—but analysts have estimated that for every Major Leaguer, there may have been eight or nine prospects who prematurely ended their careers in the Minors.

Even those pitchers with the dumb luck to make it to the highest level could rarely endure for long. Karl Spooner, Herb Score, Gary Nolan . . . there was a long, sad list of world-class talents who barely had a chance to establish themselves before something important snapped in their elbows or shoulders. Many of those who toughed it out long enough to make a big impression—Don Drysdale and Catfish Hunter, among them—were effectively finished by age 32.

It's true that some 1960s-era pitchers were blessed with the luck or natural ability to endure overwork while going on to healthy and lengthy careers, but guys like Don Sutton and Nolan Ryan were big exceptions to the rule. Taking them as representatives of a notably durable generation would be like naming a few lottery winners and concluding that Powerball tickets represent a viable investment strategy.

To go by anecdotal evidence, even pitchers with substantial Major League careers never came close to reaching their full performance potential, if only because they battled through the kind of "pitcher's pain" that could routinely reduce grown men to tears. It was, in the truest sense, a crying shame.

None of the pain seemed to make a very big impression on the bosses, however. When overtaxed pitchers blew out their arms, the powers that be only shrugged and moved on to the next batch of disposable, naive youngsters. In the bad old days, failure was so common as to be expected.

Flash forward.

After big-money player contracts first came on to the scene in the 1970s, organizations gained a new financial incentive to protect pitcher health. Changes came in nearly every phase of the game.

Managers like Tony La Russa began to adapt in-game tactics against pitcher fatigue. Skippers began to pull tiring pitchers in favor of relievers during the late innings, secure in the knowledge that the more rested relievers were more mechanically sound and more unfamiliar to the batters. At the same time, coaches like Leo Mazzone and Dave Duncan came to realize that arm injuries could be prevented if pitchers were limited to a certain number of pitches thrown in a game, in a season, and from one season to the next. More and more coaches started tracking pitch counts in the 1980s.

Due to the various changes, complete games have sharply declined in number since the 1970s. In this way they were similar to flared collars and bell-bottom pants.

Contemporary pitchers could stand to labor some more, possibly. They could "suck it up" and "just put in the work," in the words of self-styled tough guys like Rob Dibble and Dave Stewart. It would be possible for them to do any number of things. They could keep laboring right up to the point where, in mid-throw, their arms physically detach from the torsos and hurtle off into the air.

Pitchers aren't actually worked to that point, mostly because the experts have finally learned something of the heedless, needless destruction caused by overwork. Coaches now define success in terms of the preparation and caution that can prevent injuries in the first place. They needn't sit around while underlying tissue damage reaches the point where a seemingly healthy arm finally manifests a long-building but severe injury.

It was always nonsensical to believe that the old-timers were the tough guys while the new-timers have been rendered soft by pitch counts. Pitcher usage should've been based on care and science rather than carelessness and ignorance.

It's an unalloyed positive that teams now have the incentive to make pitchers as durable as hitter-friendly times might allow. Pitch counts, like any other tactic, can be taken too far, but no one needs to learn how much additional damage would be wreaked without safeguards.

If the failures of past generations were more easily recalled, the successes of the present day would be more often appreciated. We know that a record number of pitchers are staying active and effective well into their late 30s or early 40s and that pitchers who can stick around for at least a few years in the Majors enjoy historic opportunities to register 3,500 or more career innings. These have been breakthroughs, even if they're often overshadowed by reports of curtailed careers.

It's a compliment of sorts. As the treatment of pitchers has grown more intelligent and humane, expectations have changed. Arm injuries aren't seen as a fact of life, but a waste of potential.

MYTH #19

"Young Pitchers Are Babied"

There are coaches and players who say that today's pitchers are coddled, that they should build up their arm strength from an early age and keep at it on a daily basis.

—GARTH WOOLSEY, "Is Baseball Really This Dangerous?,"
***Toronto Star*, April 14, 2008**

"They don't really push the athletes now," [Fergie] Jenkins said.

—C. L. BROWN, "Hall of Famer Jenkins Is in Bonds's Corner,"
***Louisville Courier-Journal*, May 13, 2007**

If only we did coddle our pitchers. If only we did baby our athletes.

In the old days it was a lot easier to come of age as a ballplayer. With significantly fewer outside activities to occupy them, baseball-loving kids could slip a mitt onto a bicycle handlebar; ride over to the nearest city street, sandlot, or country field, and then assemble pickup teams among nearby kids. Removed from outside influences, most youngsters heeded the painful warning signs of underlying injuries.

Much of that has now gone by the wayside. As society at large saw less safety in public spaces, youth ball games were increasingly confined to structured league settings under the supervision of volunteer coaches. The amateur coaches do well enough in supervising position players, but unfortunately, their tactics often harmed young pitchers.

Overeager to develop a million-dollar prospect or a big reputation, youth league coaches often overburdened the kids with the raw power to dominate opposition batters. The coaches started the elite youngsters too often, kept them in games too long, and put too much emphasis on the strikeouts that bypassed chancy defenses.

Many teenage boys may feel the need to show off, but their preexisting inclinations were rarely reined in by their coaches. Rather, there were situations where young pitchers were asked to deliver hundreds of pitches per week, only to go all-out in off-seasons that could include prospect tournaments, skill showcases, wooden-bat leagues, and traveling youth teams. With no rules preventing such wrong-headed usage—there were no formal limits to Little League pitch counts until 2007—many threw until it hurt and then threw some more.

No one knows exactly how many young pitchers have been overworked, but the toll has been all too apparent. The renowned Dr. James Andrews performed a total of 13 Tommy John ligament-replacement surgeries on teenagers in 2001, but seven years later he scheduled over 240 per annum. As radical shoulder and arm surgeries became more accessible to more kids, the number of surgeries increased by an estimated *700 percent* in a little over a single (new millennium) decade. A growing number of pro scouts now prefer strong-armed athletes who've never pitched in youth leagues, if only because the novices have escaped severe damage to their still-maturing ligaments and tendons.

If only we did coddle our pitchers. If only we did baby our athletes.

Hitting

MYTH #20

"Power Hitting Devalues Stolen Bases"

*I see the game is changing, that there's no place for the stolen base.
Everyone wants to be on SportsCenter and you do that by
hitting the ball in the stands.*

—NATE SILVER and WILL CARROLL, "Prospectus Q&A: Rickey Henderson,"
Baseball Prospectus, August 26, 2003, quoting former player Rickey Henderson

*To me, the stolen base is a fantastic offensive weapon that seems to
have gone by the wayside. I don't think there is any secret why:
because of the long ball.*

—SEAN DEVENEY, "Steal This Base," *The Sporting News*, May 14, 2001,
quoting former player Maury Wills

Modern times are the most potent ever in terms of home run hitting. Prior to 1998, for example, only two players had reached 60 or more home runs in a season, but in the years afterward that level was reached six times.

The numbers confirm that as Major League offenses have hit more homers, they've stolen fewer bases. Here are the stats for home-runs-per-game (HR/G) in comparison to stolen-bases-per-game (SB/G) over recent decades:

	HR/G	SB/G
1986	0.91	0.79
1990	0.79	0.36
1994	1.03	0.32
1998	1.04	0.68
2002	1.04	0.57
2006	1.11	0.57

Even as home-runs-per-game surged by 22 percent over 20 years, stolen-bases-per-game declined by 28 percent.

The increased reliance on extra-base hits over stolen bases was sound baseball reasoning. More doubles and triples have allowed more runners to reach scoring position without risking a throw-out from a steal attempt. Why run when you can trot?

Other factors contributed to the decline in stolen bases. Improved defenses, for example. After guys like Rickey Henderson and Vince Coleman began stealing 100 or more bags per year in the 1980s, hurlers learned to hold runners closer with pitch-outs, pickoff moves, step-offs, quick tosses, and slide-step motions. Successful steals could take double plays out of order, but they also allowed pitchers to neutralize follow-up sluggers with intentional or semi-intentional walks to unoccupied bases.

At the same time, as teams upgraded defenses, others began to question the inherent worth of stolen bases. Conventional wisdom has long held that likely base stealers can disrupt pitch selections and infield positioning, but studies that quantified such effects found that likely base stealers only added about 11 points to the on-base plus slugging numbers of follow-up batters. The disruptive effect from steals was, at best, not good, probably because follow-up batters were so often required to protect base runners by going after unfavorable pitches.

Other than the fact that stealing has been largely neutralized, the tactic has little positive impact because it demands a high success rate. Bill James was among the first analysts to observe that caught-stealing failures are doubly hurtful to offenses in that they give away outs while simultaneously erasing base runners, so runners can only negate the tactic's downside by taking bases at an estimated 65–70 percent rate. Most would-be base thieves simply cannot sustain that kind of success over dozens of attempts; even Henderson's record-breaking 130 swipes in the 1982 season were offset by a record 42 pickoffs.

The relatively puny edge to be gained in stolen bases can look all the more insignificant because it can only be gained at the risk of runner injuries ranging from deep bruises to broken bones. Hitting the dirt at full speed while simultaneously evading a fielder's hard tag and a speeding, mid-air baseball is always a punishing task and is, very often, an injurious task.

Taking all of the above into consideration, the tactic's trajectory comes into better focus. An upgraded power game played a part in the decline of stolen bases, yes, but so did upgraded defenses and fuller evaluations. They revealed that, very often, theft didn't pay.

MYTH #21

"Power Hitting Devalues Bunts"

I become frustrated watching players, so lacking in fundamentals, unable to execute something as simple and important as a sacrifice bunt.

—HAL BODLEY, "Ichiro's Run Rivals Wee Willie's,"
MLB.com, September 11, 2009

After years of reliance on home runs, baseball teams this spring are sweating the small stuff. . . . The Philadelphia Phillies want pitchers to bunt better.

—MEL ANTONEN, "Teams Go Back to Basics without Reliance on Home Runs," *USA Today*, March 29, 2006

Bunts are adorable. They are adorable.

Even grade-schoolers know that if you push the ball in just the right spot some 20 feet into the infield, you just might register a single. Diminutive David Eckstein loved to bunt. If Smurfs could play ball, they would bunt their little blue tails off. "Bunt" has the same pronunciation as "bundt," as in "delicious bundt cake."

And yet, adorable as they may be, bunts are frequently useless.

As authors like Michael Lewis have pointed out, today's fielders can cut down mini-hits with such pitiless efficiency that, almost always, to bunt is to forfeit an out. Particularly proficient fielders can erase base runners from second base, even. The limited effectiveness of the bunt was a prime reason why Hall of Fame manager Earl Weaver was known for avoiding the tactic. ("I've got nothing against it, in its place. Most of the time that place is in the bottom of a long-forgotten closet.") Weaver's teams won by launching the ball, not slapping it.

The managers, coaches, and players who now make their living based on sound, Weaver-style play have long embraced power hitting at the expense of push-'em-over tactics. At the same time, most commentators chose to lament the infrequency of sacrifice hits.

There's a validity in this. Some players have gone overboard by completely ignoring bunting skills, which can render them incapable of taking their opponents out of a double play situation or playing for a single run in the late innings of close contests. Sometime batters ignore situations where infielders are playing too far back and National League pitchers have little choice but to bunt well, if only because they're such weak batters when swinging away.

Apart from that, though, the criticism is mostly based on some blend of ignorance and pique. A good number of the naysayers have no idea how and why bunting is, most often, useless, instead assuming that those in the broadcast booth bring more due diligence than a Hall of Famer like Weaver.

The pro-bunting view is also inflated by the likelihood that bunts were one of the few accomplishments of low-skill players. Almost none of the critics were capable of knocking shots over the fence, but almost all of them could tap out a small, smurfy bunt. Guess which plays they now call crude and brutish? Home runs. Guess which plays they now hold up as deft and wholesome? Bunts.

MYTH #22

Snapshots from an Alternative Universe in which Bunts Are Important

1938: Gabby Hartnett's famed "Bunt in the Gloamin" breaks open the pennant race . . .

1945: Hank Greenberg nudges a ball down the line after his dramatic return from wartime service . . .

1951: Mickey Mantle's rookie season hints of an utterly unique combination of lightning-fast speed and ultra-slow bunting . . .

1954: Dusty Rhodes shocks the mighty Cleveland Indians by producing two "short balls" en route to a World Series sweep . . .

1960: Ted Williams ends his career by squaring up in his last official at-bat . . .

1964: Ken Boyer's four-run squibber helps seal a championship for the Cardinals . . .

1971: Historians argue whether Reggie Jackson's bunt off Dock Ellis is the shortest, tiniest hit in All-Star Game history . . .

1975: Carlton Fisk waves a ten-footer fair as the Red Sox take Game Six of the World Series . . .

1981: Rick Monday breaks hearts in Montreal by slapping a Steve Rogers pitch just short of the third baseman . . .

1988: A hobbled Kirk Gibson pokes Dennis Eckersley's slider just past the mound, thereby inducing Jack Buck's classic broadcasting call: "This is gonna be . . . a bunt! I don't believe what I just saw! . . ."

1993: Joe Carter shocks the Philadelphia Phillies and the world by tapping a game-winning bunt . . .

1998: An out-of-nowhere Shane Spencer lays out a bunch of anti-homers during the playoff run . . .

2000: Ken Griffey Jr. reportedly bunts a ball so hard that it kills an earthworm . . .

2007: Controversy dogs the chase for the career bunting record, as many question how Barry Bonds grew so weak as to be incapable of slugging his way onto the bases . . .

MYTH #23

"Home Runs Dumb Down the Game"

Power helped dumb down the game—think how little base-running and defense matter in slow-pitch softball.

—TOM VERDUCCI, "When Bigger Gets Smaller, Small Gets Big,"
Sports Illustrated, May 30, 2005

Baseball, when it first became popular, was more of a cerebral game. You could sit there and think about whether they were going to hit-and-run or bunt. You could really get involved in inside baseball. Now people don't want to take the time for that. They want to see power hitters and power pitchers. It's the SportsCenter mentality.

—MARK HERRMANN, "A Hitter's Game," *Baseball Digest*, July 2003,
quoting former player Jim Kaat

Among all the major team sports, baseball has a singular identity as the "thinking man's game," and it's not hard to see the reasons why.

In football there's room for athletic technique, but no one seriously believes that fancy moves are going to stop a barreling, 260-pound slab of muscle as he comes in for a crushing tackle; the subtleties end when the collisions start. In basketball, too, game smarts can be helpful, but there isn't enough guile in the world to stop a flying seven-footer's slam dunks; that sport also comes down to size and strength.

Baseball, in contrast, has far more room for learned skills. Well-timed flicks of the wrists can defeat 100-mile-an-hour heaters, just as sneaky pitch movements can elude big swings. Baseball performance can be about brains as well as brawn, which is why guys like Tony Gwynn and Tim Lincecum earned multiple awards despite their resemblances to a cupcake addict and a 19-year-old skateboarder, respectively.

Long-term declines in bunting and stolen bases can seem negative because they appear to go against the game's intricate nature. They seem to make on-field baseball dumber, but that's not the case.

Bunting, for instance, derives from expert bat control and that's still a vital ingredient to all kinds of contributions: hitting behind runners, executing on hit-and-run plays, generating sacrifice flies. Bat control is vital to fouling off tough strikes and that helps produce walks. Fewer batters go so far as to lay down on bunts but they're hardly giving up on situational hitting.

Bunts themselves are also being deployed in more heady ways. When facing shut-down pitching in the late innings, a lineup may be so ineffective that it uses bunts to force fielding errors. Batters have also been known to square up for bunts because even bluffs can cause fielders to play shallow and thereby increase the likelihood of legitimate hits through the gaps. On the occasions when bunts are used, they are used effectively.

The outlook for stolen bases is much the same. Exceptional base stealers display a knowledge of pitching motions and outfield throws, elements that are still displayed among all those creating long leads off the bags or taking extra bases on outfield throws. Those advantages, in turn, help those seeking to break up double plays, to go from first base to third on a single, or to advance bases on sacrifice flies. While stolen bases aren't as popular as once before, the aggression and awareness behind stealing them are still prized.

Like bunts, actual stolen bases are still deployed, too. When base runners are matched up against awkward pitchers and rag-armed catchers, they go for steals. When clubs are desperate for late-inning scores, they attempt steals. In recent years the stolen-base success rate has actually reached historical levels and that's not dumb at all.

MYTH #24

"Sillyball"

The game went power mad.

—HOWARD BRYANT, "Out at Home," *ESPN The Magazine*, June 19, 2012

It's rare for the mainstream media to come right out and call the fans stupid, but they express the same sentiment by deeming a homer-happy era to be "silly-ball." Very often sportswriters tut-tut about how 1990s/new millennium home run levels were so bloated as to "make a mockery of the game," at least as far as it existed back in the 1980s or before.

It's true that the offenses of the 2000s reached new heights, but that ascent was premised on a time-tested belief: fans are more interested in seeing things occur than in seeing things prevented. Otherwise the Home Run Derby would give way to Pitching and Defense Derby and groundouts to second base would routinely garner massive ovations.

Homers were entertaining enough in themselves, but the rising numbers of the homer-ic era have had additional in-game benefits. More scores inevitably lead to more lead changes, which can lend wider possibilities to all at-bats and innings. When more clubs are one or two powerful swings away from a late-inning comeback there's a more lively promise that "it ain't over 'til it's over." On a purely aesthetic level, there's an anticipation that someone might launch a ball high or far enough to create a breathtaking sight.

Home run appeal was only affirmed in the 1990s and new millennium. Attendance levels increased neatly in tandem with the increased power levels and their interconnection only carry on a pastime tradition that has played out for more than 130 years. In fact fans have never rejected transitions to homer-friendly conditions, even in the 1930s and 1970s, when the transitions from previous eras were quite stark. No one found Lou Gehrig and Frank Robinson very tiresome when they rewrote power-hitting thresholds established not long before their heydays. Those who insisted on fretting over discontinuities in offensive eras could see that statistics like "ERA+" and "OPS+" (on-base plus slugging) adjust numbers for different league contexts, thus rendering player comparison relatively linear.

Cheering fans and a long line of tradition . . . the only potential mockery would be in ignoring their importance. In the way that the current era measures up, "sillyball" is more accurately called "seriousball."

The Numbers

Stat(s) of Clarity

Tradition can be taken too far.

It's all right to study vintage automobiles but it's not wise to commute to work in a Model T. One can settle into cool weather without giving up on central heating. Wooden clogs are best used as cultural curios, not casual footwear.

Tradition can be taken too far in baseball statistics as well. Many of the most familiar pastime numbers, including pitching wins and batting average, date back to the 1800s. They now carry on as mathematical relics, based on little more than blunt incomplete views of on-field action.

Starting in the 1970s, statisticians like Steve Mann and Pete Palmer undertook challenges to 19th-century stats, with their technical work later being popularized by Bill James, Craig Wright, and others associated with the Society for American Baseball Research (SABR). Their "sabermetrics" de-emphasized certain numbers while offering alternative measures of pitching, hitting, and fielding. Here are some of their revisions on traditions:

STARTER PITCHING
The Stat: Earned Run Average
What It Shows: It's the rate of earned runs surrendered for every nine innings pitched. ERA seeks to measure a pitcher's core task, which is to deny opponent scoring with the assistance of his teammates' reasonable fielding efforts.

What It Doesn't Show: ERA can be unduly skewed by a pitcher's home ballpark and the run-scoring emphasis of his era. Giving up two runs per game is outstanding if it comes in a ballpark/league that typically sees four or five runs per game, but two runs per game is more mediocre in a context where the average pitcher gives up two or three runs per game.

Statheads want to control for outside factors, so they convert raw ERA numbers into ERA+ numbers and place them on a scale with a 100 median. ERA+ ratings are useful because they don't reward pitchers who merely work with outside advantages and don't punish those who happen to toil in tougher conditions.

The Stat: Wins

What It Shows: A starter is awarded a win when he pitches at least five innings, exits with the lead, and his team holds the lead throughout the remainder of the game. Wins are often treated as the ultimate pitcher statistic; those who put up big win totals are often taken to be big winners, period.

What It Doesn't Show: A starter's win totals are highly dependent on bullpen help, run support, and defense, so it's possible for relatively mediocre pitchers to be credited with cheap wins even as superior hurlers are punished with hard-luck losses or no-decisions. That's to say that the win stat can unfairly assign a single individual with an outcome that comes about through team effort.

RELIEVER PITCHING
The Stat: Reliever Earned Run Average (ERA)

What It Shows: Like starters, relievers are expected to deny opponent scores.

What It Doesn't Show: The ERA number has especially limited utility for relievers because they pitch relatively few innings and aren't docked for the scoring of inherited runners. It's possible for a strong pitcher to display a deceptively high ERA due to a handful of bad outings or for a weak pitcher to put up a low ERA even as he consistently gives up scores through inherited runners.

The Stat: Saves

What It Shows: There are various scenarios involved in the number but it basically asks a relief pitcher to come into a reasonably close game and finish it off

without surrendering a preexisting lead. Save numbers are intended to show
how many times a reliever nails down the final inning(s).

What It Doesn't Show: A reliever can pick up a relatively easy save by coming into
a ball game with no men on base or with a multi-run lead. Generally speaking,
bullpen guys are more accurately judged by how they prevent runs, even when
those runs are produced by inherited runners or when they're blunted by big leads.

HITTING
The Stat: Batting Average (BA)

What It Shows: Batting average counts base hits in relation to official at-bats.
The stat reflects one of a hitter's most valuable contributions—the ability to put
balls into play while avoiding outs.

What It Doesn't Show: It's vital for a batter to avoid outs, of course, but that
goal can be served through bases-on-balls and hit-by-pitch totals as well as base
hits. Since on-base percentage (OBP) accounts for all three categories, it can be
more useful than raw batting average.

A side note: An emphasis on the OBP stat doesn't necessarily convey that "a
walk is as good as a hit." Walks are clearly inferior to hits. They cannot force
fielding errors, drive in runs from second base, or allow base runners to advance
by two or more bases. The statisticians who mention walks mostly do so because
walks are often overlooked as offensive contributions.

The Stat: Runs Batted In (RBI)

What It Shows: RBI tallies reflect runs scored as a result of a batter's clean base
hits. A batter's fundamental task is to help produce the runs needed to win ball
games and RBI numbers have a direct relationship to run totals.

What It Doesn't Show: Absent home runs, a batter cannot drive himself in for
a run scored but must rely on lineup support that can unfairly skew RBI totals.
A superior hitter can compile relatively low RBI numbers because preceding
batters aren't getting on base at a high rate, for example, while a more middling
hitter can put up relatively high numbers because he comes up to bat with plenty
of teammates in scoring position.

The Stat: Home runs, also known as big flies, blasts, bombs, dingers, four-baggers, goners, gopher balls, jacks, long balls, round-trippers, shots, slams, 'taters

What It Shows: Those who hit homers can yield as many as four runs through a single swing. Hitting a home run is the single most important thing someone can do to win a game.

What It Doesn't Show: Homers are very important, but power hitting also includes doubles and triples. Slugging percentage, which tallies all extra base hits, can provide a more accurate power picture.

FIELDING

The Stat: Fielding Percentage (FP)

What It Shows: This number reflects a fielder's success in registering outs and assists on balls in play, as long as those balls can be handled without extraordinary effort. It then places those outs and assists in relation to the total chances.

What It Doesn't Show: The fielding percentage number doesn't reflect failures to reach batted balls, lapses that can be just as damaging as errors in that they also allow opponents to get on base. Run prevention can be better assessed through range factor, which is based on the number of putouts (and assists) logged for every inning played.

BASE RUNNING

The Stat: Stolen Bases

What It Doesn't Show: As described in a previous chapter, high theft totals are great, but their impacts can be largely offset by failed steals. It can be more useful to judge runner effectiveness through caught stealing percentages and, to a lesser extent, advances made through passed balls, wild pitches, and sacrifice flies.

The Stat: Runs Scored

What It Doesn't Show: Runs scored is the base-running equivalent of the RBI category; its totals can be heavily skewed by a player's lineup support. Because they aren't completely fair they don't deserve complete attention.

MYTH #26

Stat(s) of Confusion

The statistics in the preceding myth gained loyal followings over the years. They were less than perfect, but at least they were secured to straightforward on-field actions. They produced numbers that were relatively necessary and uncomplicated.

Unfortunately, more exotic stats arrived over the years. Few of the "advanced metrics" won substantial followings, mostly because they were founded on theories that grew so disconnected as to render their numbers ever-more unnecessary and complicated:

PITCHING
The Stat: Runs Allowed (RA)
What It Is: Turning more than 100 years of conventional wisdom upsidedown, *Baseball Prospectus* declares that pitchers should be graded by all the runs allowed, including scores that result from fielding errors.

What?!: The conventional wisdom should stay rightside up. It's true that umpires sometimes make bad calls on bang-bang plays and that scorers can mess up the designation of errors, but such mistakes should even out over the ordinary, if imperfect, action that takes place over the long run, and no one believes that there's some kind of systematic bias against any one pitcher or group of pitchers. In the absence of massive information failures it's only fair to judge pitchers in conjunction with the ordinary fielding efforts of their teammates, judgments that can come through simple ERA and ERA+ measures.

Fair is good, simple is good.

The Stat: Fielding Independent Pitching (FIP)
What It Is: FIP is a measure of every action that the pitcher can accomplish without the ready assistance of his fielders (apart from the catcher). The stat counts only home runs, bases on balls, hit batsmen, and strikeouts, without any account for singles, doubles, and triples.

What?!: Yes, we have the perfect stat for those who believe that the fate of almost all batted balls within the field of play are irrelevant to pitcher performance.

Meanwhile, back on our home planet . . .

The Stat: Batting Average on Balls in Play (BABIP)

What It Is: Like FIP, BABIP is an attempt to measure a pitcher's skill without reference to fielding support. In theory, batted balls within the field of play should be converted into base hits at a certain average rate. If an unusually high percentage of balls fall in for base hits, BABIP places the blame on bad fielding or bad luck, not bad pitching.

What?!: Is it possible for one pitcher to fail largely because he gives up hard line drives within the ballpark? Is it possible for a different pitcher to succeed because he mostly gives up hits through soft contact? The former pitcher could easily give up fewer hits than the latter but would allow such quality hits that he ultimately allows more earned runs. Both quantity and quality matter. In BABIP quality doesn't matter.

HITTING

The Stat: Runs Created (RC)

What It Is: An attempt to calculate a hitter's run contributions both at the plate and on the base paths. There are at least 20 variations on RC, with a typical equation reading $(H + BB - CS + HBP - GIDP) \times (TB + [.26 \times (BB - IBB + HBP)] + [.52 \times (SH + SF + SB)]) / AB + BB + HBP + SH + SF$. Old-line statistics bear their biases, but so do new ones: they often imitate NASA's entrance exam questions.

What?!: As indicated by the sundry variations, the "runs created" associated with any particular player can vary widely based on how different analysts choose to define on-base, advancement, and opportunity elements or how the statisticians choose to place them within various equations. It's as if various speakers use the same "feline" word, only some of them are referring to tabby cats while others are referring to the Siamese breed and yet others are discussing Dr. Evil's hairless little cats with the pointy ears.

The Stat: Offensive Win Percentage (OWP)

What It Is: It estimates how many team wins would be produced by a lineup consisting entirely of one particular player's statistical clones.

What?!: To date we don't possess the know-how needed to produce even one statistical clone and until we reach that lofty goal the OWP scenario will stand out as the most far-fetched of far-fetched hypotheticals.

The Stat: Equivalent Average (EA)

What It Is: To quote *Baseball Prospectus*: "A measure of total offensive value per out, with corrections for league offensive level, home park and team pitching." EA is distilled from this formula, among others: $H + TB + 1.5 (BB + HBP) + SB + SH + SF / AB + BB + HBP + SH + SF + CS + (SB / 3)$.

What?!: In EA, analysts mash up ten numerical terms in order to reach a single (scaled) number, thus raising a conceptual question: how can you complicate your way into simplicity?

FIELDING

The Stat: Zone Rating (ZR)

What It Is: In this stat the playing field is divided into areas of fielding responsibility for the various defenders. A good fielder is defined by an ability to handle batted balls within his assigned "zone." In theory ZR can define fielder range to the minutest degree.

What?!: Again, here we see a clever concept with confusing definitions, mostly because the exact areas of fielder responsibilities can vary based on the batters' handedness (right or left), their hitting tendencies, ballpark conditions, and on-base/out scenarios. There can be many other factors at play. Even wind directions can make important differences in positioning.

Even if the "F/X" zones could be reliably defined they couldn't be reliably applied. There will always be a subjective call in assigning a batted ball to the invisible line dividing a center fielder's zone from a right fielder's zone, for example. A scorer—typically a college kid or an avid amateur—might believe a sharp left-side grounder was in the third baseman's zone while the scorer would've placed the ball in the shortstop's zone. In this manner we might find an "advanced" metric that mostly advances its way into fuzziness.

OVERALL PLAYER NUMBERS

The Stat: Replacement Player stats, including Value over Replacement Player (VORP) and Wins above Replacement Player (WARP)

What It Is: The various stats are all based on the expected output of a "readily available replacement player" who has been obtained "at minimal cost." It's an attempt to create the grand unified numbers that will allow comparisons among all players and for all time.

What ?!: How to identify "readily available replacements" and "minimal costs"? Are we to assume that they become readily available through Minor League call-ups, waivers, or free agency? Perhaps we should contemplate how we might find replacements through trades involving one or more of the 30 clubs within the Majors? Which fictional methods should we deploy before we come to our fictional roster needs?

As questions go on and on all their possible answers grow so contingent as to lose coherence. In practice, talk of "replacement players" is about as useful as "replacement car" talk:

"Hey, buddy, should I buy this Camry?"

"Maybe. I give it four 'replacement car units.'"

"Uh-huh. Four replacement car units. What are they?"

"They're twice as many as two replacement car units but only one-half as many as eight replacement car units, quite naturally."

"Granted, but I have no idea about the term's definition."

"Oh! 'Replacement car units' are produced by a made-up, intricate algorithm involving 13 different ways of buying 19 different cars. If you have two or three hours free I'll happily explain . . . "

"Hey, buddy, should I buy this Camry?"

The Stat: Win Shares (WS)

What It Is: Proponents believe that WS stats apportion credit for regular season team wins according to every on-field contribution from every player. The numbers are derived from dozens of steps, all with their own calculations and assumptions.

What?!: Professor Stephen Hawking once wrote a bestseller outlining advanced astrophysics in less than 200 pages while a 2002 book on WS ran significantly longer. More than three and a half times longer. In this manner "throw the ball/hit the ball/catch the ball" has taken on a complexity more daunting than time-space curvatures, speed-of-light travel, and antimatter. The world still awaits a publication implying that the pastime is more bewildering than the federal tax code.

OVERALL TEAM NUMBERS
The Stat: Pythagorean Score (PS)
What It Is: Bill James, the score's inventor, calculates a team's expected seasonal wins based on the team's total runs scored and total runs allowed. In theory the gap between a team's Pythagorean score and a team's actual win total reveals that the team is either overperforming or underperforming in some way.

What?!: Unfortunately PS predicts little more than the general vicinity of a team's final standings. Clubs can finish with as many as ten wins better than their score would indicate, with new-millennium playoff teams like the Twins, Cardinals, and White Sox overperforming by five games or more.

How did those clubs produce greater results with lesser parts? Was it because they utilized superior managerial moves and, if so, which tactics did they use? Did the overperforming clubs participate in an unusual number of blowout games and, if so, why?

Finally we come to the biggest question of all: why should we guess *what* should add up when we can't understand *why* it should add up?

Intangibility

MYTH #27

"The Little Things"

To appreciate game performances it isn't necessary to watch all the ball games. It would be impossible, anyway.

Firsthand evaluation of players in comparison to their fellow Major Leaguers would require observation of a regular season day that typically features about 135 innings, 4,300 pitches, and nearly 45 hours of game time. That is in any given day, and there are many given days. A six-month regular season adds up to about 21,800 innings, 702,000 pitches, and 6,800 or so hours.

It's hardly possible to observe a fraction of the action of a single day, much less a year, but then again, there's no need for firsthand observation. In baseball there are statistics.

As Professor Dan Brodie once noted, the pastime is "the most statistically perfect game ever invented." Because all plays can be expressed in binary terms like outs or non-outs, they produce clear numbers, and because clear numbers are linked to their authors, they're easily assigned. To contrast this construct to basketball's intertwined scrums is to realize that baseball stats are uniquely lucid.

The prototypical "numbers game" is even more fluent in the way its stats can be utilized. As mentioned in the previous chapter, the math-minded still argue over the details but, in broad strokes, a superior hitter is known for an ability to reach base and hit for extra-base power, while a fine fielder reaches batted balls and puts them away as outs.

If baseball's vast amount of action represents a highly inconvenient problem for would-be watchers, then the game's statistics present a highly convenient solution. The fact that the fans cannot eyeball everything is largely negated by the fact that tangible results are expressed in tangible numbers.

Little Leaguers know this but some assert that statistics must frequently make way for "intangible" factors.

A distrust for stats has merit; some on-field contributions cannot be easily quantified. For instance, some selfless batters make "productive outs" that advance base runners, some savvy fielders hustle to back up relay throws, and other athletes have a special willingness to play through aches and pains. Since there's no easy way to reduce these events into black-and-white figures, there's a role for factors taken in only through firsthand observation.

Unfortunately, statistical skepticism can be taken so far as to make mole-hills into mountains and mountains into Himalayas.

Take our preceding examples involving selfless batters and savvy fielders. Their skills can be helpful and don't easily translate into spreadsheets, true, but "the little things" represent relatively minor contributions. Almost all player value comes through the familiar tasks that are recorded on the backs of baseball cards. If occasional, unquantifiable actions add perhaps a few wins to a playoff club's win total, 90 or 95 wins can be reliably attributed to more easily counted successes. A few wins are not nothing but they are not nearly as important as 90, 95 wins. "The little things that don't show up in the box score" are not nearly as important as the big things that do show up in the box score.

Anyone doubting the relative value of "the little things" might notice that there are uncounted thousands of AAA players—and amateurs, for that matter—who are willing to make all kinds of outs and back up every toss in sight. They may play their hearts out right up to the moment they receive last rites, even, but they won't succeed unless their noble efforts manifest themselves in tangible results like power hitting and shut-down defense. The win column tallies only the ends, not the means, and as John J. McGraw once said, in the end it's about winning.

MYTH #28

"Thinking Outside the Box"

A great physicist once said that "prediction is difficult, especially about the future."* Dr. Niels Bohr would have understood baseball statistics.

---

*The quotation has often been misattributed to Yogi Berra but reliable sources link it to Bohr. It must have been the first and last time Yogi was closely associated with a Nobel Prize laureate.

The pastime's numbers are, by their nature, self-contained and backward-looking assessments, but game-time decisions are better made through more holistic and forward-thinking methods.

For instance, a slugger is coming up to bat, and the opposing manager has the option of bringing in a lefty reliever. The stat sheet says that the batter's on-base percentage is 50 points lower against lefties and that he's gone a measly 2 for 11 in previous at-bats against the opposition's bullpen guy. To go by nothing but the past, we can expect the reliever to win in their next matchup.

The numbers that seem to compel such a clear-cut prediction do not reveal all relevant factors at work, however. Our batter may have retooled his swing in the weeks before his next matchup against the reliever, for example, or the matchup might occur on a rain-slicked infield that neutralizes the reliever's groundball pitches. The new factors can be relatively subtle or temporary but, nonetheless, there can be an impact in the here and now.

Unquantifiable elements can make an impact. Prediction can be difficult but that doesn't mean that thinking should be entirely surrendered to feeling.

Those seeking to contradict past numbers (to "go outside the box") must still use facts, even if they involve very close observations. Casey Stengel was a master of such managerial tactics, as he would make seemingly inexplicable moves based on factors as discrete as a home plate umpire's idiosyncratic strike zone or an opponent's body language. Stengel's choices didn't necessarily rely on stats but were still within the realm of verifiable insights and testable causes and effects. Casey remained in that box.

The heavy reliance on more ill-defined factors, though, can lead to more shaky results. However expressed—as gut feelings, instincts, or hunches—such bases can easily drift into whatever whims might rule the moment, whether the whims lead into unnecessary panics or unfounded wishes. When an "outside the box" decision comes down to free-floating opinion, the intangibles can prove to be nonexistent.

A Leading Question, or "Presence," "Will," "Gallantry," and "Magic"

On every ball club there are emotional leaders.

They contribute so much. Through them inspiration intermingles with per-spiration, motivation with desperation, solemnity with levity, respect with responsibility. They are so special that they have their own titles: we call them "coaches."

Beyond the coaches, there are other leaders. In them ballplayers find relax-ation without laxity, toughness without roughness, and a "we" not "me." A sense of benevolence is generated. They are special, too, and carry their own titles: they are "managers."

Apart from the coaches and managers who are expected to be leaders, how-ever, there are few emotive roles left over for ballplayers.

To the extent that some ballplayers can become emotional leaders, they mostly avoid negative qualities. Recognizable leaders cannot be as moody as Albert Belle or as troubled as Milton Bradley. Would-be leaders don't form cliques, blame teammates, antagonize umpires, or taunt opponents. Their names shouldn't appear on police blotters or terrorist watch lists. "Leading" candidates shouldn't do bad things, in short.

A player who avoids severe disruption while providing on-field production can stand out as "a leader by example" but "a leader by example" isn't an emo-tional leader. The latter calls for ballplayers to lead mostly (or entirely) through force of personality, and such beings do not dwell among us. That is to say, sportswriters are far too imaginative when they dutifully claim that flannel-clad Churchills deliver "presence," "will," "gallantry," "magic," et cetera.

Such pixie dust isn't credible, first, because its ostensible possessors always deny its existence. Whenever veterans like Chipper Jones or Roy Halladay are asked about their leadership roles, for example, they frequently answer with well-tested clichés about giving full effort and sometimes mention that they are leading the way to plentiful homers and skimpy ERAs. At some point a captain may refer to himself as a leader by example but at no point does he treat himself as an auxiliary coach or carry himself as if his innate charm "makes everyone around him better."

Many commentators take such denials as backhanded confirmations—"a-ha, leadership is too ethereal as to be expressed in mere words."

If emotional leadership was real we would see all sorts of phenomena. Someone would provide step-by-step explanations on the ways amiable dinner outings transform mediocrities into stars. General managers might describe exactly why it's all right that members of their clubhouse are highly overpaid in relation to their actual, on-field performance. Second- and third-line players would be seen as make-or-break influences rather than useful supplements. Commentators might prove how chemistry creates winning and that winning does not create chemistry. There would be all sorts of coherent explanations why great players don't necessarily establish themselves by great play. These things never happen.

No, Major Leaguers deny emotional leadership because the notion is, in practice, an insult. Athletes who run actively attempting to gin up good vibrations end up slighting the leadership position of their coaches or end up depleting mental resources better devoted to their own performances. Would-be leaders would also remember that even the Major Leaguers established themselves many years before. When they struggle, they need only look into mirrors to find presence, will, gallantry, and magic.

Clutched

"Clutch Situations Exist"

*Clutch Hitting and Strong Pitching Are Keys
to First-Place Padres's Success.*

—NATHANIEL UY, Associated Press, May 5, 2010

There are such things as clutch hits.

—TOM VERDUCCI, "Does Clutch Hitting Truly Exist?,"
Sports Illustrated, April 5, 2004

A confession: I've never understood "clutch" situations.

I do know that there is a belief that some moments are more important than others in deciding a baseball game. The parameters can vary a tad but the clutch consensus says:

- The late innings of a ball game are more important than the early ones.
- At-bats with runners in scoring position are more important than at-bats with the bases empty or with a runner on first base.
- At-bats in close ball games are more important than at-bats during blowouts.
- Late-season ball games are more important than early season contests.

I hear that clutch numbers involve extra contributions in the late innings, with guys on base, in close games, and in September playoff runs. I hear it but I don't understand it.

One of the interesting aspects of the game is in the way that any given moment might be a turning point. This is a main source of game surprises, and the clutch notion, by implying that many situations aren't so important, seems nonsensical.

The specifics of the crunch-time concept seem inherently flawed, too, and in ways that make sense to anyone who knows a foul line from a checkout line:

- Early innings or middle innings may be more important than the latter ones because early leads tend to demoralize opposing pitchers, pressure hitters, and deplete bullpens. Managers have maneuvered to gain initial scores for at least a century.
- Since the deciding margin in most ball games comes through one or two multi-run innings, at-bats with the bases empty can be as important as at-bats with the bases occupied. The presence of a base runner doubles the run-scoring value of a follow-up homer and in any case, it's impossible to clear the bases if there's no one on base.
- At-bats during games with big run differentials can be just as important as those with close games. This is especially relevant in today's relatively high-scoring times, when few leads are completely safe.
- Like early inning scores, early season wins are crucial in the way that they can deny realistic opportunities for opponent comebacks. "Pennants can be won or lost in April," some say.

To me, the main reason many still hold on to the clutch concept is because certain baseball moments are inherently more dramatic and, therefore, more memorable than others. It's very tempting to take a further, shakier step by concluding that such moments deliver an impact far beyond their true importance.

To see how critics tend to overlook worthy contributions while focusing on more dramatic spots, consider the following scenarios:

- A run-scoring hit in the middle innings may make the all-important difference in a one-run game, even if its importance is obscured by the hard-fought innings that followed. In Game Seven of the 2001 World Series, for example, Danny Bautista drove in a run that eventually proved to be the winning differential in the game, but it came at a point when no one knew if the later action would represent a pitcher's duel or a slugfest; it was Luis Gonzalez's ninth-inning hit that was remembered, if only because its impact was obvious in the moment.

• The runners who get on base in front of a home run hitter may represent the tying or winning runs in a ball game, even if contributions are easily lost in the luster of a successive shot. That's what happened in Game Six of the 1993 World Series; few remember how Rickey Henderson walked and Paul Molitor singled early in the ninth inning, but everyone remembered how Joe Carter cleared the bases with a game-winning homer. The Henderson base-on balls and the Molitor single tripled the value of the later home run—what would have been a solo shot became a three-run clout—but only Carter's singular drive took the clutch label.

• For Game Seven of the 1960 World Series, only the most die-hard fans remember that Rocky Nelson, Bill Virdon, Dick Groat, Roberto Clemente, and Hal Smith drove in the runs that the Pirates eventually needed to overcome the Yankees's nine runs. After Bill Mazeroski's walk-off homer won all the headlines, however, it was "Rocky, Bill, Dick, Roberto, and Hal who?"

• Many remember that the 1949 pennant race between the Yanks and Red Sox wasn't settled until the last game of the season. That was true, but the pennant's single-game margin was made possible by the 27-21 Yankee record in one-run games over the preceding months. The finale's fame was, again, in the theatrical angle, in the way that it represented New York's one last challenge.

In sum, the clutch notion bypasses key moments in favor of showy moments. There is a big difference between the two.

MYTH #31

"Clutch Players Exist"

Some players thrive on pressure situations, some can't deal with them.

—MURRAY CHASS, "Pampered Pitchers and Their Enablers,"
MurrayChass.com, March 6, 2011

Jack Clark: Clutch Hitter for Life.

—ANNA MCDONALD, *The Hardball Times*, August 10, 2010

An everyday person would never thrive in the rigors of baseball. It would be impossible.

Forget the unrelenting physical demands of the game or its many distractions. Ignore how every on-field move can be witnessed by tens of thousands of screaming spectators, how every quotation can be captured by outlets from Boston to Tokyo, and how every move might be scrutinized by tens of millions. Leave all that off to one side.

The greatest pressure in the sport may be in the way it demands that athletes constantly apply themselves through every game, all with the certain knowledge that most any pitch might turn the tide in a ball game, any game might turn around a season, and any season might define a career.

An Ordinary Joe couldn't easily handle such constant demands. He might give in during an early at-bat, just so he can lock in when there are men on base. Maybe he would take it easy until the late innings or slack off until the final weeks of a very long season.

It would be tempting for ordinary athletes to try to coast in these ways, but that's why ordinary athletes are ordinary. The extraordinary few who reach the Major League level know that a save-your-strength strategy can never work.

Professionals realize that the difference between a 3.00 ERA champion and a more run-of-the-mill 4.00 ERA pitcher can come down to a single (home run) mistake for about every 140 pitches thrown. They are certain that the difference between a .333 batting champion and a mediocre .293 average is an additional hit or so per week, assuming 600 at-bats on the season. They also comprehend the fact that the difference between an above-average outfielder (.990 fielding percentage) and a more ordinary defender (.980) is in a single error for every 100 putouts and assists.

With those tissue-thin differences separating stardom from mediocrity, players have little choice but to give their best whether it's the fourth inning or the fourteenth, whether the bases are empty or loaded, whether the score is 10–0 or 0–0, or whether their team is in first place or last place.

In the way that pastime excellence is defined by sustained effort, any clutch cliché can be turned on its ear. For those involved, the game is always on the line, all moments are defining moments, the pressure is always on, their backs are always to the wall, et cetera.

The insistence on steady effort is probably what essayist John Updike had in mind when he wrote that "baseball's interest can be maintained not by the occasional heroics that sportswriters feed upon but by players who always care; who care, that is to say, about themselves and their art." During interviews, star players invoke the word "consistency" like a mantra and never say that they are reaching for occasional heroics "when it matters most." It may be wise to credit them by their own self-understanding.

Those who claim that intangibles are unfairly overlooked may well turn reality upside down. If anything, nonquantifiable factors are probably *overemphasized* by the media, since those factors can hint at a personal zeal or bravado that imparts human-interest angles to otherwise humdrum stories. Executives are ever eager to affirm the storytelling, if only to justify player salaries that are not nearly justified by numbers alone. Everyone can read box scores but only a select few are granted the insider access needed to wax rhapsodic about "the stuff that no one talks about," so insiders constantly talk up the stuff that no one talks about.

MYTH #32

A Tiny Problem with the Clutch

Dozens of statistical studies, starting with Richard D. Cramer's groundbreaking work, have backed the commonsense view that individual ballplayers succeed in "ordinary" situations at about the same level they succeed in "high-leverage" situations; the extra edge attributed to "clutch" players can be explained by random variation.

Then why the persistent belief in clutch hitters? As described in the preceding chapter, the belief can be based on a misunderstanding of the sustained effort needed to succeed in the Majors. In addition, the concept seems to linger because it usually encompasses relatively small data samples.

About two-thirds of all at-bats come in the first six innings and about three-quarters of all at-bats take place without men in scoring position. As many as 525 out of 600 at-bats in a season come up in situations where a ball game isn't close in the late innings, and by the time September rolls around about five-sixths of the season is already in the books.

Of course, all the above assume perfect opportunities in a far-from-perfect world. Depending on their places in the lineup and the on-base abilities of preceding batters, some players may receive significantly fewer opportunities to hit with men on base and pitchers may issue intentional or semi-intentional walks to especially dangerous batters. Those playing on second-division clubs are less likely to play in close games throughout the year and in the late season, might not play in any meaningful games. It's always possible to lose at-bats through random injuries.

In whatever scenario, "defining moments" are so relatively infrequent as to become relatively unimportant. By the time those rare clutch moments come around, there have been many other opportunities to determine ball games and seasons, and in them, truly great players put in the contributions needed to produce winners.

MYTH #33

Another Tiny Problem with the Clutch

The previous chapter described how the clutch concept can put an overemphasis on relatively small data samples and how big moments can be emphasized to the detriment of the many other moments that make up a season. The relatively small samples involved can be deceiving for another reason—they can easily produce outliers.

Over a relatively small slice of the season Player A's numbers might be noticeably greater than they are in other situations while Player B's numbers might be noticeably lower. When a given portion of the season happens to coincide with clutch situations, it's not hard to conclude that Player A warms up in the spotlight while Player B freezes.

The conclusion isn't without a certain degree of validity. Baseball is a strange game in that strange things can happen over clutch situations that amount to a few days or weeks. Manny Alexander can put up better numbers than Manny Ramirez owing to whatever fleeting factors allow certain players to shine; maybe Alexander is playing over his head for a little while by dinking a few more hits into the defensive gaps, facing weaker pitchers, or playing on fully healthy legs.

In whatever ways they come about, however, short-term flukes eventually trend back to the results that can be repeated over a 162-game season or a years-long career. Coincidences give way to causes and when they do, clutch results disappear.

MYTH #34

Oh Captain, My Captain! (Sigh)

The mainstream media pundits believe in the clutch and they believe in the legend of Derek Sanderson Jeter.

Newsday has hailed him as "the greatest clutch player ever." The official *Yankeeography* view says, "No one thrives on the big stage more than Derek Jeter."

In 2011 *The Sporting News* represented how "guts are what define his longevity, his consistency and, especially, his greatness when the moments and the spotlights are at their brightest." *Sports Illustrated* gave the world a worshipful piece entitled "Mr. Clutch." One could wallpaper the Empire State Building with that kind of copy; if anyone alive today is a clutch player, it's Derek Jeter.

The lionization seems to stem, firstly, from D. J.'s excellence as a hitter. Over the first 16 full seasons of his career, Jeter established himself among the best offensive shortstops of all time. In addition, he's durable and is an above-average runner. Barring some kind of unforeseeable scandal involving a dog-fighting ring, Jeter will be named a first-ballot Hall of Famer.

Jeter is an excellent hitter but, in the case of the clutch, excellence isn't enough; if excellence was enough it would just be called "excellence." No, the clutch sees one *doing even better than usual* in scenarios involving late innings, runners in scoring position, close ball games, and late-season contests. Many seem to believe that Jeter somehow possesses the higher consciousness necessary to elevate himself in select situations.

In putting Mr. Clutch to the test, we can first examine late-game situations. Due to the tireless efforts of Sean Forman and Baseball-Reference.com, we have the data needed to contrast Jeter's on-base percentage, slugging (SLG), and on-base plus slugging in various innings:

	OBP	SLG	OPS
Innings 1–3	.383	.469	.852
Innings 4–6	.394	.466	.860
Innings 7–9	.368	.405	.773

The Derek Jeter Appreciation Society can only hope that late-inning at-bats are not the occasions when the great players must step up, as their main man actually steps down in such situations. He is still a very good batter in innings seven through nine—as usual, his numbers are high—but Jeter doesn't reach a higher level in the late going.

On the next clutch criterion, the one related to at-bats with runners in scoring position, it's much the same story:

	OBP	SLG	OPS
Without runners in scoring pos.	.383	.412	.795
Runners in scoring pos.	.395	.424	.818

Jeter is good in prime RBI opportunities, by the equivalent of a few extra base hits for every 162 games played, but the improvement is within what might be expected through random variation.

Moving on, we can look at the D. J. at-bats in all situations in contrast to those situations when his club is either tied or within a couple runs after the sixth inning:

	OBP	SLG	OPS
Normal (not tied or late and close)	.384	.449	.832
Tied	.380	.458	.837
Late and close	.384	.412	.796

To be as generous, it's a wash. While D. J.'s on-base performance is slightly better in tie ball games his slugging takes a noticeable drop-off in late and close situations.

Last, we can contrast Jeter's overall numbers to his performance in late-season contests:

	OBP	SLG	OPS
All other months	.379	.448	.827
September	.401	.461	.862

Well, give him that one—Jeet does pick it up in September, when the leaves can start falling and the audiences start growing. It picks up only a few extra bases over what might be expected from other months, though a smallish improvement is there.

In sum, Derek Jeter neither slumps nor shines in prototypical clutch situations. If one is to include the playoffs in the analysis, it's much the same mixed bag.

Here's how D. J.'s regular season numbers compared to his postseason stats in terms of OBP, slugging, and OPS through 2011:

	OBP	SLG	OPS
Regular season	.383	.449	.832
Playoffs	.374	.465	.839

In keeping with a couple precedents, Jeter improved by a smidge in clutch-y postseasons. Breaking down those playoff numbers a bit further, we can see that Jeter's seemingly unflappable nature can suddenly become very flappable.

On the positive side, there were times that Jeter has been just as good as advertised. During the American League Championship Series (ALCS) of 1996, for instance, Jeter made his case as the most outstanding hitter on the field and he had every right to win the Most Valuable Player (MVP) trophy for his terrific (9 for 22) line in the 2000 World Series, too.

On the negative side, however, there were times when Jeter's gone from cool to ice-cold. In the 1998 American League Division Series (ALDS), the 2001 ALCS, and the 2007 ALDS, for example, Jeter was among the worst hitters in either lineup. The numbers definitely didn't display evidence of a "spectacular talent for doing the right thing at the right time."

The only constant in Jeter's playoff numbers has been the inconsistency. He has had years (1996, 2000, 2001) when a stepping-up series alternated with a stepping-down series in the same year, plus occasions (1997/1998) when a good year has been followed by a bad one. In the last seven years when Yankees won pennants, their captain had only three seasons when he didn't flop in at least one series along the way.

The more you look at Jeter's October performances, the more you realize that they don't surpass his regular-season norms and haven't been especially consistent. The only real question left is why so many still seem so intent on hanging on to the "big stage" notion.

In all probability, on-field reputation is closely linked to off-field reputation. Jeter is a genuinely nice guy, by all reports. He signs autographs, shakes hands, and gives speeches. His Turn 2 Foundation is among the most generous charities in sports and his beaming parents are never far from view. Bland but reassuring postgame comments are received by a media clique that is almost cultish in its devotion. He was a more-than-capable *Saturday Night Live* host.

Taken in totality it's easy to believe that a consistently nice fellow is a consistently unique player in some way or another.

If a positive persona has contributed to Jeter's clutch image, good luck may have played an even more important role. D. J. played his first full season just when the Yankees assembled enough talent to win the team's first championship in over a decade, in 1996, then he rode along on a 14-2 playoff series run over the next six years. After that 1996–2001 period, Jeter became the unassailable symbol of success—when he did well the Yankees won and when he didn't do well, heck, the Yankees still won. It was no great leap to assume that he was 6'3" worth of game change at shortstop, which directly contributed to a cascade of clichés about his "coming through when it mattered most" and so on.

By now, somehow, everyone is so invested in the clutch notion that it can be awkward to point out its contradictions. Having seen the 14-2 run, it's inconvenient to note that Jeter's teams staggered through a 3-6 playoff series record in the years afterward. Still comfortable with the winner tag, few were eager to point out that Jeter has also played in the most *losing* playoff games of all time. His lead in career postseason hits is a well-known achievement, so it can be unsettling to note that #2 is also #1 for October strikeouts.

There is an ease in emphasizing Jeter's poetic turns over his more prosaic moments. Fans interpret the "Jeffrey Maier homer" as a semi-comedic episode on the march to the 1996 championship, not a blatant umpiring mistake. It's easy to remember "the flip" play that helped win the 2001 ALDS, but difficult to remember that Jeter's extraordinary effort only paid off because of his opponent's lackadaisical amble toward home plate. Likewise there was a distinction in D. J.'s hitting the first official homer in the month of November, but no great distinction in his going 4-for-27 as the Yanks lost that same series.

So many enjoy storylines about "the greatest clutch player ever." So many still believe in the legend.

Moneyball

"*Moneyball* Is about On-Base Percentage, Stolen Bases, College Pitchers, Et Cetera"

Another Moneyball *notion is the extreme emphasis on stats,
particularly walks, on-base percentage and home runs,
which were sold as keys to success.*

—JON HEYMAN, "Beyond *Moneyball,*" SportsIllustrated.com,
September 11, 2006

On-base percentage, the gold standard of Beane's player evaluation . . .

—MURRAY CHASS, "When *Moneyball* No Longer Pays Off,"
New York Times, February 7, 2006

A Tale of Two Cities was not a mere travelogue involving Paris and London. Sophomore term papers are misguided when they reduce *Hamlet* to a depressed Dane with mommy issues. On its most basic level *Moby Dick* is a dire warning against whale-watching, but Melville's novel represents much more.

With great works of literature, one must go well beyond surface to find substance. And so it was with *Moneyball.*

At first glance, the Michael Lewis book focuses on Billy Beane's tactics in assembling a low-budget, high-performance winner with the Oakland Athletics in the 2002 season.

Readers were told that the general manager (GM) downplayed the value of established closers. He valued hitters who could reach base through walks.

Beane didn't put much weight on fielding or stolen base totals. The exec favored college players in the amateur draft and passed on big-name free agents.

That was an accurate snapshot of Beane and the Athletics in one season, but it would be a mistake to see such style as the book's substance.

As Lewis explained, the GM wasn't fascinating so much for what he did but for how he worked. The front office's reliance on certain stats and players were timely responses to the ways that their rivals undervalued certain outputs and overvalued certain others; not unlike a Wall Street investor, Beane found bargains by approaching the market in a different way.

Beane's disdain for convention was so great, in fact, that it soon extended to the very tactics chronicled in *Moneyball*. In the wake of the bestseller an increasing number of ball clubs imitated Beane's style, leading them to bid some players beyond Oakland's modest means. In response, Beane found ways to rearrange his methods:

After nearly a decade of acquiring primary relievers exclusively through trades, Beane chose to draft Huston Street in 2004 and then quickly installed him as a lights-out closer.

The organization's strict methods regarding bases-on-balls were quietly dropped a few years later.

The 2002 A's finished tenth in league double plays and eighth in errors. Within five years, the team had significantly boosted its defense, with marked improvements in double plays and errors (16 percent changes in each).

Oakland went from rock-bottom stolen base totals (46 in 2002) to a more respectable sum in 2006 (61) and by 2009, they had Rajai Davis stealing 41 bases on the year.

When rival teams started drafting more and more college players in the first round, Beane began using early draft picks for high-schoolers like Vin Mazzaro and Jared Lansford.

After avoiding prominent free agents in the early 2000s, the club picked up aging-but-valuable sluggers like Frank Thomas and Mike Piazza in 2006 and 2007.

In every one of those instances, what looked like inconsistency wasn't inconsistent. In one well-chronicled season, Beane favored certain approaches toward innovation and then, as the times changed, he found other means toward the same end.

MYTH #36

"*Moneyball* Is about Numbers"

Moneyball *focused on statistical analysis and how it is changing the game.*

—MICHAEL PATRICK NELSON, "Two for the Books,"
Long Island Press, March 9, 2006

At the core of the Moneyball *philosophy promoted by Beane and his disciples is continuous statistical analysis designed to reveal a player's worth.*

—STEVE FAINARU, "White Sox Way Is to Win,"
Washington Post, March 5, 2006

Billy Beane hasn't earned an academic degree in mathematics and doesn't enjoy regression analyses. In his spare time, he listens to the Ramones and avoids calculators.

Beane has never claimed to be an innovator in statistical analysis. For the majority of his adult life he generated stats rather than studying them. Beane was unaware of *The Bill James Historical Baseball Abstract* until the landmark stat book had been widely circulated for a decade and a half.

Beane wasn't the first Athletics general manger to utilize more objective stats. His predecessor, Sandy Alderson, introduced Beane to the concepts when the younger man was first starting out as a scout.

Some might imagine that Beane had a comprehensive reliance on statistical scouting. They would be mistaken. In fact, he used conventional scouting methods to draft mainstay pitchers like Tim Hudson and Mark Mulder (and then turned them over to longtime coach Rick Peterson). No, Billy Beane's success was based less on statistical acumen than managerial masteries.

Beane didn't have a fondness for algorithms but was crafty enough to recognize the ways that stats could clarify talent evaluations. He wasn't a trailblazer but was secure enough to enlist young assistants familiar with contemporary ideas. He didn't possess ultra-exclusive databases but was ambitious enough to take full advantage of the numbers that were at his disposal.

Beane displayed other sharp judgments unrelated to numbers. He asked his key evaluators simple, if unexpected, questions. ("If he's that good of a hitter, why doesn't he hit better?") He remained skeptical of tradition for its own sake but welcomed new methods. Never fearful of personal clashes, he nonetheless retained key personnel. Optimism and long hours were staples within the front office. As biographer Michael Lewis has conceded, Beane's chair-tossing tantrums were attention grabbing but relatively rare.

To clearly perceive Beane's managerial ability, contrast his fate to those who faltered since *Moneyball* was published in 2003:

- "Stat Gurus": The *Moneyball* movement paved the way for big league organizations to hire stat-heads like Voros McCracken and Ron Shandler, but professional discontent soon pushed them from front offices to home offices.
- Meanwhile, Beane has held the same job since 1997, back when television was recorded on VHS, most pictures were taken on film, and Internet sites were accessed from dial-up connections.
- Paul DePodesta: Beane's able assistant was hired as a big-budget general manager in Los Angeles but frequently clashed with an antagonistic media and a lost-in-space ownership. "DePo" was fired from the Dodgers after two seasons and perhaps an ulcer or two.
- Meanwhile, Beane turned down all offers to leave from his low-pressure setup in Oakland. He was eventually granted a lucrative stake in team ownership.
- J. P. Ricciardi: After Beane's bargain-seeking lieutenant was hired by the Blue Jays in 2001, Toronto soon splurged on big-ticket free agents like A. J. Burnett and B. J. Ryan, who signed deals soaking up about

$20 million per year. J. P., A. J., and B. J. were all gone within a few years.

- Meanwhile, Beane's clubs continued to hew to no-frills, initials-free methods in averaging over 90 wins per year from 2000 through 2008.

In the end, Billy Beane simply proved himself more flexible, affable, and disciplined than others. He wasn't a numbers man but a baseball man.

The October Revolution

"The Wild Card System Diminishes the Regular Season" (Pt. 1)

The wild card takes a toll on the import attached to the six months of baseball we call the regular season.

—GARY THORNE, "Baseball's Regular Season Becoming Less and Less Significant," *USA Today*, September 7, 2006

We have to keep the integrity of the regular season. Fans should want the best baseball teams playing in the World Series.

—BOB NIGHTENGALE, "Format Blurs the Picture," *USA Today*, October 7, 2009

When Major League Baseball introduced the wild card playoff format in 1995, the move was met with some skepticism. The game had just been dragged through an ugly labor war in the previous year, so it was easy to believe that a dysfunctional leadership was finding new ways into dysfunction.

One of the most understandable complaints was that the wild card would devalue the regular season. The way the critics saw it, doubling the number of qualifiers (from four teams to eight) inevitably put less emphasis on the 162 games that came before October. While pre-1995 teams had no choice but to earn their way into division crowns through kill-or-be-killed races, the new-era teams would face the temptation to relax their way into second-place consolation slots.

In the years since its unveiling, however, the new playoff structure established itself as a great improvement. Not only did the wild card idea fail to mess up the game, but it answered airy fears with solid achievements.

The wild card, first, provided contenders with more hope. The alignment in place from 1969 to 1993 saw an average of only eight teams within a doable five games of a playoff spot on September 1. In years like 1976 and 1986, there were no substantial playoff races at all because the division leaders ran away from the field. Virtually all MLB teams were playing less-than-meaningful late-season games, either because they had built up unassailable leads or because they had fallen behind unassailable leads.

In the first ten full seasons of the October Revolution, however, the increased number of playoff slots led to an increased number of contending teams. The 1996 to 2005 era saw about 13 teams per year with five games of a playoff slot on September 1. As many as 18 teams were involved in a given year, and on average, the number of serious September clubs increased by 63 percent.

Under the old system the many noncontenders often ran up a white flag by promoting scrubs and trading off frontline players. In extreme situations, second-division teams would semi-intentionally tank the season in order to improve in future draft positioning. These were regrettable, but understandable, responses to weak standings.

The wild card changed those anticompetitive impulses, however. Thanks to the new system's possibilities, many underdogs attempted to regroup in time for some of the most dramatic games of the late season.

To see an example of the new incentives at work, consider how the wild card slot motivated the 2001 Athletics. In late June of that year, Oakland was trudging along with a 38-41 record, even as their division rivals were cruising to a 116-win campaign. Under the old system they would've been "overwhelming underdogs," in Yogi Berra's words. Oakland's lack of realistic playoff hopes would've led it to passively play out the string over the following months.

The 2001 A's were playing under the new format, however, and the system's additional hope changed everything. The *Moneyball*-inspired front office decided on a full-season, all-hands-on-deck push to take the wild card position and, with the aid of late-coming luck, good health, and key player streaks, the team got hot enough to win 102 games.

The Athletics weren't alone in their wild card pushes. In virtually every year, teams chasing wild card slots made big news; the also-rans found reason to become me-toos. The 2007 Rockies, for example, reached the playoffs through a weeks-long comeback. The Marlins of 2003 were in last place as late as June 18 but persevered long enough to win a wild card and, in time, a world championship. During the postgame celebration, Andy Fox said, "We're just a great example of the importance of never giving up. When a team has talent and starts believing in itself, it's amazing what can happen."

Sheer persistence played a role, as did attention-grabbing trades. The 2004 Astros, for instance, acquired Carlos Beltran en route to a wild card berth and the franchise's first-ever playoff series win. In 2008 C. C. Sabathia was the centerpiece of a trade that carried the Brewers into October play for the first time in more than 20 years. Time and again, revamped rosters shook up league standings and fan expectations.

Little League coaches are known to say "don't give up" and "always look to improve." As it turns out, these can be keys for both players and teams. Because the wild card system gave teams reasons to hold on and to improve, the system brought a new excitement to the game.

MYTH #38

"The Wild Card System Diminishes the Regular Season" (Pt. 2)

"The wild card format has diminished and disrespected the importance of the regular season," says Bob Costas.

—MIKE DODD, "Wild Card Turns Ten," *USA Today*, October 5, 2004

The prelude has always been more important than the playoffs.

Among the big three team sports, the national pastime has always placed the most importance on the regular season, with any team's regular season lasting at least eight times longer than its postseason schedule. In contrast, a pro football team's regular season can be only four times longer than its playoff run while any team's NBA regular season schedule can be little more than twice as long as its playoff run. Through 2011 the Majors also allowed a smaller percentage of playoff qualifiers (27 percent) than either the NFL (38 percent) or the NBA (a ridiculous 53 percent).

With the use of the wild card system, baseball still stands alone in both the proportion and importance attached to its regular season. Through the wild cards, the regular season has actually enhanced the importance attached to its 162-game slate.

Under the previous playoff alignment, the one in place from 1969 to 1993, it was common for the team with the second-best regular season record in the league to be denied shots only because it happened to play in the same division as a powerhouse team. In fact, this injustice happened in most every year (18 times in the 24 non-strike seasons). At the extremes, in years like 1980 and 1993, even 100- and 103-win teams were left on the outside looking in.

On the other side, the old system had relatively weak teams sneaking into the postseason solely because they happened to play in relatively feeble divisions. In years like 1987 and 1973, for instance, teams took their division with 85- and 82-win records that would've qualified for *fifth* place in the stronger division.

The previous playoff system was unfair in the way that team accomplishments were oft overruled by arbitrary divisional groupings. It was as if two equal students applied to the same college and one candidate was rejected due to nothing more than their middle initial.

The new wild card format de-emphasized those divisional groupings and, in the process, enhanced fairness. Through 2011 all ball clubs that finished with the best, second-best, or third-best league records were almost always granted playoff slots, while markedly less-accomplished finishers were almost always denied entries. By effectively recognizing team accomplishments and punishing team failures, the wild card system elevated the regular season.

MYTH #39

"The Wild Cards Are Mediocre"

By definition, any team that isn't the best of a subdivision of the whole can't then be the best of the whole.

—"Questions With Lee Sinins," WasWatching.com, April 2, 2012

The wild card means more mediocre teams are making the playoffs.

—MARK ZUCKERMAN, "A Major Downside to Parity," *Washington Times*, September 1, 2008

When you let more teams into the playoffs you must lessen the distinction involved, too. The critics said that when the Majors introduced the wild card system back in 1995, and the critics were correct. Kinda.

There has, indeed, been a drop-off in regular season records of playoff teams, but it was a very slight drop-off. Under the divisional arrangement used from 1969 to 1993, playoff clubs averaged 96 regular season wins in full (162-game) seasons while the wild card system of 1995 to 2006 produced qualifiers with an average of 95 wins in full seasons.

The one-game decline in the regular season average represented six-tenths of one percent of the total schedule. Even at that, the wild card–era teams averaged win totals greater than those achieved by old-style champions like the 1990 Reds (91 wins), 1987 Twins (87 wins), and 1974 Athletics (90 wins). With this in mind, Professor Andrew Zimbalist may have overstated a warning about the new era's "muddle of mediocrity."

The wild card–era teams were actually more impressive than the previous system's playoff teams because the wild cards played against more contenders in important September games.

To see how that worked out in practice, consider the 2003 Red Sox. By August 11, with about three-quarters of the season finished, the 2003 Sox were in second place in the AL East with a 68-50 record, three games behind the first-place Yankees. Under the old (two-division) setup, the Sox would have only faced playoff hopefuls in New York, Oakland, and Seattle over the remaining seven weeks. Every other club in the league would have been eight or more games away from an available playoff spot, so they had no incentive to act as anything more than spoilers.

As it was, however, the 2003 Sox were playing under the new wild card format, which allowed teams like the Athletics, Royals, White Sox, and Twins realistic shots at the playoffs. They were close enough to playoffs that they gave their very best in the games against Boston. When the Red Sox made it into October that year, it was because they won hard fights against multiple, intense competitors.

The wild card system placed good-to-great teams into more competitive regular seasons. The system put more fizz in the champagne, more excitement in baseball.

MYTH #40

"Wild Cards Win Because Anything Can Happen in a Short Series"

Because a short series is so unpredictable we've seen wild card teams advance over much better teams.

—JOE AIELLO, "Sweet Spot," ESPN.com, February 2, 2011

As the adage goes, anything can happen in a short series

—MARTIN B. SCHMIDT, "When It Comes to the World Series, Luck Conquers All," *New York Times*, November 5, 2006

To this day, most baseball writers still believe the teams with the superior regular-season records are superior teams, end of sentence, period. Division winners, by definition, prove themselves through the 162-game season, so when they lose to wild card teams, it's easy to say that the best team doesn't always win.

There is an appeal to the notion. One of the things that makes baseball so compelling is that a less talented team *can* beat its opponents with the right combination of slumps and streaks or extrinsic factors like injuries, weather, and lucky hops. Random luck can determine a few games, and if those few games happen to arrive in October it's possible for lesser teams to advance once in a rare while.

The possibility exists but doesn't match the wild card results.

First off, wild card teams have seen success far more often than once in a rare while. In their first 13 years, from 1995 to 2007, wild cards won on a consistent basis:

	APPEARANCES	WINS	WINNING %
Division Series	25	15	.600
League Championship Series	15	9	.600
World Series	8	4	.500
Overall	48	28	.583

Despite facing division winners that usually benefited from more rested rosters and more set rotations, the wild cards forged winning records in every playoff round.

On the opposite side, division titles didn't count for much. In the 12 postseasons from 1995 to 2006, only one team (the 1998 Yankees) won a championship in the year they boasted the best regular season record in their league. Regular-season powerhouses like the 2001 Mariners (116 wins) and 2004 Cardinals (105 wins), among others, faltered against teams with lesser regular season win totals. In years like 1995, 2003, and 2006, division winners lost to opponents with ten fewer regular season wins.

Both the wild card successes and the non–wild card non-successes must've been fairly curious developments to those who regarded wild cards as less than fully legitimate. These weren't results encompassing a few contests or a few days but many series and many years. It seems wildly improbable that a random "anything" can favor one side so often. No one group stays lucky for 13 straight years.

The more you look at it, the harder it is to see isolated aberrations and the easier it is to perceive an integrated pattern.

The wild card teams apparently found effective ways to go from early season inferiority to autumnal superiority. Maybe their younger players matured and their older players rejuvenated; perhaps their front offices found new blood or cleared out deadwood. Possibly the wild cards were so well prepared for play-off pressures because they had already steeled themselves under the pressures involved in earning wild card berths.

One way or the other, we might look for more than a crapshoot playoffs. We might give due credit to the "inferior" wild cards who prove themselves so often and repeat a simple conclusion: the inferior teams are the ones who pack their bags in the early going and the superior teams are the ones who hoist their hardware at the end. It's the winners who win.

The Drug Problem

Bad Chemistry

"Steroids Make Players Better"

My biggest problem, and I'm so sick of hearing it, is that steroids don't help you hit. That's the most bald-faced lie ever.

—TOM VERDUCCI, "From Games to Gaming, Schilling On, Well,
Pretty Much Everything," SportsIllustrated.com, January 31, 2012,
quoting former player Curt Schilling

Steroid users gained an unfair competitive advantage.

—KEN ROSENTHAL, "McGwire Thankful in Giving Back to Baseball,"
Fox Sports, March 31, 2012

Athletes are practical people. They go with what works. Many athletes take steroids because, for them, steroids work.

Bicycling, weightlifting, and sprinting are contests in which the more powerful, explosive, and enduring athletes almost always win out. No one triumphs in the Tour de France or in an Olympic track meet because they've mastered a complex bicycle-riding technique or an innovative running method. In the overwhelming number of cases, the battles go to the strong and the races go to the swift.

In contests coming down to muscle, there is no doubt that steroids can be of help. Decades after their widespread introduction, the chemicals have been scientifically proven to increase muscle mass, so, in the many sports based on muscle, steroid users can become better athletes.

Baseball is a whole different ball game. In its need for precision and complexity, its play is akin to golfing rather than biking or sprinting.

Leave aside, for the moment, the determination needed to shake off near-constant failures, the smarts needed to address perpetual opponent adjustments, the composure to ignore the live sound levels that can approximate Led Zeppelin concerts, et cetera. Leave aside everything on the mental side.

In its physical demands alone, the pastime is defined by "kinetic chains" whereby strict, sequential movements must take place at just the right positions and at the right times, much like dominoes falling in prearranged patterns.

For example, consider the mechanics needed by batters:

In the four-tenths of a second between its departure from the pitcher's fingertips to the ball's arrival at home plate, a hitter must react to (1) pitch velocities that can range anywhere from 70 to 100 miles per hour plus (2) ball movements that can range from darting slides to off-the-table dips and then (3) match the ball's speed and trajectory to an invisible strike zone's boundaries while (4) maintaining the balance, hand positioning, and stride needed to initiate a swing that (5) instantaneously generates more than 70 miles per hour in bat speed while (6) creating bat placement on the ball and then (7) fully following through on all the above movements.

Baseball is sometimes labeled a game of moments or inches but the phrase doesn't do it justice. Dr. Robert Watts Jr. found that less than one-quarter of one second in timing or one-eighth of an inch in bat surface can add 50 feet in line-drive distance. As a practical matter, the difference between a routine pop-up and a game-changing homer can be measured in the blink of the eye or in the thickness of a McDonald's nutritional pamphlet.

Now consider pitching.

An effective pitcher must (1) coordinate control of everything from torso rotation to limb flexion while (2) maintaining a very exact hand grip, (3) finger pressure, and (4) wrist snap through the (5) arm slot, (6) release point, and (7) foot strike needed to generate (8) several different combinations of (9) velocity and (10) deceptive ball movement at corner targets (11) perhaps nine square inches in size and (12) nearly 60 feet in the distance.

Here, again, small mistakes are harshly punished. Dr. Tom House of the National Pitching Association has stated that a split second in forward acceleration or one inch in angular positioning can make all the difference between a breaking pitch and a broken pitch.

Hitting and pitching may look simple enough from up in the press boxes but baseball athletes don't belong in a category with French cyclists or Canadian runners. Ballplayers must play with skills that can never be ingested in a pill or injected by a syringe.

MYTH #42

"Steroids Make Players Stronger"

Yes, steroids make you bigger, faster and stronger. Yes, they work.

—RICHARD JUSTICE, "Real Hype Shouldn't Be about Bonds,"
Houston Chronicle, May 15, 2006

"This is what our sport is up against," one baseball executive said to me on Friday. "We are up against the fact that the [steroids] we are fighting against WORK."

—MIKE LUPICA, "Welcome to the Club, Gary,"
New York Daily News, March 4, 2007

Imagine an aspiring ballplayer.

He has gone through the hundreds of games and thousands of practice hours needed to sharpen his hand-eye coordination, master the details within on-field situations, and anticipate opponent actions. He has developed multiple strikeout pitches or an ability to switch-hit. His hopes have taken him as far as hard work will allow.

Imagine, further, that our hypothetical player decides that he still isn't good enough. He might be a Minor Leaguer who wants a shot at the next level, a bench player looking for a starting job, or a star looking for the promotion into superstardom.

If the player in our example is suddenly confronted with the choice of using anabolic steroids, he may be intrigued. He knows that drugs are no substitute for learned motor behavior but then again, he's already made those commitments. Our young player may be tempted to take muscle builders in order to increase pitch velocities or to push line drives over the fences.

A player may be tempted to use steroids, but he should never follow through on the temptation. While it's well established that steroids can add muscle, it's just as well established that the drugs demand terrible trade-offs.

Mainstream medical professionals declare that steroid-fueled muscles can strain the body's fragile joints past their natural limits, with users frequently snapping tendons in the quadriceps, rotator cuffs, biceps, and hamstrings. It's not rare for ligaments to be torn from bones. Steroids have also been connected to kidney disease, liver damage, and other unpleasantries.

This kind of trauma would be bad news in the best of circumstances but baseball athletes don't face the best of circumstances. Their finely tuned limbs must endure a six-month regular season with almost daily contests, a grind that leaves even the most limber of athletes vulnerable to breakdowns. Ken Caminiti, an admitted steroid user, once said that anabolics made him feel like a "superman" but overconfidence is kryptonite when it comes to overloaded knees and shoulder joints.

The discrete injuries from steroids are bad enough, but the systematic harms can be worse still. Artificial testosterone levels tend to shut down the hormones that regulate normal chemistry throughout the human body, resulting in side effects like hyperactive aggression ('roid rage), psychosis, depression, and other maladies listed in the *Diagnostic and Statistical Manual of Mental Disorders*.

There may be users unfazed by the possibility of having their muscles torn from their bones, perhaps because they are already suffering from psychosis. These brave few may, instead, yearn to look buff with their shirts off, but they should be aware that steroid usage can also lead to shriveled testicles, impotence, and the growth of breast tissue. Long story short—guys seeking to impress the ladies can be in for surprises.

Since steroid use is illegal in the United States without a prescription, those who seek out the black market for badly administered or counterfeit drugs can only add to the frequency and severity of their ordeals. Attempts to cycle off the worst of the side effects can, likewise, provide a false assurance that sets up more damage in the long term.

At the risk of stating the obvious, players cannot enhance on-field performances through drugs that can easily render ballplayers unfit for everyday functioning, let alone everyday playing. This is a primary reason why Dr. Gary Wadler, an expert on sports drugs, has joined virtually all reputable doctors in referring to nonprescribed steroids as "dangerous snake oil."

Performance enhancers? Steroids are performance debilitators. An aspiring ballplayer would be better off doing just about anything else. Crocodile wrestling. Plague testing. Grenade juggling may be safer.

When an aspiring player learns the facts, either through prudence or pain, there is no way he would use steroids.

MYTH #43

Caminiti, Canseco, and Giambi: A Case Study, or The Not-Good, the Bad, and the Ugly

You hear it all the time. It's the standard back-and-forth in the steroids debate.

It all starts when someone contends that steroids don't aid baseball's essential requirements and cause many more health troubles than they're worth. Since even the dumbest of dumb jocks come to know their own self-interest, it's fairly safe to assume that smart ballplayers either don't try them or don't use them for very long.

The response from the steroids critics is predictable. Sluggers like Ken Caminiti, Jose Canseco, and Jason Giambi admitted to steroid use. Since the trio won awards while they were on the stuff, they supposedly affirmed steroids as performance enhancers.

Let us think that over a few minutes.

Caminiti, Canseco, and Giambi certainly took chemical assistance with the thought they would gain a competitive edge. They surely *wanted* to cheat, but they didn't succeed, and their career arcs proved as much.

First, Caminiti, Canseco, and Giambi started off on steroids when they were at or near their career peaks.

In the years before Caminiti started using in 1996, he had already made his only league leaderboard appearances in hits, doubles, walks, and fielding percentage. By the time he began using steroids during the 1996 season he was also on his way to career highs in home runs and slugging.

Canseco's pre-steroid time frame is open to debate but Oakland's general manager has said that he first noticed a difference at the beginning of the 1989 season. If that's true, almost all of Canseco's best days had already come and gone; he had already topped out in full-season hits, on-base percentage, slugging, and home runs.

Finally, Giambi was on his own roll before steroids came along. By the time he began using during the 2001 season, he was already among a handful of Major Leaguers to improve in on-base plus slugging every year for six straight years and had also achieved career highs in home runs and walks.

The second characteristic among the trio was strong interim results. Caminiti was named Most Valuable Player in his initial season on steroids while Giambi and Canseco were All-Stars.

The third, most striking, element among the three users was in the way that they quickly endured repeated injuries and production drop-offs.

The pre-steroids Caminiti was an iron man, playing 998 of 1,069 possible games (93 percent) through his first seven full years in the Majors. After he started on anabolics at age 33, though, he went from averaging 149 games in non-strike years to less than 105, and predictably enough, Caminiti never matched his previous production in terms of slugging or hits. Not good.

Canseco's collapse was even more complete. In his first three seasons (1986 to 1988) Canseco averaged 158 games played per year but after he initiated steroid usage he spent extended periods on the disabled list in 11 of the next 13 years. In the relatively few games when Canseco limped onto the diamond, he never did match the production levels he established before the drug abuse. His seasonal stolen base totals diminished by two-thirds, his so-so glovework degenerated to the point where he "fielded" a fly ball with his head, and his once-strong arm blew out after one inning pitched. Widely considered a clown, "Mistake-o" bounced through eight clubs in nine years. Bad.

Finally we had Jason Giambi. Readers might remember Giambi as the superstar whose departure from the Oakland Athletics was a sign of the franchise's dire lack of finances. Little did Oakland realize that Giambi, like Caminiti and Canseco, would soon see his numbers decline in tandem with his drug dalliance. Three years into his use, in 2003, his slugging dropped more than 100 points off his previous high, and in the next year, at age 32, he missed more than half the Yankees season with the severe muscle strains and infections often linked to steroid abuse. He was still a shell of his former self in 2004, four years after he began sabotaging a once-promising career. Ugly.

Caminiti, Canseco, and Giambi represented more than media stories on steroids; the trio presented a case study on how limited, short-term benefits came only at the expense of ruinous, long-term problems. They tried to cheat but got cheated.

MYTH #44

"The Jose Canseco Revelations"

Hall of Fame voters, take a hard look at Canseco: he's the most honest man in baseball.

—JON GALLO, "Canseco Deserves the Hall," *(Baltimore) Examiner*, December 18, 2007

Like him or not, [Canseco] is telling the truth.

—ANDREW MARCHAND, "Gossage Targets Roger Clemens," *ESPN New York*, June 21, 2012, quoting former player Goose Gossage

Jose Canseco says that he started using steroids in the mid-1980s, but the previous chapter is premised on a belief that he didn't start until 1989. I highly doubt most anything that he has to say about the subject, mostly because Canseco and facts have never been close friends.

The *Juiced* autobiography credited steroids for Canseco's on-field successes and thus worked as a bizarre denunciation of his own talent. However, former teammates Dave Parker and Don Baylor, who played for a combined 38 seasons, said he was "the greatest talent I've ever played with" and possessed "the most natural ability of any player I've ever seen."

Canseco says his autobiography should be considered nonfiction but fact-checkers have pointed out that he routinely trafficked in doltish non-truths. He bragged about breaking a rookie home run record that existed only in his imagination, for example. He said he went 0 for 40 following the 1986 All Star Game, which would have been valid but for the fact that he went 2 for 4 in his first game back. He said that he played in the sixth game of a 2000 World Series that lasted only five games. In a bold venture into surrealism, he also claimed that he ran the 40 yard dash at the fastest time in recorded human history (3.9 seconds).

Canseco has conceded that trouble seems to seek him out, leading to an involvement in several regrettable misunderstandings. His rap sheet lists spousal abuse, aggravated battery, possession of an unlicensed handgun, a moving violation clocked at 125 miles per hour, a 15-mile police chase, an incident in which he rammed a parked car with his sports car, and another incident in which he rammed a parked car with his sports car. He once attempted to defraud boxing promoters by sending his brother to fight in his place. In retrospect the most regrettable misunderstanding was in his decision to become a one-man crime wave.

On the subject of crime . . .

Canseco holds himself out as a steroid expert because he regularly used illegal drugs and has insisted that "juicing" is so healthy that it can allow a person to live to be "a healthy 120 or 130 years old." Physicians, who hold themselves out as steroid experts because they graduate from medical schools, have insisted that juicing is only healthy when it involves mixed-fruit drinks, and that nonprescribed drugs, like unlicensed handguns, can kill people quite a long time before they reach age 120.

Canseco lied for more than a decade before a troubled conscience, and a six-figure book contract, inspired his ostensible revelations. *Publishers Weekly* said he was "a disgraced ex-player who so desperately wants respect that he casts his own extraordinary recklessness as perfectly commonplace" and that he wanted "to raise his own legend by bringing the game—and some of its great players—down to his level."

Finally, Canseco insisted he started abusing steroids as a teenager. Others draw their own conclusions.

MYTH #45

Mark McGwire, Rafael Palmeiro, and What No One Knows

Besides Ken Caminiti, Jose Canseco, and Jason Giambi, another couple of high-profile homer hitters were implicated in steroid use during the 1990s and 2000s. Did steroid use enable Rafael Palmeiro and Mark McGwire to both compile more than 500 career home runs?

I have no idea. Only Mark McGwire and Rafael Palmeiro possess complete knowledge on the steroid use of Mark McGwire and Rafael Palmeiro.

McGwire has remained vague on the specifics of his usage, while Palmeiro has always denied intentional steroid use, even after a positive drug test in 2005. The duo's silence and forced disclosure have been in marked contrast to Caminiti and Canseco, who volunteered for tell-all interviews, and to Giambi, who was compelled by a subpoena.

Without reliable evidence, the McGwire and Palmeiro stories produce far more questions than answers. Maybe McGwire mostly took steroids in the early to mid-1990s, when he missed most of several seasons with the kind of recurring injury problems often linked to steroids. Or not. Maybe Palmeiro was only desperate enough to take the drugs in the last year or two of his career, when he was on the wrong side of 40. Or maybe not.

And there are the other elephants in the room, other nonsense passed off under the phrase "everyone knows that . . . "

There have never been clinical studies on day-to-day steroid effects on ballplayers, so no one really knows if the drugs provide *any* net benefit on the diamond. If we are to pretend that this benefit has been proven, we don't know which offensive accomplishments, if any, can be attributed to steroid use. We don't know if pitching usage ever nullified hitting usage or the extent of the counterbalancing. Wannabe muckrakers don't know how many users actually made their way onto rosters in any given year and certainly don't have any certain numbers on an entire generation. No one has ever explained why so many virulent accusations should be aimed at individuals who've never been penalized via arbitration, litigation, or adjudication.

Finally, no one has ever answered—or addressed, even—the biggest uncertainty: how a barrage of wild suppositions and unproven charges can ever be used in service of a better-understood, more positive sport.

Moral Dilemmas

MYTH #46

"Steroids ~ Evil"

The mere sight of [a syringe] makes me feel as though I am looking straight at evil, like a weapon somebody left behind at a crime scene.

—ADAM RUBIN, "R. A. Dickey's Book Reveals Abuse," ESPN.com, March 27, 2012, quoting player R. A. Dickey

Every writer and every player knows that using steroids to pump up your numbers is flat-out immoral, unethical and wrong.

—RICK REILLY, "Gutless Wonders," *Sports Illustrated*, August 15, 2005

There was a time when everyone knew what baseball cheating was all about.

There was an unambiguous, forbidden status for the various black arts. For time out of mind, foreign substances like grease and nail files weren't allowed on baseballs, just as cork was disallowed in bats. According to the rule book, the on-field aids were always wrong.

That was then. Today we have off-field enhancements, and off-field enhancements have always been allowed.

There have been invasive surgeries, for example. Over the course of more than 30 years we have seen ligament reconstruction procedures save the careers of hundreds of pro pitchers, including guys like Adam Wainwright and John Smoltz, while Greg Maddux, Jeff Conine, and many others have undergone Lasik eye surgeries. The radical procedures were never associated with the slightest impropriety, much less betrayals, stigmas, or desecrations. What's the opposite of zero tolerance? Is it 100 percent acceptance? There was a policy of 100 percent acceptance.

There has been a long history of performance-enhancing drugs in baseball, too. Very potent painkillers and anti-inflammatories enabled Sandy Koufax's no-hitter in 1965, Kirk Gibson's game-winning homer in the 1988 World Series, and Curt Schilling's "bloody sock" performance in the 2004 American League Championship Series, to name but a few landmark moments. No one has ever hinted how modern baseball could survive *without* performance enhancers, but no one has ever thundered on about how painkillers and anti-inflammatories left us tarnished, corrupt, fraudulent, disgraced, or otherwise saddened.

Everyone seemed to agree that *some* unnatural help should be allowed, but few can agree on what is *too much* unnatural assistance. Nowadays, for some strange reason, forms and labels seem to make all-important differences. We're told that it's always okay to use scalpels with the intent of healing injuries but it's never okay to use steroids in the hope of preventing injuries. Take a well-known steroid called cortisone and you're conscientious but take a relatively unfamiliar steroid called Winstrol and you're unconscionable. The therapies that make you a patient in the Caribbean can render you a criminal in the United States. A whole lot of legwork was assigned to prescription tabs and short plane rides.

Some have tried to draw a bright line by saying "rehabilitation" measures are legitimate while "enhancement" measures are illegitimate, but such a distinction is incoherent. *All rehabilitations are enhancements*; they enhance bodies right up to the point where athletes are capable of taking the field of play. Both rehabilitations and enhancements can be provided in secrecy and both are unavailable to those without serious financial resources. All outside interventions serve as substitutes for innate talent, hard work, and luck. They produce rosters, standings, and records that wouldn't exist in their absence.

These types of contradictions may be most obvious in connection to the human growth hormone (HGH) issue. HGH can be easily obtained but belongs in the same ill-defined category as steroids, which presumably makes a user both "right" (according to federal law) and "wrong" (according to the Major League rule book). *The American Journal of Sports Medicine* has also found that HGH's chief effect is to replace hormones that would otherwise decrease over one's adult lifespan, so it's simultaneously "clean" (for rehabilitation against impairments) and "dirty" (for enhancement against "all-natural" aging).

The incoherence comes up time and again, including the shifting legal/social context involved.

Amphetamines have long been known as addictive drugs, yet many old-timers, from Willie Stargell and Mike Schmidt on down, saw the pills as a completely acceptable means to maintain energy throughout a 162-game MLB season. It was the players who didn't take the stay-awakes who were shunned as wusses; they let everyone down by "playing naked."

In 2006, amphetamines' chemistry was unchanged but the political winds had shifted enough for the drugs to move from the condoned to the condemned. What other substances will violate "the spirit of sport" in the future? Maybe a, b, and c nutritional supplements or x, y, and z medications. Maybe anything.

Virtually any aid can move from "right" to "wrong" or from "wrong" to "right." Today's drugs will probably look like Flintstone vitamins in comparison to the designer chemicals of the 2030s, and at that point every drug that's now considered dangerously powerful will be acceptably mild.

With no logic or facts to anchor the debate, it can only spin into circular arguments. "Steroids are wrong." Oh, why are they wrong? "Because they're against the rules." Why are they against the rules? "Because steroids are wrong." Around and around we go. Wash, rinse, repeat.

MYTH #47

"Users Are as Corrupt as the Black Sox"

Steroids are the most serious challenge that baseball has faced since the 1919 Black Sox scandal.

—LARRY FINE, "Mitchell Steroid Report Spreads Baseball Guilt," Reuters, December 13, 2007, quoting former commissioner Fay Vincent

It has become almost a cliché to draw parallels between the steroids scandal and the 1919 Black Sox scandal but one would be remiss not to mention that moment because of a lesson learned: the sport of baseball ought not to have room for cheaters.

—DAVID FRENKIL, "Send a Strong Message to Baseball's Cheaters," *Baltimore Sun*, December 28, 2007

On the murky evening of September 19, 1919, a professional gambler named Sport Sullivan met with a professional baseball player named Chick Gandil in Boston's Buckminster Hotel. In this meeting Sullivan proposed that Gandil and his White Sox teammates intentionally lose their upcoming World Series contests against the Cincinnati Reds. The ballplayers did pocket the gambler's money and proceeded to throw the 1919 Series, only to be caught out and, in time, banned from the Major Leagues.

The Black Sox scandal is still invoked as baseball's single worst chapter, as it should be. The sport is expected to mean something more than balls and strikes, wins and losses, players and teams. It's expected to represent competitive pride. When Gandil and his co-conspirators turned the World Series into a charade they betrayed a promise to offer their best efforts.

Steroid users are at the exact opposite end of the moral spectrum. Those who took steroids may have attempted improvement by self-destructive means—condemn that—but their end goal was completely defensible. In Tennyson's phrase, they sought "to strive, to seek, to find, and not to yield." Like the fans, the players wanted to win.

The commonality between baseball fans and baseball players may explain why the so-called steroid scandal has been accompanied by record levels of public interest in the game. Those who hold themselves out as the heralds of an outraged American public rarely notice that there is no outraged American public, not as it can be measured in real-world behavior.

Finally, a brief comment on those sportswriters who would sit in judgment of pro athletes. They cry that arrogant individuals should be taken down.

Let us contemplate the typical sportswriter—a middle-aged sort with a thickening waistband and thinning hairline—and let us further imagine that this cranky individual was suddenly given the choice to take magic beans enabling him to become an average Major Leaguer. Leaving aside the benefits of professional pride and female attentions, an assent would lead to about $3.4 million in salary for a single year. Otherwise law-abiding citizens have killed for far less. It's wealth enough to buy a fully stocked mansion in Southampton, Martha's Vineyard, South Beach, Sun Valley, Mercer Island, or any other tony locale.

Can there be any doubt that our thickening/thinning sportswriter would take up our magic beans? He definitely would, and in exchange for far less than a fully stocked mansion; he would probably ingest a lifetime supply in exchange for a fully stocked mini-bar. The only thing unique about the scribe would be in the way he would feel free to attack those who might face similar choices.

To observe these people is to observe arrogance. They are the ones who should be taken down.

The Bonds Issue

MYTH #48

"Barry Bonds Was Too Big"

Bonds used a shocking array of banned substances, notably steroids, to transform himself into a grotesquely overstuffed behemoth.

—Steve Buckley, "Giant Cheater Shouldn't Prosper,"
Boston Herald, March 9, 2006

Bonds looked like a WWE [World Wrestling Entertainment] wrestler or a toy superhuman action figure.

—Mark Fainaru-Wada and Lance Williams, *Game of Shadows*, 2006

Barry Bonds was supposed to be too big.

As he reached for new season and career power hitting records in the years after 2000, he was described as "a redwood," "Godzilla," and a "muscled-up monster." In one print piece he was called "grotesque" and "thick." Fans were told that he "just doesn't look right."

Bonds was supposedly so big that his body, in itself, was taken as a convincing sign of steroid use. If there was a push beyond authentic boundaries, the counterfeit came into view.

That is what some concluded about Barry Bonds. Others, who know a fuller context, concluded otherwise.

It was true that the late-career Bonds was, objectively speaking, one of the most powerful baseball athletes of all time. Among adult males, body mass is measured in terms of pounds per inch in height, and according to research from Professor Ben Rader, the Major League hitters of 2006 averaged 2.65 pounds/inch while Bonds averaged 3.11 pounds/inch (weight/height ratio). While the typical position player at Bonds's 6'2" could be expected to come in at 196 pounds, the star's official weight (228 pounds) surpassed that figure with more than 30 pounds of muscle.

In baseball Bonds was a man among boys but baseball wasn't the only team sport in America. Basketball and football also attracted some pretty big athletes, and if Bonds's 3.11 weight/height ratio was so incriminatingly muscular, he should have been bigger than those guys, too.

Let's consider the members of All-NBA teams and the NFL Pro Bowl's "skill position" players (quarterbacks, wide receivers, running backs, and defensive backs). Even if we leave aside NFL linemen, who are behemoths even by football standards, the following pro athletes matched or surpassed Barry Bonds's 3.11 weight/height ratio in the 2002 to 2006 time frame:

	LEAGUE	POSITION	WEIGHT	HEIGHT	RATIO
Shaquille O'Neal	NBA	C	300	7'3"	3.45
Yao Ming	NBA	C	310	7'6"	3.44
Elton Brand	NBA	PF	275	6'8"	3.44
Ron Artest	NBA	SF	244	6'6"	3.13
Daunte Culpepper	NFL	QB	265	6'4"	3.49
Jamal Lewis	NFL	RB	245	5'11"	3.45
Donovan McNabb	NFL	QB	240	6'2"	3.24
LaDainian Tomlinson	NFL	RB	221	5'10"	3.16
Travis Henry	NFL	RB	215	5'9"	3.12
Steve McNair	NFL	QB	230	6'2"	3.11

The list included famous names, and an additional 13 NBA and NFL stars who were even more muscle-bound. Bonds may have been big by baseball standards but wasn't among *the top 20* team athletes of his era. At the same height as Brett Favre, Bonds was three pounds over Favre's listed weight.

It's very difficult to explain that away. If steroids were the most likely explanation for Bonds-type muscles, then those others must have been guilty, too. Donovan McNabb must have been Godzilla. LaDainian Tomlinson must have been grotesque. At one glance you could tell that Steve McNair was a 'roider.

No one has ever made such ludicrous accusations, of course. With the exception of Barry Bonds, it's taken for granted that star athletes are unusually big and that they work to build themselves up even further. With one exception, they're congratulated for this.

MYTH #49

"Steroids Were a Likely Explanation for Bonds's Size"

Bonds insisted that his transformed physique resulted from weight-lifting and legal supplements, which is an insult to the intelligence of sports fans.

—"No Joy in Mudville," *San Diego Union-Tribune*, August 9, 2007

I don't believe in coincidences or physical transformations so stark that you do a double-take.

—Gene Wojciechowski, "Latest Revelations Seal the Deal for Bonds's Legacy," ESPN.com, March 8, 2006

The fact that Barry Bonds was far from the biggest, most muscle-bound athlete in the three major team sports didn't let him off the hook, not with some critics. Even though nearly two dozen basketball and football stars displayed more massive physiques, Bonds was still under a steroids suspicion for the way that he bulked up. This was because the buildup wasn't gradual but fairly sudden, as the San Francisco slugger gained about 38 pounds in lean muscle from the ages of 32 to 35 (1997 to 2000).

Many in the media believed that Bonds pumped up so fast due to anabolic steroid use, a condemnation that conveniently fit into their pre-existing belief that Bonds was, personality-wise, an ogre. The hostility was not unnoticed, as Bonds often went after mediocre pitchers and pundits with an equal relish; he feuded with the NBC network long before volunteering the opinion that Bob Costas is "a midget" who "knows absolutely jack shit about baseball."*

There were so many strong feelings swirling about. If only they were matched by facts. First, the media commentators who would have the public believe that they could spy out the telling signs of steroid use had medical cre-

---

*Costas is short and once declared that the 1988 Dodgers lineup was too weak to win the World Series, but he isn't a midget and does know more than absolutely jack shit. Bonds was exaggerating.

dentials equal to those of Dr Pepper. Those who spoke with such assurance about Barry's hat sizes spoke in the lingo of pseudoscience minus the "science" part. Last, definitive body-type judgments were rendered by sportswriters who had, themselves, never lifted anything heavier than jelly donuts.

Even if they didn't loathe Bonds beforehand, the media's opinions on his physique had a credibility equal to Don Zimmer's views on hairstyling. The utterly empty say-so was, interestingly enough, almost never backed by outside experts. The solitary attempt along those lines came from authors Lance Williams and Mark Fainaru-Wada, who cited a 1995 study published by Dr. Harrison Pope; they get points for effort but Pope was a practicing psychiatrist, not an endocrinologist.

On the other side, there were several experts who believed that Bonds built himself without steroids. Jim Warren, a trainer to the stars, said, "In 25 years, I've never found anyone who trained with as much passion and commitment as Barry. I've never had anyone show up early, work hard, stay on task, do the shit nobody wants to do, and stick with it every day." Tony Cooper of the *San Francisco Chronicle* called the steroid accusations "ludicrous" and added that Bonds "merely looks like a man who keeps himself in condition."

The most obvious explanations for the size increase came in conditioning, albeit legendary levels of conditioning. During his late career Bonds was known to begin his training day before 6 a.m., end it more than 12 hours later, and fill the time in between with workouts that would have exhausted men half his age. He didn't believe in the off-season, either, as he held year-round workouts documented by the *New York Times Magazine*, among other publications.

Bonds's exertions were supplemented, of course, but the help wasn't necessarily illegal or illicit in nature. As it happened, his career neatly coincided with the most dramatic fitness revolution in human history and Bonds employed three full-time assistants to maximize the benefits of state-of-the-art nutrition, exercise equipment, and training schedules. Asking how many home runs Bonds "should" have hit without those tools is like asking how a 21st-century jet "should" fly based on Orville Wright's knowledge of aerodynamics.

MYTH #50

"Bonds Improved Too Much"

[Bonds] put up inflated, dishonest numbers.
—HOWARD BRYANT, "Out at Home," *ESPN The Magazine*, June 19, 2012

The eye-popping stats that Bonds has accrued stand as too good to be true.
—TOM VERDUCCI, "The Consequences," *Sports Illustrated*, March 13, 2006

"I think one day Barry will put up numbers no one can believe." So said R. J. Reynolds back in 1990 but, for a long time, Reynolds was one of the few to hold such a high opinion.

Oh, to be sure, Barry Bonds was, on some level, always bound for greatness. His father, Bobby, was a spectacular, four-sport athlete who set a still-standing long jump record for California high schools. As a young All-Star, Bobby Bonds enlisted teammates like Willie McCovey to act as his son's tutors. To get an idea of Barry's childhood, try to imagine a boy with immense physical gifts and the most capable teachers in the world.

For all his gifts and training, Bonds was rarely free from the kind of insecurities that saddled his father and brother with substance abuse problems. In part, it was because everything came too easily for the younger Barry; the high school player who once hit 15 straight homers eventually became a Major League rookie notorious for half-hearted practices and full-throated tantrums. One scout said, "He's got all the tools in the world but he's a showboat who doesn't want to play."

By all accounts, it was only later in life that everything came together for Bonds. Through 1998, at age 33, his one home run for every 16.1 at-bats established him as one of the most outstanding power hitters of our time, but in the five years beginning in 1999 his homer/at-bat ratio of 8.2 established him as one of the most outstanding power hitters of *anyone's* time.

As with Bonds's physical buildup, the performance improvement was taken as an occasion for finger-pointing. *Game of Shadows* baldly claimed that the latter period, from 1999 to 2003, represented the years when Bonds was using steroids.

The accusation has now been repeated to the point where it's nearly unassailable, which is a shame, because it should be assailed. Barry's latter career improvements were very impressive but weren't so impressive as to completely redefine pastime history.

WAS BARRY BONDS SLUGGING AT AN UNPRECEDENTED RATE IN HIS LATTER CAREER?

Several other Major Leaguers increased their production as they aged, as confirmed by data assembled by Sean Forman of Baseball Reference. Forman studied Major Leaguers who compiled at least 1,000 official at-bats from ages 30 to 34 and again from ages 35 to 39, then found those whose home-runs-per-at-bat (HR/AB) ratios dropped in such a way as to indicate more efficient production. Here were his findings:

	HR/AB (AGES 30–34)	HR/AB (AGES 35–39)	IMPROVEMENT
Carlton Fisk	32	8	300%
Tony Phillips	60	34	76%
Tony Gwynn	84	35	71%
Barry Bonds	13	8	63%

Until someone explains how Fisk, Phillips, and Gwynn were aided by steroids, the Bonds improvements had no necessary links to the stuff.

DID BONDS'S BEST SLUGGING SEASON COME AT AN UNPRECEDENTED AGE?

Bonds reached his personal-best slugging at age 36 (in 2001) but he wasn't the oldest player to peak at around that age. Hank Sauer had his best power year at age 37 (in 1954), for example, and Ted Williams came within a few points of his personal-best slugging when he was 38 years old (1957). Fisk was the oldest player to slug at a career best rate, as he was 40 years old in 1988.

Analysts are free to explain how Sauer and Williams were hooked on steroids in the 1950s, but until they do there's no reason to believe that Bonds got too good when he was too old.

DID BONDS PRODUCE AN UNPRECEDENTED ONE-YEAR SPIKE IN HOME RUNS?

It goes without saying that Bonds did something stupendous when he hit a record 73 home runs during the 2001 season. In the process of besting everyone else's single-season total, Bonds bested his own previous high (46 homers) by a remarkable 59 percent.

While Bonds's improvement was age inappropriate, again, it wasn't unprecedented. Howard Johnson, for instance, went from a career high of 12 homers all the way up to 36 in 1987 (a 200 percent improvement). Davey Johnson went from a previous high of 18 to 43 in 1973 (a 138 percent improvement). Many other well-established players produced single-season homer totals that defied their previous career patterns—Andre Dawson, Davey Lopes.

Bonds wasn't the first home run king with a surprising year—even Roger Maris set his single-season record by going from a career-best 39 homers all the way up to 61 (a nearly 61 percent increase that, appropriately enough, occurred in '61).

DID BONDS GET TOO GOOD, PERIOD, END OF SENTENCE, NEW PARAGRAPH?

This goes to the heart of the matter. Even without completely unprecedented improvements in his latter years, the final Bonds numbers were, indeed, peerless. Unlike Phillips, Bonds toiled in an exceptional offensive era. Unlike Sauer, Bonds set a glamorous record. The jump in performance didn't come from a solid contributor like Howard Johnson, but a star who had already earned enough awards to stock a trophy store. There are those who suspected Bonds because he improved so much compared to already-impressive standards.

The problem with that criticism is in its pinched understanding of baseball potential, which is to say human potential. All-time greats have always been defined by broken barriers, including age-related barriers, and who's to say what Bonds was capable of all along? Maybe Bonds didn't overachieve as a veteran as much as he underachieved as a younger man. Maybe R. J. Reynolds was right.

MYTH #51

"Steroids Were a Likely Explanation for Bonds's Improvement"

Bonds went from a terrific hitter into arguably the most productive in baseball history when biological law essentially dictates that was impossible.

—PAT CAPUTO, "Why I Won't Vote for Bonds for the Hall of Fame," *Michigan News-Herald*, January 15, 2012

When you're 36, 37, and 38 years old is not when you peak in your home run production. You're supposed to do that when you're 26, 27, and 28 years old.

—"Van Slyke Believes Bonds Took 'Roids," *The Sporting News*, March 4, 2004, quoting former player Andy Van Slyke

Saying that Barry Bonds was a superb veteran player because of home runs is like saying Albert Einstein was a preeminent physicist due to a distinctive haircut. Memorable features aren't necessarily important features.

To be sure, the Bonds homers, like the Einstein hairstyle, were hard to overlook. In 2001, Bonds set the single-season home run record as part of a multi-year power spree that put him in position to break Hank Aaron's career home run record in 2007. He was first or second in the National League in slugging for the five straight full seasons after his 35th birthday. When most players were winding down, Bonds was warming up.

Barry's latter-day value as an offensive force went far beyond home run power, however. He was a great performer because he excelled in several areas:

- At the same time he was proving himself to be the most explosive hitter in the game, Bonds was establishing himself as the most patient one, too. From ages 34 to 39 (1999 to 2004), Bonds was getting on base at a .535 clip that surpassed the best performances of Ted Williams. His swing was so controlled that his homers exceeded his strikeouts in 2004, an achievement rarely seen since the days of Joe DiMaggio and Johnny Mize.

- The late-career power and patience matched up with durability. After an injury-plagued 102-game season in 1999, the San Francisco star's 143-game-per-season average from 2000 to 2004 placed him among the most resilient outfielders of all time. Bonds earned it the hard way, too, without any breathers as a designated hitter or as a first baseman.
- The new-millennium Bonds also became a terrific playoff performer. In his four postseason series with Pittsburgh and San Francisco (1990, 1991, 1992, 1997) he compiled a woeful on-base plus slugging of .613, but in his golden twilight, Bonds became the spectacular postseason hitter that he had always been in the regular season: from 2000 to 2003 he averaged a 1.217 OPS that vaulted him to a place among the top eight playoff hitters of all time.
- Finally, Bonds earned the unofficial distinction as the "smartest man in baseball" after 1998. For instance, after 2001 Bonds revamped his swing mechanics to reduce his ground-ball-to-fly-ball ratio from a career average of .75 down to .55–.62. Teammates also marveled at how he memorized pitch releases to the point where he could identify pitch selections at the split seconds they had been released. If there was a PhD for hitting knowledge, Bonds would've been first in line for a diploma.

Those who focus on Bonds's muscles risk losing sight of all the other factors in his late-career greatness. Here was a man who found new levels of patience, durability, poise, and intelligence to match a virtuoso swing. Any one of those qualities, standing alone, could have made him epic. In conjunction, they made him Barry Bonds.

The late-career improvements could be explained through loads of hard work and mental adjustments, but nothing in the steroids story explained anything.

HOW DID CHEMICALS MAKE BONDS A MORE SELECTIVE BATTER?

Anecdotes have steroid-addled batters making wild hacks in the hopes that brute force might carry balls over the fences. This was a style displayed by Ken

Caminiti, Jose Canseco, and Jason Giambi, who posted awful strikeout ratios during their chemical romances.

The fact that petrified pitchers were only willing to chance, maybe, *one* hittable pitch per game to Bonds should've been enough in itself to inhibit day-to-day timing, but Bonds only grew more disciplined as time went on.

HOW DID STEROIDS KEEP BONDS HEALTHY?

Muscle-heads like Caminiti, Canseco, and Giambi ruined their health through steroids. At ages when that bunch—and almost all their contemporaries—had retired, Bonds remained and reloaded.

HOW DID THE CHEMICALS ENABLE HIM TO OVERCOME THE PERSONAL PRESSURE?

In his record-breaking prime, Bonds was contending with . . . where to begin? The distractions included an ongoing grand jury investigation, the prolonged illness of his father, a nasty child custody battle, and an acrimonious breakup with a girlfriend. There were vicious hecklers numbering in perhaps the tens of thousands. There was a pack of retired players expressing undisguised bitterness over how they'd been surpassed by Bonds. As for the most influential columnists and broadcasters in the nation, they ardently campaigned not for failure but imprisonment. All this came down only a few years after a big-budget movie entitled *The Fan* depicted a thinly veiled Bonds character being stalked, attacked, and nearly murdered on the diamond.

A genuine druggie would've collapsed under those burdens but Barry Bonds never collapsed. To the fury of many, he always found strength.

MYTH #52

Barry and Hank

Henry Aaron's clean and scrupulous home run record . . .

—SALLY JENKINS, "Time for Bonds to Go First Class," *Washington Post*, July 16, 2007

Aaron pounded more in his career than any other player and without suspicion of chemical enhancement.

—TOM VERDUCCI, "The People's King," *Sports Illustrated*, July 17, 2007

Barry Bonds and Hank Aaron have much in common.

Bonds was a National League star who enjoyed his greatest home run seasons after age 35. His single best year for homers-per-at-bat occurred at age 36.

Aaron was a National League star who enjoyed his greatest home run seasons after age 35. His single best year for homers-per-at-bat occurred at age 39.

Bonds was subject to an avalanche of death threats by self-appointed judges who decided he didn't truly deserve the career home run record.

Aaron was subject to an avalanche of death threats by self-appointed judges who decided he didn't truly deserve the career home run record.

Bonds has also been vetted by millions of dollars in scrutiny, all aimed at the first iota of information as to his chemical engagements.

Aaron . . . gosh, the parallel only goes so far.

That Aaron story, if ever pursued, might be interesting, though.

We do know that Hank Aaron played in a 1960s–1970s period when the majority of Major Leaguers were breaking rules by taking amphetamines. The users of the time believed the drugs were performance enhancers in that they provided the near-instant energy needed to play through a rigorous 162-game schedule. The brightly colored pills were so widely accepted that they were openly dispensed on clubhouse tables as if they were jellybeans.

In addition, we also know that the federal government rates amphetamines as being more destructive than steroids, which is why their pushers are more frequently and severely punished in the court system.

We also know that Hank Aaron used amphetamines. He admitted this in a 1992 autobiography, though he didn't connect his favorite performance enhancers to the durability displayed in the late stages of his career. Sportswriter Bruce Jenkins cited sources who confirmed that Bad Henry "liked" amphetamines. Bud Selig—none other than Commissioner Bud Selig—said he was aware of amphetamine use in the Braves clubhouse as early as the 1950s.

Few fans now are aware of Aaron's drug use, however, because the reporters who devoted years and fortunes to Barry Bonds could never devote a few minutes and pocket change necessary to fully investigate Aaron's connection to illegal performance enhancers of his time.

Neither have the idolizers mused that, well, maybe Aaron never used steroids for the exact same reason he never used a jet pack to fly around the outfield: a lack of opportunity. An old-time competitor named Buck O'Neil once said, "The reason we didn't use steroids was 'cause we didn't have 'em."

It's almost as if the media decided to cast Bonds as an ignoble, undignified villain to be contrasted to Hank Aaron's role as a noble, dignified hero. It's almost as if the media was so fixated on "sullied" record breaking that they forgot to ask how sullied the record may have been in the first place.

MYTH #53

If You Must Make a Federal Case Out of It . . . (Pt. 1)

The evidence that Bonds cheated is overwhelming.

—MARK KRIEGEL, "Barry Haters, Here's What You Do,"
FoxSports.com, May 15, 2007

Bonds is a man who has denied using performance enhancers
despite a silo of evidence.

—RICK REILLY, "Giving Barry His Due," *Sports Illustrated*, July 27, 2007

1) *Game of Shadows*, the book that helped initiate the government prosecution against Barry Bonds, had the authors conducting hundreds of interviews

and reviewing more than 1,000 document pages of grand jury testimony, unredacted affidavits, and confidential federal memoranda, all without finding conclusive evidence that Bonds ever obtained steroid prescriptions, used syringes, or possessed illegal drug vials.

What is your reaction?
A)   I'm glad they didn't go after me because, with that kind of digging, they could've convicted me of the Lindbergh kidnapping.
B)   With that kind of digging *anyone* could've been convicted of the Lindbergh kidnapping.
C)   Barry Bonds should be convicted of the Lindbergh kidnapping.

2)   According to former Giants teammate Jay Canizaro, Bonds suffered from the kind of acute back acne often linked to steroid usage. According to a magazine story, Bonds confessed his usage to Ken Griffey Jr. In 2004 Andy Van Slyke said it was an "utmost certainty." However, when asked to testify under oath, Canizaro recanted the acne accusation. When Griffey was asked about the supposed Bonds confession, he said that the conversation never happened. At the time of his utmost certainty, Van Slyke hadn't played on a Bonds team for over ten years.

How do these stories stand up?
A)   Are you kidding me? None of them are true!
B)   Are you kidding me?
C)   Are you kidding me? All of them are true!

3)   Consider the following:

   • From 2005 to 2007, Bonds was subject to unannounced, random steroid tests during the regular season and the off-season alike. He never tested positive.
   • There are no witnesses to his ever buying or possessing steroids.
   • When put under penalty of perjury, Bonds denied knowingly using steroids.

Which of these facts undermine the case against Bonds?

A) All of them.

B) Most of them.

C) Let's move on.

4) Jeff Novitzky was the IRS worker who initiated the federal government's investigation by—no joke—diving into heaps of garbage. Consider the following facts about Novitzky:

- A California State drug agent said that Novitzky had openly mused about gaining a lucrative book deal out of the controversy that he had created. Novitzky, the agent said, described Bonds by a seven-letter word that began with the letter "a," ended with the letter "e," and is not "awesome."*
- Two members of a local narcotics task force told an assistant U.S. Attorney that Novitzky had lied about the investigation.
- Four witnesses contended that Novitzky lied about their conversations. For example, one witness supposedly confessed to handing steroids to athletes when, in actuality, the witness had never met the athletes in question.

Your reaction to Novitzky's probe?

A) Novitzky is the one who should be probed.

B) No, seriously, Novitzky should be probed, for being a law enforcer who's probably a lawbreaker.

C) Set aside the abuse-of-power thing and get back to the crucial issue— athletes with big muscles.

5) Consider the actions of the Bonds investigators:

- They tipped off the news media and brought an official photographer in their raid on the Bay Area Laboratory Co-Operative (BALCO).
- They also brought 25 armed agents into the suburban office.
- Their agents allegedly drew their weapons on a startled company receptionist and then knocked down office doors, much in the style of Hollywood action movies.

---

*He called Bonds an "asshole."

Do these facts cast doubt on the government?
A) That's a good question.
B) That's in question.
C) Next question.

6) Victor Conte, the central figure within BALCO, was a motormouth who had no qualms in naming nearly a dozen former clients as steroid users, including high-profile figures like Marion Jones and Bill Romanowski. He went to prison rather than implicate Bonds, however.

What should we make of this?
A) Conte knew that Bonds was using.
B) Maybe Conte didn't know.
C) Conte knew.

7) Secretly recorded conversations of a Bonds trainer, Greg Anderson, had Anderson taking credit for his client's successes. Anderson made "T," "G," and "E" notations that might have referred to doping codes. When Anderson was put under oath, however, he denied the boasts and imputed code. When prosecutors gave Anderson a choice to either give up Bonds or serve prison time, Anderson chose prison. After the feds went after his beleaguered wife and mother-in law, he still refused to surrender.

Why did Anderson go to prison?
A) Because he could not, in good conscience, frame an innocent man.
B) Because he would not betray a friend.
C) Because he wanted to catch up on some light reading.

8) For a brief time in 2003 Anderson supplied Bonds with substances called "the cream" or "the clear." Bonds applied them while in full view of milling reporters within the San Francisco clubhouse. Under penalty of perjury, Bonds denied knowledge that the substances were steroids.

What is the conclusion to draw?

A) Bonds must've thought he was using flaxseed oil and arthritis balm. No one would be stupid enough to knowingly take illegal drugs in front of a gaggle of reporters bearing a combined hostility that burned like an oil well fire.

B) Bonds didn't act guilty, anyway.

C) Steroiding was just the kind of steroid a steroider like Bonds would do, being with steroids in a steroidal manner. Steroids, steroids, steroids. And, in conclusion, steroids.

9) Bonds testified that he never questioned Anderson about the details of the workout supplements.

This claim is:

A) Believable. Clients trust their trainers and trainers hand out ointments all the time.

B) Kinda believable. Clients trust trainers, trainers hand out ointments all the time, and athletes don't conduct independent tests for everything that goes into or onto their bodies.

C) Unbelievable. Clients don't trust their trainers, trainers don't hand out ointments, and athletes do conduct independent tests for everything that goes into or onto their bodies.

If You Must Make a Federal Case Out of It . . . (Pt. 2)

"There's no more doubt that Barry Bonds used steroids than there is that the sun rises in the east and sets in the west," Bob Costas said.

—**"With Bonds and Clemens, Steroids Era on Trial,"** *Wilmington News Journal,* **February 25, 2011**

Everybody knows what he was and what he did.

—**PETER BOTTE, "Most Hall of Famers Say No to Cooperstown for Barry Bonds,"** *New York Daily News,* **December 16, 2011**

10) The chief accuser in the Bonds prosecution was Kimberly Bell, his former mistress. Shortly after Bonds dumped her and reportedly reneged on a $100,000 payment, Bell claimed verbatim, word-for-word memories of Bonds conversations from several years before. There was no independent confirmation for this, but in the interest of full disclosure, Bell did pose for *Playboy*.

Her testimony had the approximate credibility of:
A) A $3 bill.
B) Any other angry ex-mistress with money problems.
C) Clergymen pledging their honor upon holy writ.

11) Bonds accused his one-time assistant of forgery before firing him and turning him over to the FBI. Steve Hoskins was let off scot-free, teamed up with the cops investigating Bonds, and then claimed that he had numerous steroids-related conversations with Dr. Arthur Ting. The doctor testified that those conversations never happened.

Keeping in mind that federal cases aren't laughing matters, tell us about Steve Hoskins:
A) How was it possible to find someone even less credible than Jeff Novitzky or Kimberly Bell?

B) Why would anyone ever believe an ex-employee out for revenge?

C) What, me worry?

12) Starting in 2003, federal prosecutors began scrutinizing gym workouts with the kind of years-long grand jury investigation otherwise reserved for mob kingpins and war criminals.

Consider the outcomes:

- They dropped 40 of the 42 charges against Conte and Anderson for lack of evidence.
- They won three- and four-month prison sentences on the remaining counts.
- True fact: Tommy Chong got more than twice as much prison time for selling *thousands* of marijuana bongs.
- U.S. Attorney Kevin V Ryan was fired by the George W. Bush adminis-tration for being too incompetent, a fate comparable to being fired by bears for shitting too much in the woods.

Your thoughts?

A) I don't trust the government and I don't trust lawyers.

B) I harbor some doubts over both the government and lawyers.

C) I trust the government, I trust lawyers, and I trust the government's lawyers most of all.

13) An estimated $35 million was spent for government employees to investi-gate Bonds and other jocks. The same sum could've paid for five years' salary for over 140 new police officers, firefighters, and teachers or for the construction of dozens of brand-new police stations, firehouses, and schools.

Please comment:

A) What a circus.

B) Circuses don't cost $35 million.

C) I happen to enjoy circuses.

14) In 2004 the government saw fit to seize medical records that were created on the promise of doctor/patient privacy. Armed with a warrant to see ten

confidential files, the cops walked out with 4,000 files. A prosecutor in the *United States v. Barry Bonds* case stated, "You don't get in trouble unless you do something wrong." Perhaps the prosecutor's ancestors brought the same sentiment to the Salem witch trials; the little old ladies wouldn't have been put through the witch trials unless they were witches.

The constitutional rights of which nation have been built on such actions and reactions?

A) The Soviet Union.

B) Banana Republic.

C) The United States of America.

15) In 2011 the government's case eventually transitioned from the court of public opinion to a court of law, from a guilt-by-suspicion standard to a guilt-by-evidence standard, and from a guilty-until-proven-innocent presumption to an innocent-until-proven-guilty presumption.

     After all was said and done, a lot was said but almost nothing was done. The jury refused to find that Bonds knowingly took steroids. They did find that Bonds did give confusing testimony, however, for which he was required to attend probation meetings, do charity work, and spend 30 days within his Beverly Hills mansion.

Your reaction?

A) Where does Bonds go to get his name back?

B) I deserve a refund on *Game of Shadows*.

C) Fair trials are overrated.

Scoring:

Give yourself one point for every A response, two points for every B, and three for every C.

    15–25: You are a journalist reluctant to tear down a man's livelihood and liberty.

    26–35: You possess an uncommon trust in the Big Media Establishment.

    36–45: Welcome to the Big Media Establishment.

In the Markets

"Baseball Is a Big Business"

Baseball is a big business.

—BRIAN MEEHAN, "Ramirez Worth the Antics,"
Newhouse News Service, May 29, 2008

Baseball is no different from any other big business.

—CHARITA M. GOSHAY, "Baseball Goes Down Looking on Steroid Issue,"
Copley News Service, March 29, 2005

It can seem like its own religious denomination, the Church of Baseball.

We are told that the pastime is populated by immortals leaving behind hallowed records. A vintage card, bat, or jersey can be a prized artifact rather than a piece of old cardboard, lumber, or cloth. The Hall of Fame is a shrine subject to pilgrimage. Half-joking hyperbole suggests the spiritual benefits of fielding practice or explains how life can imitate the World Series.

With the national pastime surrounded by such outsized passions, it's easy to believe that it's also large in the financial sense, but that's not so. Relatively speaking, baseball doesn't boast even medium-size finances.

Though present-day baseball is awash in money as never before, with its 30 franchises combining to gross more than $6 billion in a typical year. It's a lot of money to anyone who didn't invest in early Microsoft stock, but the sum is a pittance within the context of the national economy.

Consider that the combined resources of Major League Baseball fall behind about 400 corporations on *Fortune*'s listing of the biggest businesses in the United States, including relatively low-profile outfits like Autoliv and Assurant. Even before the recession that began in 2008 the baseball industry's yearly grosses were smaller than the *weekly* grosses of mega companies like Exxon Mobil and Wal-Mart.

It's, again, a relatively modest picture when you consider teams as a part of their metro area economies. While teams like the Cardinals or the Giants might be synonymous with St. Louis and San Francisco in the popular imagination, their local impacts are no larger than large department stores. It's rare to find a Major League club among the top 100 grossers within its metro area economy or to find one that has contributed more than 1 percent to a metro area's annual wealth creation.

Even millionaire players aren't as wealthy as they seem.

Much was made of the fact that, in recent years, Alex Rodriguez and Mark Teixeira cleared average annual salaries in excess of $20 million. The salaries were oversized in comparison to everyday life but not in comparison to the nearly 60 corporate executives who made more money on an annual basis (*Forbes* estimated that 17 of the CEOs made at least twice as much as Rodriguez and Teixeira). The richest of rich players weren't pulling in much compared to Hollywood big shots, either, since *Forbes* estimated that 49 entertainers and studio execs outearned baseball's most highly paid stars (some pulled in salaries several times larger). While A-Rod and Teixeira made enough money to hang out at island resorts, others were raking in enough to *buy* island resorts.

Some see the game's relatively paltry financial standing as diminishing its standing in our national life. A combination of 30 teams should pull in more than Autoliv. The typical team's economic impact should be greater than a department store. We might expect the sport's highest-paid stars to earn more than half the yearly take of Dr. Phil.

When you think about it, though, the full context doesn't trivialize baseball's appeal; it only explains it. The pastime inspires a caring all out of proportion to its economics. At the heart of the order it's about a love for the game.

"Someone Can Define the Big Markets and Small Markets"

When it comes to Major League markets, no one can doubt that size matters. Just what size is and how much it matters—those are open questions.

There's an obvious difference between mega-metro areas like New York (18.9 million people, according to the 2010 U.S. Census) or Los Angeles (12.8 million) and significantly more modest markets like Cincinnati (2.1 million) and Milwaukee (1.6 million). Everyone says that, and everyone is right.

What is significantly less obvious is the relative size and strength among the different markets.

Greater Philadelphia, for instance, is rarely identified as one of the big markets, yet its 6.0 million population is the sixth largest in the United States, well ahead of metro areas like Boston (4.6 million). Detroit, likewise, is seldom identified among the biggies, yet it boasts an area population (4.3 million) more than double that of a mid-size town like Cleveland (2.1 million). Dallas (6.5 million) also has more than twice the number of people of middling St. Louis (2.8 million).

At the other extreme, some of the smaller-market teams are not as small as portrayed. Many call the Marlins one of the relative have nots of baseball, for example, yet Miami anchors the eighth-largest metro area in the country. Minneapolis has gained an image as some out-of-the-way cow town, but it boasts a metro population (3.3 million) more than 50 percent larger than a genuinely small place like Kansas City (2.1 million).

What's more, there's plenty of reason to question the assumption that baseball markets are synonymous with metro areas.

As far back as the 1980s the Braves and Cubs were using cable superstations to reach entire swaths of the country, and that motivated multiple franchises to expand their own outreach. The Boston Red Sox, for instance, used their NESN system to gradually transform themselves as a regional brand more accurately dubbed the "New England Red Sox." Teams like the Mariners and Twins have quietly done much the same thing, defining their sphere of influence less in terms of Seattle than the greater Northwest region, less in terms of Minneapolis than the upper Midwest. The examples go on. By 2012 nearly all MLB clubs had struck deals with cable networks reaching as far as 100 miles from their home ballparks, a reach that rendered the organizations far more resourceful than they would appear according to strict metro numbers.

If teams surely deserve credit for finding new markets, then others must deserve blame for failing to expand their fan bases.

Toronto, for instance, has a relatively modest metro area of 5.6 million, but the Blue Jays have always had the potential to become, in effect, "Canada's Team," the favorite club of more than 28 million countrymen. The fact that they still lose chunks of their expected audience to the Twins, Tigers, and Red Sox can probably be attributed to their on-field mediocrity. The Marlins, similarly, have the potential to draw a wide following, but rocky community relations have hampered that potential.

Even if we limit ourselves within the acknowledged markets, it's up for debate which fan base really belongs to which team.

New York City is commonly believed to be a Yankee town, for example, but history proves that the Mets can dominate the market whenever they are ahead of the Yanks in the standings, most recently in the late 1980s; if and when the Bombers struggle once again, they'll probably find a significantly diminished fan base. It's much the same case in Los Angeles, where the Dodgers overshadowed the Angels until the Halos won a World Championship in 2002; afterward the attendance numbers of the two clubs have often moved in tandem with their standings.

Flexible definitions of market share bring up competition questions in nearly every market. After all, if the Yankees and Dodgers can lose goodwill due to resurgent clubs across town, they must also lose out in relation to any number of local restaurants, theaters, and other attractions.

No one's really sure exactly how much big-market clubs are hurt by relatively intense market competition or how smaller-market teams can benefit from lesser competition from local attractions. We do know that teams like the Milwaukee Brewers, Colorado Rockies, and Cleveland Indians can blow away big-city rivals by more than four to one in terms of revenue per capita. We also know that the Tampa Bay Rays, Cincinnati Reds, and San Diego Padres can stand among MLB's top six teams in regional cable ratings. While their areas contain smaller fan bases, clubs apparently learn to make the most of them.

Beyond all the "lost in the market" ambiguities there are still more unanswered questions:

- How to account for status as a "baseball town"? It's well established that the Cardinals and Cubs are capable of drawing attendance beyond what their win/loss records would indicate, but is there something in St. Louis or Chicago that makes for more passionate fans? Is there something about the local culture of Atlanta that makes it less of a pastime market?
- How to account for per capita income? Do relatively high wealth levels in towns like Philadelphia and Houston always provide extra market leverage, or do they only matter when teams are winning?
- How much do fan relations matter? Can a team like the Mariners make up for mediocre win totals by courting Asian American audiences while a team like the Royals erodes its potential market through long-term futility?

And so on and so on. Everyone has good questions about the markets, but almost no one has good answers.

Take Your Tickets

MYTH #57

"We Can Define the Average Ticket Price"

Being a baseball fan means carrying an opinion and, often, it means carrying a loud and negative opinion. It's part of the game. When you pay for a ticket, you purchase the right to complain about anything from the right fielder's throwing arm to rainouts.

Booooooooooooo.

The inalienable right to jeer can get a little out of hand at times, as it does when someone cries about baseball's ticket prices.

On the surface level, the ticket price inflation can be easily verified. According to the oft-quoted Team Marketing Report, for instance, the average MLB ticket price was $8.73 in 1991 but surged by 117.5 percent (to $18.99) by 2001 and appreciated even further in the new millennium.

The numbers sound bad, but only until you realize that there's no such thing as an "average" MLB ticket. Winning teams with high-demand seats post higher prices in comparison to losing teams with lower demand, but beyond that generalization, there are too many factors at work to produce any reliable means or median.

Baseball teams have long moved past the halcyon days when they would offer fans straightforward ticket plans consisting of perhaps half a dozen different prices. Instead they have used heightened market information to divide seating inventories into multiple categories, then vary their pricing according to the number of games bought, the time of the season, the day of the week, and the opposing team, not to mention the discounts that might come into play in terms of group purchases, promotions, and season ticket packages. The Dodgers, for example, are fairly typical of today, offering two dozen seating categories and over 100 price packages. When the Mets moved into their new ballpark in 2009, they offered over 200 different price options.

From that jumble anyone trying to figure out an "average" ticket price is presenting estimates of estimates. Better to leave the mathematical mush aside and instead ask if affordable deals are available. Thankfully, the answer is an emphatic yes.

According to one recent survey, nearly 90 percent of MLB venues offer "Uecker" seats for $10 or less. Detroit's general admission tickets have gone for $2.50, and ball clubs as varied as the Arizona Diamondbacks, Oakland Athletics, and Baltimore Orioles have offered outfield seats for a dollar each. Online resellers have sometimes slashed prices to the point where Red Sox tickets with $30 face values sometimes sold for $3 each.

Ticket prices can range from champagne-and-lobster rates to soda-and-hot dog numbers. Rich folks get the best seats—always have, always will—but there are plenty of affordable seats out there, too.

MYTH #58

"Expensive Tickets Are Pricing Out the Fans"

It's no exaggeration or cliché to point out that working-class people have been priced out of attending sports events.

—DAVE ZIRIN, *Bad Sports*, 2010

High Prices Driving Away Fans at Baseball Games

—*USA Today*, **March 27, 2009**

Way back in the 19th century, an entrepreneur figured out the unique business of baseball.

The first part of the equation came from the lure of the sport's athletics. As it turned out, the schedule could allow 150 or more regular-season contests from March to October, and there were a great many athletes ready and willing to take on such an expansive schedule. There could be a great ticket supply.

The second part of the equation came from the lure of the game's spectacle. It turned out that there were a great number of working- and middle-class fans who loved it enough to fill the stands all during a lengthy schedule. There could be a great demand for tickets.

The third basic element was in low prices. Going back more than 130 years, it was clear enough that fan-friendly prices were the most effective means to drive up the daily, all-important turnstile counts. If nothing else, rock-bottom pricing could draw the consistently large crowds necessary to boost concession and merchandise revenues.

Professional baseball came into being through that neat combination of supply, demand, and pricing. Its unique business model, including its affordability, can best be seen in relation to its rivals in pro football and pro basketball.

In contrast to 81 regular-season home games per year, NFL teams work on a hyper-abbreviated schedule that allows only eight such contests. The NBA has a more reasonable 41 home games per year, but teams play in arenas with less than half the average seating of a ball club (19,800 to the baseball's 45,900-plus average). Either through their abbreviated schedules or smaller venues, football and basketball franchises offer only about 15–20 percent of the total tickets offered by MLB franchises in a given season.

With such relatively scarce ticket supplies, the NFL and NBA can best maximize profits through tickets estimated to be two or three times more expensive than Major League tickets. The exact prices are open to debate, but just about everyone agrees that there's a yawning chasm between the NBA and NFL on one side and MLB on the other.

The wide differences between the sports inevitably result in a greater inclusion in live event fans. The typical grandstand is an egalitarian place, one affordable enough for everymen to be joined by everywomen and everychildren. The seats at the typical NFL or NBA games, though, are so pricey that they pander to more adult, male, and upper-class elites. Very often their demographics match up to the membership list of the Greenwich Country Club.

There's nothing intrinsically wrong with relatively rich people gazing upon even richer athletes in the other sports leagues, of course, but it does lend baseball a special status. By including so many Americans, it's the prototypical "game of the people."

The national pastime has always been the most accessible of our national sports, but its status isn't without its qualifiers.

First off, baseball tickets aren't *always* cheaper than football or basketball tickets. Local situations dictate local prices, so it's possible for a losing NFL or NBA franchise to offer distant seats at prices cheaper than a popular ball club's best box seats. That kind of thing is relatively rare, but it does happen.

In addition, baseball's *relative* affordability doesn't apply to historical comparisons. Ticket prices, like all consumer prices, rise over time due to inflation and the presence of $6 hot dogs and $8 beers might be especially jarring to oldsters who can recall times when relatively low demand led to relatively low prices.

MYTH #59

"Payrolls Push Prices"

Money's ruined the game. Players today make more in a signing bonus than I did in my career; families can't afford to go to games.

—TIM WOODWARD, "Vern Law's 'Golden Days of Baseball,'" *Idaho Statesman*, January 16, 2011, quoting former player Vern Law

I was sitting in a backyard in Marine Park the other day, talking to my Brooklyn pals about how much it costs to go watch grown men play a kid's game in New York these days. It's gonna kill baseball.

—DENNIS HAMILL, "Ballparks Strike Out with Families," *New York Daily News*, May 5, 2009

The fans rule.

There are ironclad laws when it comes to the business of baseball. When fans are presented with exciting and winning ball clubs, they show up, bid up ticket prices, and enhance team finances. When fans find boring or losing ball clubs, meanwhile, the fans stay away in droves, driving down both ticket prices and team revenues. In either case, it's the public that makes the call about who is either rewarded or punished.

That may seem obvious enough, but many commentators never tire of insisting, implying, and inferring that it's the players who are making the decisions, chiefly by raking in astronomical salaries and then, in some never-explained way, forcing the public to pay out for them.

Back on this planet, though, baseball fans are no more forced to pay for expensive and terrible teams than they are compelled to buy expensive and terrible songs. If the fans see a $100 million team that stinks up the field, they'll stay away. If the fans see a $40 million ball club scratching its way up the standings, on the other hand, they'll show up in force.

Consumers never respond to payrolls, only products. If it were otherwise, movie buffs would allow actor salaries to dictate their ticket-buying decisions.

Fans decide the prices, and the only possible way to grow confused on this point is when ball clubs sign new free agents and immediately hike their rates. It may seem like the teams are dictating terms in those cases but they're doing no such thing. They're merely betting that their new signings will upgrade their clubs to the point where the public will buy into rate hikes. There are occasions when the execs are proven right and occasions when they're proven wrong, but there are no occasions when they dictate anything.

No, the buck stops with the fans. It has to: it's their buck.

Minor Considerations

"Pampered Players"

Today players have become pampered, spoiled celebrities.

—STEVEN MORRIS, "Baseball Injuries: Mystery Solved,"
New York Times, July 12, 2009

*Unlike, say, normal people, America's professional sports stars reside in a
universe that's pure Fantasy Island: room service is included, flights are
chartered, dollars are limitless, groupies are curvaceous. . . .*

—JEFF PEARLMAN, "Politics, Athletes Don't Mix," ESPN.com, November 7, 2006

It's often said that modern athletes are so rotten because they're so pampered.

After talented young kids prove that they can jump, run, or throw better
than their peers, they're treated like unofficial royalty. Gifted athletes are show-
ered with the kind of perks and power that would warp anyone's values, and by
the time they make it to the highest level of their pro games, the overindulged
jocks act like perpetual brats.

The "pampered young athlete" storyline is mostly true. About two-thirds
true, to put a number on it.

Football and basketball *do* bring young stars up through a twisted system
called the National Collegiate Athletic Association (the NCAA). Baseball, on
the other hand, presents a very different kind of schooling in the Minor Leagues.

RECRUITING

NCAA: When child stars are being courted by top-notch college programs they patiently receive a parade of fawning coaches and team assistants. Everyone is cozy. Players get on-campus trips complete with access to the hottest parties, introductions to the prettiest girls, and meetings with the richest school boosters. Admission standards are bent or broken for the privilege of offering the jocks free tuition.

School of Hard Knocks: Players get ten-minute conversations with grizzled scouts. The old men are constitutionally charm-deficient, and at any rate, it's not in their interest to become too chummy, lest a prospect try to leverage the connection to inflate his signing bonus. If the process involves hot parties, cute babes, sly payoffs, or free rides, it's a very well-kept secret.

SIGNING OPTIONS

NCAA: Top high schoolers can choose to sign with any one of multiple colleges, then jet off to most any locale they like. In many cases, they pick a ritzy campus fairly close to home, maybe in beauteous Los Angeles or Charlottesville, Virginia.

School of Hard Knocks: Players must sign with their drafting team, then ship off to a town like Bluefield, West Virginia (population: about 10,400). Almost all the rookie league or low-A towns are located in rural areas where the "farm team" label is highly appropriate.

FAME

NCAA: The "Big Man on Campus" may become the biggest celebrity in the region or the state. Seasons can feature sellout crowds, nationwide TV appearances and blanket media coverage. In select cases *Sports Illustrated* and Nike issue proclamations of "The Chosen One."

School of Hard Knocks: Minor Leaguers are barely household names in their own households. None of them have ever been compared to Jesus Christ or Neo.

FORTUNE

NCAA: The bosses want star athletes to stay around as long as possible, so they glide between exclusive dorms, all-you-can-eat cafeterias, best-of-everything stadiums/arenas, and chartered jets. Boosters slip cash under the table, just in case a little more luxury is in order.

School of Hard Knocks: The bosses want athletes to move either up or out of the Minors just as soon as possible, so life on the farm includes transient rooms, greasy-spoon diners, second-rate clubhouses, and hours-long bus trips. Someone once said, "It's called the Minors for a reason."

OFF-SEASON

NCAA: Local boosters routinely set up star college players with make-work or no-show jobs.

School of Hard Knocks: Minor Leaguers take whatever all-too-real jobs they can scrape up during the winter months. These can include short-order cooking or truck driving but never include anything fun or fascinating.

TEAMMATES

NCAA: BFF.

School of Hard Knocks: None. By the time a guy gets to know a teammate in the Minors, one of the two is on the next bus out of town.

ENTOURAGE

NCAA: The world owes them everything. Teenage jocks are given trainers to run workouts, tutors to do homework, fraternities to set up parties, minders to cover up misadventures, and it can only be a matter of time before they're given Impressionists to paint landscapes.

School of Hard Knocks: The world owes them nothing. Players must do laundry, balance checkbooks, lug bags, and sometimes serve as unofficial bat boys and clubhouse attendants. With any luck, a harried young Mrs. Prospect helps haul all his worldly possessions from one small town to the next.

DISCIPLINE

NCAA: It takes something egregious for an otherwise sheltered player to show up in the disciplinary system, something along the lines of rape, drug trafficking, or grand larceny. Even then, the athletes are indispensable to the next big game/revenue check, so most punishments vary from slaps on the wrist to nothing at all.

School of Hard Knocks: May heaven help those who step out of line, because no one else will. Minor Leaguers aren't union members, so they're powerless against disciplinary actions that can range from severe to "good-bye."

TIMELINE

NCAA: Off to the pro leagues after a few dozen college games. By the time players reach the NFL or NBA, a plush sporting life is all they've ever known.

School of Hard Knocks: There's no outside limit to how hard they'll have to work. Even All-Rookie players average over 400 games in the sticks and guys like R. A. Dickey can slog through the Minors for six years or more.

Add it all up and there's a different picture for young baseball players. Spared the ludicrous self-importance to be found in big-time NCAA football and basketball, a down-to-earth upbringing molds youngsters into approximations of mature adults. They've never been perfect but they aren't pampered.

MYTH #61

"Obscene Salaries"

Ballplayer salaries are troubling when things are good,
obscene when they're bad.

—TIM DAHLBERG, "Baseball Salaries Should Outrage, but Don't,"
Associated Press, December 13, 2008

Obscene salaries just keep on ticking in professional sports.
As we try to figure out not just what's fundamentally wrong with the
American economy but with America itself, look no further than what's
being shelled out to the men who play with bats and balls.

—BUZZ BISSINGER, "All Stars and Layoffs," *New York Times*, July 26, 2008

An Open Letter from A. Realist

Some say pro baseball players have dream jobs. They look more like nightmares to me.

Oh, sure, I know the headlines. If a guy makes it to the very top of the game, he can make eight figures per year, maybe pull in a guaranteed contract worth nine figures.

That's all fine and dandy for the lucky-duck superstars but that's not the case for most. Most pro players are destined not for Major League riches but Minor League rags.

The average Minors player puts in eight- or nine-hour days, with maybe one day a month off during the regular season. First-year lawyers deal with more reasonable schedules. The young players are also living hundreds of miles from home, making a few dozen road trips in the space of six months or so. Traveling salesmen have it better. Almost all of their time is spent outdoors in conditions that can range from freezing nights to blazing after-noons. Manual laborers work in more comfort.

Baseball athletes are told to never complain about the work itself, but it requires a tremendous amount of pain resistance. Position players endure seasons full of the slides, dives, and dashes that inevitably result in count-less bumps and bruises, stiffness and soreness, spasms and sprains, tweaks and tenderness. Pitchers have it even worse; in mid-windup their arms move with such momentum that, in photograph stills, the limbs appear to be snapping at torturous angles.

The need for courage is ever-present. Guys might be struck in the face by rock-hard spheres traveling at 100 miles per hour or make full-speed col-lisions with 225-pound men, but those are only the most spectacular episodes in careers full of dangers. On routine plays, and through no fault of their own, athletes have suffered injuries necessitating months of ago-nizing rehabilitation. Intermediate cases can wipe out a year and the worst cases see permanent joint damage.

There's an inevitable mental, even spiritual, cost to that ugliness. Just imagine how well you can concentrate if you had the full knowledge that, in the process of completing your earnings report or plumbing repair, there's an outstanding chance that you will suddenly suffer a severe injury. Imagine how well your sense of motivation can hold up against the pos-sibility that your lifelong dream will be snatched away with little or no warning.

All this is bound up in the work of play. The business involved is even harsher. Since nonproductive Minor Leaguers are only costing their teams money, their bosses are just looking for excuses to cut players from the active rosters. The players are never allowed to be comfortable. Those who aren't kicked to the streets must rise up through six organizational levels with steadily improving competition.

Oh, and the competition. It's the hardest in American team sports.

Great players hail from all around the world, with most foreign-born stars coming from economic backgrounds so desperate that they're working to transform the lives of everyone they love. It's hard to conceive of more motivated competitors.

I try to help these kids. I tell 'em to go with a better option. Which is the same as saying, "Go with *any* other option." They can work in a grocery, where they aren't asked to risk life and limb on a daily basis. Accounting departments provide job security. Those shooting for big money might go into work with less competitive pressure, which is the same as saying, "Go into *any* other work."

The kids never listen. I may as well talk to batting tees.

"I love the game," one prospect told me. "Someone's gonna tear the uniform off my back before I quit," said another. "This is my life." Once, I heard a young man say, "I don't care about the money."

Can you imagine that kind of attitude in this day and age? It's obscene.

A. Realist

Major Salaries

"Back Then They Played Harder"

I would've liked to have played when they played. Not that guys don't play hard now, but it seems they played harder back then.

—DAVE ANDERSON, "A Respectful Aftermath to the Zimmer-Martinez Bout,"
New York Times, June 30, 2004, quoting player Tim Wakefield

It's certainly true that the athletes of the 1950s and previous were tougher than the athletes of today.

—"The Bill James Interview," *American Enterprise*, April–May 2004

The sun was slowly setting over picturesque midwestern skies as the teenager and his father played catch.

The young man, Johnny, bore an uncanny resemblance to Roy Hobbs's son from *The Natural*, while his father, Jim, had a certain cinematic look about him, too, via Dennis Quaid in *The Rookie*. Their catch took place between a sweeping front lawn and a cornfield, a tableau not unlike the one from *Field of Dreams*.

It was a very baseball-y setting.

As the daylight faded, Jim grimaced just a little. He had been tossing with Johnny long enough to feel the worse for wear. The kid looked like he could go on forever but his father's 50-year-old body wasn't what it used to be.

Just as his son zipped yet another fastball into the glove, Jim had to grimace and speak up. "Great job, great job, what an arm, but tomorrow's another day. How about some of your mom's lemonade?"

The younger man was just getting warmed up but he could see his dad slowing down. "Sure," Johnny said as he bounded over to the porch. His father's gait was more of a limp. "Boy, I *am* getting older," he thought.

The lady of the house had thoughtfully set out some lemonade, ice cubes, and drinking glasses by the porch table just a few minutes before. Her husband and son eagerly helped themselves. "Ahhhh," they sighed at once.

Jim could tell his 18-year-old had been growing stronger over the last few months. He said, "Keeping up with your workouts, huh?"

Johnny was proud that the hours at the high school gym were starting to pay off. "No doubt about it. Coach said we have to stay in top condition to fulfill our potential."

Jim could only chortle.

Johnny took another sip as he asked, "What's so funny, Dad?"

"Nothing, really," was the answer. "There was a different attitude when we were first coming up. In the 1970s, all that conditioning was mostly unheard of."

Johnny was puzzled. "You were an athlete. Of course you worked out. Everybody did."

Another good-natured chortle.

"Not exactly." Jim knew his son was interested in baseball history but didn't know much about this particular subject. "What if I told you that no more than a handful of Major Leaguers—Major Leaguers!—were lifting weights back then?"

Johnny knew his father had a healthy sense of humor but couldn't make out any joke. "C'mon, Pop. Our *J.V. team* practically lives in the weight room. The best in the world didn't lift?"

Jim grinned. "Until guys like Tom Seaver came along in the 1970s, managers and coaches assumed that strength training was counterproductive. Players were told that they would become too stiff and bulky, so they never bothered."

Johnny said, "It *is* possible to overtrain."

Jim laughed. "Have you ever seen pictures of those guys? They had to worry about overtraining like they had to worry about bumping their heads against the moon."

Now it was Johnny's turn to laugh. "How did players stay in shape?"

"Well, apart from their game schedule, they did pregame stretches and wind sprints," replied Jim.

"That was it?" said his boy.

"They would sometimes run after cocktail waitresses."

"Wow."

Jim said, "Most any exercise was considered suspicious in those days. Reporters laughed when they found out that Steve Carlton was keeping in shape with martial arts and resistance training."

"That is unbelievable."

"Like I said, it was a different world back then. Most professionals barely ate better than the sportswriters, or anyone else, for that matter. That was back when Denny McLain said that 'the only thing running and exercise do is make you healthy.'"

Johnny shot Jim a highly skeptical look. "In the old days, Harmon Killebrew and Tony Perez were as strong as anyone."

"That was true," said the older man. "Those guys were strong, but only because they had to do manual labor on off-season farms. Most of their team-mates were nowhere close. George Brett, one of the best extra base hitters of all time, said he *never* lifted a weight. Never. He lifted weights as often as Santa Claus mugged little old ladies."

Johnny slumped back in amazement. He stated (rather than asked), "Today's high school players work harder than *the professionals* of your day."

"Today's high school players work far harder than the Major Leaguers of my day." Jim took another sip of that lemonade. "You and your buddies keep up your balance and agility drills throughout the calendar year, which is fantastic and historically unprecedented. Back when, the off-season was the off-season; athletes went off to work ordinary 9-to-5 jobs during the winter. Ken McMullen pumped gas. Phil Rizzuto sold suits. Richie Hebner dug graves."

"I thought they called him the Gravedigger because he buried pitchers," said the young man.

"It was because he worked in a cemetery."

Johnny asked, "Well, if they worked all these off-season jobs, how did they stay in shape?" Before his father could respond he answered his own question. "They didn't!"

Jim had to smile. "Yeah. Some played a few weeks in the Caribbean but most put on rust for three, four months at a time and then did their best to round back into shape during spring training."

He continued after taking another sip. It was good lemonade.

Jim continued, "Back then, if you told them that star players like Cal Ripken Jr. would someday build their own home gyms for constant workouts, they would've thought you were nuts."

It was Johnny's turn to talk. "I work my tail off at the gym but I keep hearing about all these other guys hiring baseball-only conditioning coaches. They can tailor exercises to the sport's specialized movements."

"I cannot get over how advanced and sophisticated the game has become," Jim said. "The scientifically proven biomechanics, aerobics, yoga, the works."

Johnny spoke up. "Well, that would explain why so many players are sticking around well past age 40."

"The new conditioning regimes can explain a lot of things. Many players are displaying the kind of foot speed, arm strength, and stamina rarely seen in the past. I remember when Goose Gossage was treated as superhuman for consistently throwing in the high 90s, but today almost every staff has a guy with that kind of ability. Do you know what I'd love?"

"What?"

"I'd love to take a time machine and match up a 1960s ball club against a contemporary team. They can have the never-met-a-dumbbell crowd on their side and I'd take the world-class athletes for my side. The old-timers would look like beer leaguers, I think."

Johnny whistled in agreement.

"The funny thing is that no one seems to mention their fanatical commitment to the game, not without complaint. Sports writers keep nattering on about how players strive *too* hard nowadays." Jim shrugged again. "I always thought it was the old guys who cheated."

"What do you mean?"

"They cheated the fans by failing to keep themselves in condition. Many players smoked cigarettes between innings of official games."

"They smoked *during* the games?"

Jim nodded. "Joe DiMaggio smoked during games. Dick Allen. Dave Parker. There were many others and I wish that was the worst of it. In the old days the standard belief was that teammates who drank together also won together. One player said that in the early 1960s maybe one-third of all players were hung over when they showed up for work, which was a problem, because teams like the Yankees refused to discipline falling-down drunks."

"What did the managers have to say about that?"

"Very little, since managers were some of the biggest drunks going. Here's a story: one manager stole team equipment to pay for booze, was so drunk that he started a hotel fire, jumped out a hotel window, hurt his knee, and ended up in a hospital, where he didn't write apology notes because he wasn't allowed to be around sharp objects."

His son asked, "Was that really true?"

"No. That was from *A League of Their Own*, but the nonfiction was almost as bad. Sometimes managers encouraged slumping players to go out on benders, as a means to snap back. It was common knowledge that Pirates managers would look the other way as Paul Waner gulped whiskey in the dugout. In 1945 Leo Durocher went out of his way to give a slumping player whiskey as if it was a medicine."

"Hard to believe," said Johnny.

"Believe it, son. The drinking culture, as destructive as it was, pervaded things to the point where it isn't too difficult to forgive someone like Mickey Mantle for becoming an alcoholic. He was barely out of his teens and living thousands of miles from home while those around him encouraged a belief that alcohol was a big part of team camaraderie. The habit, unfortunately, stuck with him, and it erased a lot of natural skill. We'll never know what entire generations might've been if they had stayed somewhat clean and sober."

Johnny stared out into the western panorama. The sun was just about over the horizon, placing him in a more philosophical frame of mind. "I always heard that the old timers hustled more. Mickey often played with a limp, I saw the newsreels."

Jim smiled and went on. "Chain-smokers and problem drinkers have a hard time hustling, kid. A lot of times, Mickey was still limping because he passed up physical rehabilitation needed to get back to 100 percent, and that was because he'd been out drinking."

The younger man nodded, as if to silently agree. Jim took it as a permission to continue.

"Really, John, I always thought that today's athletes play far harder than the old guys. A lot harder. Money makes the *new*-timers play far harder."

Johnny nodded along but piped up, too. "I hear you, okay, but players are imperfect. A championship-level manager says that J. D. Drew is a prime example of a modern-day player without the best work ethic."

Jim heard out his son and responded, "That might be true. Maybe Drew and some others don't get the most out of their gifts, but keep in mind that there have *always* been players that have gotten by on physical gifts. 'Million-dollar arms and five-cent heads,' is what they used to say. Years ago, that was the chatter around 'Sudden' Sam McDowell and Bo Belinsky and there are still a careless or unconditioned few around, OK."

Jim paused for a moment, still feeling a low ache in his throwing arm. He continued, "Now, more than ever, they're rare. Given modern conditions, most Major Leaguers bring a work ethic and focus more in line with guys like Albert Pujols or Roy Halladay."

Father and son could sense that dinner was coming up inside. As they got up from the porch table, Johnny couldn't resist kidding his father. "So it's getting harder and harder to make it to the Majors, eh, Dad?"

Jim gave Johnny a playful tap on the head with his fielding glove. "Well, yeah, it is! But, son, I'm rooting for you."

MYTH #63

"Re: Too Many Rich Kids with No Fire"

Once a player is guaranteed $60 million over five years maybe he starts to think that, given the financial security, he doesn't have to try as hard to improve. With money comes a sense of entitlement, something too many young guys have today.

—TIM KURKJIAN, "Mental Mistakes a Real Drag on the Game," *ESPN The Magazine*, April 30, 2010

Intensity is desperately needed in today's game—"too many rich kids with no fire," says an executive.

— JEFF PEARLMAN, "Despite Verdict, Clemens Doesn't Belong in Player Development," SportsIllustrated.com, June 21, 2012

There have always been tall tales floating around baseball and usually they're harmless enough. No one truly believes that Cool Papa Bell was so fast that he could turn out the light switch and then get back into bed before the room went dark or that Jimmie Foxx hit a ball that Neil Armstrong later found on the moon. The stories were colorful little compliments, benign ways of saying "that man could run" or "he really knew how to hit."

There's another old story still making the rounds, though, and it does harm through misinformation; the story has older generations of ballplayers motivated to play harder than the ballplayers of today.

In a certain way old-time baseball did effectively spur players. Before the free agency system came about in the 1970s even big stars were forced to sign for modest bonuses and to play for single-year contracts on owner-dictated wages, so they were forced to give their best efforts. Desperation led to perspiration.

As times changed, players faced a new set of financial rules.

Today's system ensures that some young ballplayers can become rich from their earliest years in the game. High draft choices can receive multimillion-dollar signing bonuses, earn no less than $480,000 per year as Major League rookies, and become eligible for seven-figure arbitration awards in their third to sixth years. In this, it's said, some young players can be tempted to become lazy, entitlement-minded bums.

Those are the origins of the "old-timers worked hard but the new guys don't" theory, but the theory has a couple gaping holes.

First, players tend to measure themselves by their own potential, including their financial potential, and they're well aware that money garnered in a signing bonus is slight compared to a future free agent contract that might be worth $10 million per year or a career that can yield $100 million or more. Until he reaches a later payday, a born perfectionist may consider himself not a contented millionaire but a frustrated multimillionaire. In this way early rewards can make players even *more* motivated.

Ordinary people would certainly be tempted to hit cruise control after a big initial bonus but, at the risk of stating the obvious, pro athletes aren't ordinary people.

Major Leaguers are an elite among elites. The young athletes selected in the first round of the MLB draft have already outplayed millions of would-be competitors, and those who eventually reach the highest level beat out about 90 percent of Minor Leaguers. "Many are called but few are called up," someone once said. Those in position to win free agent contracts are the most exceptional ones of all, since they've passed a "job interview" lasting, on average, about ten pro seasons and 1,500 pro contests.

By the time they reach the Majors, ballplayers have fought through a process that makes MIT admissions look like elementary school sign-ups. It seems very unlikely that the select few capable of such achievement might suddenly abandon their competitive spirit at the sight of one or two big checks. It seems very likely that an unprecedented vetting process has demanded an unprecedented appetite for success.

Lest anyone think this a too-rosy view of the competitiveness involved in the game, consider some hard numbers. Tom Van Riper of *Forbes* did a study that considered 177 Major Leaguers who were playing in the last year of their contracts from 2001 to 2009, then compared those last-year stats to the immediately preceding years. If most players were actually driven by money they could've been expected to give more, and achieve more, in contract years. They didn't.

Here were Van Riper's findings in terms of home runs and on base plus slugging for every 500 at-bats:

	HR	OPS
Contract Year	19	.824
Preceding Year	19	.821

Those supposedly being motivated by the immediate prospect of big free agency money didn't play any better (or worse) than they did beforehand. Since the financial motivation didn't change overall results, it's safe to assume that it didn't affect the blood, sweat, and tears involved.

Certain cynics seem blind to both the selection process and the contract year data, only to miss out on wonders.

They don't appreciate how guys like Jamie Moyer and Julio Franco stayed in the game well into their 40s, a decade or more after they had banked tens of millions. They cannot see how guys like Vlad Guerrero and Edgar Renteria still dived after balls and crashed into walls as if they were still cash-strapped rook-ies rather than rich veterans. They forget that guys like Gil Meche and Andy Pettitte turned down eight-figure contracts rather than give diminished per-formances in their late careers. They overlook how guys like Dustin Pedroia and Johnny Damon played in pain for months on end, even when they were enti-tled to collect guaranteed salaries from their hospital beds.

To cynics those stories can sound like tall tales, but they're true.

Agency

"Free Agency Destroys Player Loyalty"

*Now, don't think I'm against free agency! Oh no, not at all.
I'm pointing out one of the negatives: guys move around so much that
they aren't as loyal to teams as the guys who stayed with teams
during their entire careers. That's just a fact.*

**—"Trust, Loyalty among Teammates a Thing of the Past," *CBC News*,
February 19, 2008, quoting former player Jesse Barfield**

*What makes free agency objectionable to many fans is the
disloyalty that's bred by success.*

**—LOREN STEFFY, "Free Agency Has Become a Way of Life,"
Houston Chronicle, October 25, 2005**

Jerry Seinfeld jokes that players move around so often that we can only root for the uniforms, not the players. The background noise for every big-money trade or signing can include world-weary complaints about how baseball has been wracked by demanding agents and their clients, those mercenaries in stirrup socks. Whenever a star departs for a better deal, even today, "SELLOUT" and "GREED" signs sprout up in the stands.

If only athletes were more connected to a more humane world. If we could only return to that land of yesteryear . . .

As Jim Bouton would say, "Yeah, suuuure."

A number of those hearing the chatter may be only vaguely aware that the players only stayed with their teams because they could hardly do otherwise. No matter how unhappy their situation, they played under their organization's complete control, including control of movement among the various teams, and anyone who objected could only abandon their lifelong training. If loyalty were defined by a free choice to return an employer's goodwill, then there was no loyalty at all; the system *outlawed* the bilateral agreements that define the concept.

Only complete outsiders saw anything like personal allegiance at work in former times. The players, certainly, harbored no such illusions. They were painfully aware that they lacked the mobility taken for granted by most all other American workers. They played for a love of the game, no doubt, but they would've loved the game even more if it offered them some rudimentary freedoms.

It was only in the 1970s, as the union matured from a little puppy into a watchdog, that more established players won the right to move on to new organizations and new hometowns. It was a pivotal change but it could hardly destroy "loyalties" that never existed.

MYTH #65

"Free Agency Erodes Team Identity"

*Back in the 1950s players usually stayed with a team
on a fairly permanent basis.*

**—MAUREEN MULLEN, *Yogi Was Up with a Guy on Third . . .*, 2009,
quoting former player Ralph Kiner**

*There was a time in baseball's past when players routinely stuck with one
team for most, if not all, of their careers and nobody thought twice about
it. In the age of free agency that notion quickly became a thing of the past
as players moved through teams as if through a revolving door.*

**—SUSAN KELLY, "How Do You Solve a Problem Like Jeff Bagwell?,"
All-Baseball, January 27, 2006**

Joe McCarthy once said he would release his own brother to make his team better, and he wasn't alone in that mind-set.

At one point the Dodgers' general manager had his only son signed as a Minor Leaguer in the L.A. organization but the young man couldn't handle curveballs, so Al Campanis traded Jim Campanis. Athletics owner Connie Mack also sold off his son. Senators owner Clark Griffith sold off his sons-in-law twice, as if to prove that the first time was no accident.* Family, shamily.

Players could only hope that team execs wouldn't treat them as sons, but, alas, those hopes were often dashed. Front offices always made moves in regard to their own win/loss records or profit/loss statements, never in regard to the wishes of the players and their loved ones, and they made moves quite often. In fact, more than two-thirds of all Hall of Famers were sold, traded, or released at least once. Before they reached age 30, all-time greats like Lou Brock and Joe Morgan were shipped off like cattle.

It was only with the advent of the new free agency system of the 1970s that players gained some input over their own fates, some power to stop the heedless shuffling. No one had to sell family members to Cleveland. Few could argue with the moral good in this but some believed that star players moved to new clubs at a rate that would erode the public's attachment to familiar rosters. It was said that "team identity" would erode.

Thankfully, though, that never happened. The data proves as much.

David Vincent of the Society for American Baseball Research conducted a 2003 study on players who stayed with their teams for at least nine years. Vincent found 51 such players during the pre–free agency era of 1951 to 1975, while 48 players fit that category during the free agency era of 1976 to 2002. Another study, done by ESPN.com, took a look at the longest tenured players among the different clubs in 1975 and in 2004 and found that, in 1975, the marquee players averaged 11.2 seasons with their teams, a number that stayed at virtually the exact same level (11.1 seasons) in 2004.

---

*If you think that *your* family's Thanksgiving dinner can get awkward just contemplate the conversations around those dinner tables: Mom is asking Dad why he sold their son halfway across the country; a child is asking why he's never been good enough for the family business; Daddy is telling his daughter that there was nothing personal in the deal to ship out her husband, et cetera. So sad. Baseball should bring families *together.*

In the historic transition to free agency, then, the number of long-term/single-team stars went from 51 all the way down to . . . 48. In terms of long club tenures, the drop was from 11.2 all the way down to . . . 11.1. The changes were so slight that they were barely noticeable. Heck, if baseball was to be graded relative to the NFL's churning rosters, the baseball displayed *far more* stability than ever.

MYTH #66

"It's Always about the Money"

Baseball has devolved into a bottom-line business. Or so say many old-timers. Nowadays "it's all about the money," says Hall of Fame pitcher Bob Feller, who retired 20 years before free agency. "All professional sports are built on greed."

—STAN MCNEAL, "Has Free Agency Damaged Baseball?,"
The Sporting News, January 22, 2009

Let this be lesson # 1,087,042 that players only care about money. They say the right things but greed is good and players don't care about their towns. They're only passing through.

—RICK SNIDER, "It's Always about the Money,"
Washington Examiner, November 21, 2006

People say ballplayers are greedy. People are mostly right.

Professional baseball is a competition that demands a constant hunger. The very greatest of hitters aren't satisfied by four-hit nights, not if they can attain five, six, or seven hits per night. The best pitchers in the world aren't satisfied with giving up a mere two runs in a game, since a one-run effort would be even better and a shutout best of all. Those good enough to win their first Most Valuable Player are also competitive enough to sense that they're only halfway to winning two awards and one-third of the way to three.

Baseball, it never ends. There's always another at-bat, another game, and another season, and competitors never seem to win enough of them. They're greedy. Because they might go for victories at the bargaining table, too, they can be tempted to accept contracts with top dollars.

For all that, though, baseball athletes are also capable of leaving a lot of money on the table. Examples abound. When Jake Westbrook signed his Indians contract he may have passed on $10 million or more in a future free agent contract. When Jake Peavy signed a four-year, $15 million deal with the Padres he probably would've doubled the money if he'd gone for free agency. When young players like Johan Santana and Eric Chavez signed extensions with the Twins and Athletics in recent years, they, too, took contracts estimated to be at least $10 million less than those that would've been available in free agency.

It's tempting to blame temporary insanity for such atypical, uncompetitive behavior, yet a long-term sanity was at work.

Financial security, for instance, was an explanation for the hometown discounts. Injury risks are a constant in pastime play and a player who accepts a lower-bid contract prior to free agency is thereby eliminating the risk that an injury will erode, maybe destroy, his future value. If it's better to have a bird in hand than two in the bush surely it's wise to take a sure thing over a big contract that may never arrive.

In addition, players can settle for less money due to the familiarity factor. From the time they are first signed in their teens or early twenties, they're shipped off to teams located hundreds, if not thousands, of miles from their homes and then asked to move through at least six different home bases in the Minor Leagues. If one is to count road destinations, they've lived in and through dozens of towns.

After years of being so far from home and far from rooted, many of those who finally make it up to the Majors develop an understandable yearning to find a home. The discounts extended to current employers can provide the peace of mind to be found in settled neighborhoods and social lives.

Other factors lead young players into less-than-maximum salaries. Those who remain connected to home can also establish endorsement deals and announcing gigs that can last decades into the future. Like Kent Hrbek in Minneapolis and Frank White in Kansas City, they can become local heroes.

Finally, there's another factor in the un-greedy choices. Call it enlightened self-interest.

Pro baseball players live with their organizations on a day-to-day basis for years on end, giving them the time to develop lines of communication with the front office, close-knit friendships with teammates, and agreeable community ties. All those down-home positives can stand in contrast to the bigger markets where more whispers are passed, factions are formed, reporters are worked, egos are inflamed, and backs are stabbed.

Anyone who might doubt the unintended consequences of free agent dollars need only examine how Kevin Brown became a media piñata in L.A., how Alex Rodriguez became a scapegoat for organization-wide failures in Texas, or how Miguel Tejada faded into obscurity amid Baltimore's chaos. The catalogue of misfortune is longer than George Steinbrenner's old enemies list.

Even among die-hard competitors, success isn't always about money; it can be defined by the fullest sense of security, familiarity, and comfort. One can get rich in various ways.

Payroll

"You Get What You Pay For" (Pt. 1)

Ultimately the only numbers that matter are the ones that follow the dollar sign.

—FRANK DEFORD, "Baseball's Sure Thing: Big Money Wins Big," National Public Radio, April 7, 2010

The major-league free-agent market is generally full of knowns. . . . Generally, you get what you pay for.

—JEFF PASSAN, "Rethinking the MLB Draft," Yahoo Sports, June 5, 2006

In Hollywood, it's said, nobody knows anything.

Every year, it seems, another would-be blockbuster fails to bust blocks. Movies like *Battlefield Earth* and *John Carter* came along with nine figure price tags and all they could buy, including the most expensive talent, the flashiest effects, the splashiest promotions. They flopped nevertheless, chiefly because no amount of dollar bills could paper over shortcomings in clunky characters, plot holes, clumsy dialogue, and so forth. Instead, financial successes came from upstarts like *The Blair Witch Project* or *Paranormal Activity*, projects that tied small budgets to big returns.

In baseball, as in Hollywood, there can be vast inefficiencies in terms of inputs and returns. Consider, at one extreme, some of the most expensive failures in the pastime's recent history:

- *Catcher*: Jason Varitek (2005, received a 4-year contract for a total of $40 million). The Red Sox re-signed their catcher in the warm afterglow of the 2004 World Championship, only to see Varitek struggle against both opposing pitchers (he was roadkill away from Fenway) and opposing runners (with less than a one-third assist rate, he had one of the worst throwing arms in the game). Interviewers and bartenders loved him, though.
- *First base*: Mo Vaughn (1999, 6 years/$88 million). The no-necked Vaughn was a multidimensional threat with the Angels and Mets because he killed his teams with strikeouts (three appearances among the league leaders), low on-base percentage (never higher than .365), and "fielding" that had to be witnessed to be believed. Before long television producers began to refer to super-slow-motion replays as "Mo Vaughns."
- *Second base*: Kaz Matsui (2004, 3 years/$20.1 million). He was huge in Japan but it turned out that the "little" part in "Little Matsui" referred to his contributions in terms of hitting, fielding, and durability.
- *Shortstop*: Alex Rodriguez (2002, 10 years/$252 million). Texas overbid rivals by an estimated $100 million to sign A-Rod to the richest contract in team sports, devoted a similar level of judgment to other deals, and then landed the club into last place. The deal was a perfect demonstration of how a high-powered player could fail in a badly built roster, or put another way, it showed what happens when a "splashy" signing involves a very long dive into a very shallow pool.
- *Third base*: Adrián Beltré (2005, 5 years/$64 million). Beltré was a Most Valuable Player candidate in 2004, a big-time free agent in 2004–2005, and a Least Valuable Player candidate in 2005. The Beltré deal *did* address the Mariners's run-producer question, but the answer was "No, Beltré can't fulfill that role."

- *Outfield*: Raul Mondesi (1998, 6 years/$60 million). In Mondesi the Blue Jays paid for a slick-fielding, hard-hitting superstar but got an increasingly sluggish malcontent who failed to show up among league leaders in any important offensive category. It may have presented the worst Canadian disappointment since the death of Gen. James Wolfe on the Plains of Abraham in 1759.
- *Outfield*: Shawn Green (2000, 7 years/$84 million). In his first five years in L.A., Green hit 162 home runs in exchange for $67.4 million, meaning, on a per unit basis, his bombs may have been more costly than functional nuclear bombs.
- *Outfield*: Damion Easley (2000, 5 years/$29.9 million). The Tigers wanted to buy a "respectable" ball club in 2000 but Easley chipped in .250 on-base percentage/.350 slugging years that evoked Rodney Dangerfield. In 2003 the club released him despite all the money the club still owed on the contract; in effect the Tigers paid Easley more than $14 million to go away. Would a Major League team pay you that kind of scratch *not* to play for them? Then you're at least as good as Damion Easley.
- *Designated hitter*: Mike Sweeney (2002, 5 years/$55 million). Sweeney was so fragile that he barely played more than 100 games per year from 2002 to 2006. To waste more money you would need a pile of cash, a kerosene can, and a matchbox.
- *Pitcher*: Mike Hampton (2001, 8 years/$121 million). Hampton signed a contract that lasted as long as two presidential terms but couldn't stay effective (averaging a 4.80 ERA), mostly because he could not stay healthy (averaging about 111 innings per campaign). It was a complete debacle but did inspire Jeff Passan's immortal poem: "Hamstring, elbow, Tommy John / Disabled list you're always on / Mr. Hampton, you're the best / Working on three years' rest."

In recent years the game saw more than enough busts to stock a full lineup. Of course, such overpaid players had opposite numbers in a little roster that could:

- *Catcher*: Joe Mauer (2004–2006, average annual value of $342,000). Scouts swooned over Mauer's batting title and Gold Glove–quality defense, reporters touted his hometown-boy storyline, and fashionistas hailed his long sideburns. Mauer was a markedly better catcher than Varitek while earning about 1/29th the annual salary.

- *First base*: Ryan Howard (2005–2006, $355,000/year). After winning the National League Rookie of the Year Award in 2005, Howard became known as a "gentle giant" figure. The "gentle" part related to his YouTube comedy sketches and friendly interviews while the "giant" connected to his 6'4", 240-pound frame and a sophomore MVP campaign that featured a .425 on-base percentage and .625 slugging. Howard was significantly funnier and more productive than Vaughn but made 1/41 as much money per year.

- *Second base*: Alfonso Soriano (2001–2003, $687,000/year). The young Yankee did a convincing Rickey Henderson impersonation in his first three years, appearing on the leader boards in categories like hits, slugging, doubles, home runs, and stolen bases. Soriano was very similar to Matsui, aside from his nationality, his far superior numbers and, oh yeah, the ninefold difference in annual salary.

- *Shortstop*: Troy Tulowitzki (2007–2009, $1.75 million/year). Over his first three seasons in Colorado Tulo's offensive production and tracked with A-Rod's league-leading numbers over the American League, but his production only yielded about 1/14th as much in average annual salary.

- *Third base*: David Wright (2005–2006, $349,000/year). At the ages of 22 and 23, Wright hit for average (.306, .311) and extra-base power (82 total doubles) while driving in buckets of runs (218) and starring in several commercials. Any general manager would've taken Mr. Wright over Beltré, even before considering that Wright's salary was 37 times smaller.

- *Outfield*: Miguel Cabrera (2003–2006, $332,000/year). According to Baseball Reference, Cabrera's first four seasons blended patience and power on a Hall of Fame level. He was about 30 pounds heavier than Mondesi was but his annual paychecks were 35 times lighter.

- *Outfield*: Jason Bay (2004–2006, $553,000/year). Bay's first three years in a Pirates uniform were good for both power (30–35 home runs per year) and patience (.400 on-base percentage.) He was very much a

Green-type player, as long as you overlook the 21-fold difference in their salaries.

- *Outfield*: Andre Ethier (2006, $387,000/year). L.A.'s highly touted prospect became a highly respected rookie in 2006, putting up the kind of early numbers (.278, .330, .440) that promised even more spectacular things to come. Ethier started off with Easley's high level of production and hoped to multiply his salary 15 times over, so that he might finish off with Easley's high finances, too.
- *Starting pitcher*: Brandon Webb (2003–2006, $1.18 million/year). Arizona's ace had multiple finishes on the NL leaderboards for ERA, walks-plus-hits per inning, and innings pitched. Webb pitched down in the desert while Hampton lived high up in the mountains, a geographic difference almost as sheer as the 12-fold difference in their annual salaries.

MYTH #68

"You Get What You Pay For" (Pt. 2)

If money isn't the answer in sports, you're not asking the right question.

—JEROME SOLOMON, "Mr. Crane, You Get What You Pay For,"
Houston Chronicle, June 26, 2011

Like most everything else in life, you get what you pay for in baseball.

—TOM HAUDRICOURT, "Brewers Just Can't Win," *Milwaukee Journal Sentinel*, September 6, 2004

One thing that stands out in a survey of the most overpaid and underpaid ballplayers is how process can determine outcome. As it turned out, free agency produced every one of the big busts while team options or arbitration led to nearly all the big bargains.

It was no coincidence. The two different salary mechanisms virtually guarantee that, at different times in their careers, players can be either vastly overpaid or vastly underpaid. Teams can get both far less and far more than they pay for.

The first part relates to free agent deals given to players with about six years or more of MLB experience. The deals are struck through auctions involving two or more teams, where general managers are not only attempting to predict future player performance but the numbers involved in rival contract bids. Even when there are no alternative bidders, teams can end up bidding against themselves due to the phantom offers conjured up by cagey agents. There's a psychological pressure in bidding, too, because executives know that the failure to land high-profile, well-accomplished free agents can lead to unsettled team rosters, bolstered oppositions, angered media members, and angry fan bases.

Given all the panic-inducing factors at work, execs are perpetually goaded into contracts featuring far-too-generous terms. Those who submit such high auction bids often "lose" by drastically overestimating their future returns, a mistake common enough for economists to refer to "the winners curse."

Younger player deals, on the other hand, come through distinctly more team-friendly situations. In roughly their first three years in the Majors, player salaries can be set by teams without any negotiation whatsoever. In their third to sixth years players can go into salary arbitration but teams can bypass the process by refusing to tender contract offers. Those teams that do go ahead with the process are adept enough to win a fair number of decisions, and even when they lose, the stakes are most often measured in a few million dollars and a couple of years, as opposed to the nine-figure, multiyear debacles that can be produced by free agent auctions.

When considering that kind of increased leverage, certainty, and room for error, arbitration can provide great bargains. Teams can get far more than what they pay for.

MYTH #69

"You Get What You Pay For" (Pt. 3)

It's undeniably true that big market teams are at an advantage.

—JONATHAN MAHLER, "Smaller Markets and Smarter Thinking,"
New York Times, October 14, 2011

*When you get the best free agents, that's what makes for a better team.
The more money you can spend the better you get.*

—DAVID LENNON, "Rice Blames Boss, Yanks on Never Winning a Series,"
Newsday, January 18, 2009

As seen in previous chapters, baseball's salary structure can produce bizarre outcomes; some of the best young players in the Majors can work for salaries dozens of times smaller than the monies lavished on big-ticket free agents. Appropriately enough, vast efficiency differences can also play themselves out in entire team payrolls.

When Dr. Alan Abramowitz studied the correlation between overall team payrolls and win totals between 1996 and 2005, he found that well-run teams like the Twins, Braves, and Cardinals could expect to win eight or more games per year beyond what would've been predicted by their budgets while teams like the Devil Rays and Tigers underperformed by ten losses or more. Smarts, or lack thereof, could make more than enough difference to place clubs in or out of playoff contention.

The vast disparities in team spending allowed sharp-minded, low-spending clubs to compete with more dim-witted, big-spending rivals for years on end. We saw this in the Oakland Athletics and New York Yankees, the respective heroes and villains of the *Moneyball* movie. From 2001 to 2006 the A's were outspent by the Y's by more than three to one ($301.3 million versus $971.2 million) but finished only 19 games behind the Yanks in regular season wins (573 wins to 592). In another example, the Marlins won more than the Mets from 2001 to 2010 (812 wins versus 800) despite spending $741 million less in payroll (Florida was outspent by a ratio of 2.9 to 1). So much was produced by so little. The smaller-market teams that hired general managers like Miami's Larry Beinfest at a salary of $1 million or so could find competitive advantages equivalent to tens of millions of payroll dollars per year.

These examples relate to payroll efficiencies that were sustained over several years but smart-spending teams can make even bigger impacts over the short term. When analyst Bill Felber broke down the 1996 to 2005 time frame, for instance, he found that inexpensive teams like the Reds and the White Sox had individual seasons when they won 18 to 30 more games than their payrolls would've predicted while dum-dums like the Rangers or Dodgers could lose 20 or more per season.

Looking at the Major Leagues as a whole, Dr. Abramowitz found that opening day payrolls only explained about 20 percent to 30 percent of the variance in team wins for the 2001 to 2005 period. That's to say, anywhere from *70 percent to 80 percent* of the results seen in the standings were explained by largely nonfinancial factors that include amateurs drafting, prospect development, and low-level trades.

Such facts surely shocked the famous broadcaster who devoted a 2001 book to his theory that two-thirds of all teams were out of serious contention before the seasons even begin but, in the spirit of understanding, let it be said that baseball outcomes have had no obvious analogs in the outside world. No one would ever expect experienced buyers to consistently overpay for cars by far more than 200 percent, for example, and no one could rightly expect a computer company to significantly outperform a rival's ten-year results while profiting significantly less.

Certainly, baseball's payroll structures wouldn't have produced such variable results in other team sports. In the NFL or NBA executives with overwhelming budgets might assemble all-but-unstoppable juggernauts. There, again, vastly differing payrolls would be considered symptoms of an inherently unfair game.

Baseball stands as a world apart in its finances, as in other respects, and that incredible fact is largely taken for granted. If it were otherwise, serious analysts would claim that $100 million teams should win twice as many games as $50 million clubs, or blaring headlines would greet pennant-winners like the 2008 Rays (second-lowest payroll) or the 2010 Rangers (fourth-lowest payroll). This doesn't happen; it's only to be expected that big spenders can fall on their faces even as small spenders vault into postseasons. Fantasy operators heed performances rather than paychecks in building their rosters.

One can pick any upside-down platitude by way of explanation. In the pastime, at least, money doesn't change everything. Financial might doesn't necessarily make right. You don't always get what you pay for.

Money for Nothing

Revenue Sharing . . .

". . . Connects to Competitive Balance"

*Team owners spent most of the summer on revenue sharing, all in the
interest of restoring competitive balance to a game gone awry.*

—TONY MASSAROTTI, "Owners Finally Figure It All Out,"
Boston Herald, December 18, 2002

MLB officials instituted revenue for the sake of competitive balance.

—ALAN SNEL, "Forbes List Compares Baseball's Apples to Oranges,"
Tampa Tribune, April 21, 2006

Accountability is part of the beauty in baseball. If you want to be Major League,
you must prove yourself among the very best.

It all starts on the playing fields. No one plays a single game at the highest
level without putting in years of excellence, where their every on-field move is
studied, examined, and compared to the last one-thousandth place of a decimal
point. Only those who pay their dues can access Major League moneybags.

Virtually everyone working in the game, from front office personnel on
down, must validate themselves through years of sacrifice and success. A perfect system ensures that great results are always linked to great rewards.

Well, an *almost* perfect system where great results are *almost* always linked to great rewards.

For a perfect case study in dysfunction, look no further than Kevin S. McClatchy.

After making his money the old-fashioned way—by inheriting it—the 33-year-old McClatchy headed a group that bought the struggling Pittsburgh Pirates in 1996. As their chief executive officer from 1996 to 2007, he was an oddity—one who consistently delivered rotten results only to receive lavish rewards in return.

McClatchy's Pirates were the lowliest of doormat franchises, failing to achieve so much as a winning record, much less a playoff spot, in more than a decade. The typical year saw them staggering through the season with a 71-91 record, which meant that of the 28 MLB teams in existence when McClatchy started out, the Pirates finished 28th in team wins. Granted, the franchise fielded sorry teams before and after his 12-year tenure, but in over a century of MLB history only a handful of owners matched Mr. 28th's string of unbroken futility; McClatchy was to losing what perfect-game winners were to winning.

If the Pirates' standings didn't present pretty pictures, the views got even worse in their details. In one vista were the train wrecks that represented the big-ticket signings of guys like Pat Meares and Kevin Young. Elsewhere was the flaming rubble representing the trades of Aramis Ramirez, Jason Schmidt, and others. All around was the barren wasteland created by the drafting of John Van Benschoten, Bryan Bullington, and dozens of other guys no one's ever heard of.

To mix metaphors, McClatchy was to managerial excellence what the *Titanic* was to nautical safety but, unlike that doomed old boat, he kept afloat. His life raft was the 2002 Collective Bargaining Agreement (CBA) that mandated that bigger-market teams like the Yankees and the Red Sox contribute local-market monies into a central fund to be divided among the smaller-market teams. Out of that setup, the Pirates were suddenly flush with cash, going from a pre-CBA assistance of $1.8 million per year to about $35 million per year. This revenue-sharing money was in addition to the nearly $40 million per year the team automatically collected through national sources like MLB.com, satellite radio, and the like.

Free money was good to McClatchy's Pirates. According to recent stories by the *Pittsburgh Post-Gazette*, one of the sport's worst franchises in on-field results consistently stood out among the best franchises in off-field finances, pulling in tidy profits nearly three times greater than the MLB average. In 2008 a *Forbes* estimate had the franchise's value standing at more than $292 million, a figure that represented an astounding increase of more than $197 million (207 percent) during the McClatchian reign of error. After a decade of both ineptitude and riches, young Kevin existed as a strange loser/winner hybrid, as if a fourth outfielder had won an MVP trophy or a 5.00 ERA pitcher took home a Cy Young award.

Revenue sharing has been an utter disaster for Pittsburgh, as it has been for Kansas City and, until recently, Tampa Bay and Milwaukee. In each of those cases, piteously incompetent owners were met with more than generous rewards, thus encouraging their clubs to coast through ever more failure. Unless Wall Street bankers start taking taxpayer bailouts *every* year, it'll always stand out as one of the worst wealth-transfer systems of all time.

The CBA's supporters tend to acknowledge that revenue sharing has introduced perverse incentives but sometimes insist that the flaws might be ironed out in the future. Theoretically, the leadership can enforce a requirement that ne're-do-wells use the revenues to "improve performance on the field." (This piece of paper is known as Article XXIV-B-5-a of the Basic Agreement.)

The first stumbling block in the CBA requirement is practical; nearly anything can count as a team effort to "improve performance," be it in capital projects, loans, or interest expenses. An owner might pay lucrative salaries to sit on a so-called advisory board, for example, or can shuffle monies into related companies. One way or another, accounting trickery can ensure that money intended for the team coffers can find its way into owner pockets.

Even assuming that the spending guidelines were functional, no one had a real incentive to enforce them. Bud Selig came into the commissioner's office as "Bud the Buddy," one of the oldest boys in the old boys' club. For over 20 years, as the managing general partner of the Milwaukee Brewers, Selig was known for little more than glad-handing and backslapping among his fellow owners; he was in office *because* he was unwilling to take on multimillionaires capable of fighting regulations through expensive, multiyear lawsuits.

Not surprising, Selig has never called out the dozens of revenue-sharing recipients for failures to "improve performance on the field." There was one year when a payee club slashed payroll by more than $45 million. There was another club that raised its payrolls by 6 percent in a term when its revenue-sharing money more than doubled. There were other recipients who received more in annual revenue-sharing monies than they paid out in annual salaries. None of them were ever called out; the only owner ever to be publicly fined in connection to the revenue-sharing system has been John Henry of the Red Sox, who publicly doubted the wisdom in funding habitual losers. Henry was punished for speaking out, not for lying.

For MLB to instill some new competition into a noncompetitive framework, drastic measures may be necessary. The sport could institute highly specific rules for the use of the revenue checks, for example, and give independent boards the power to dock freeloaders like McClatchy. Independent boards can also give public grades on the recipient's discreet efforts to improve, be that in Minor League development or off-season training or international signings. Lower-revenue teams may be allowed the leeway to draft additional amateurs or select from a pool of unprotected Major Leaguers.

There are various ways baseball might direct its revenue-sharing system away from handouts and toward helping hands. It wouldn't be easy but it would be necessary.

"... Encourages Competitive Balance"

As long as there's no salary cap to equalize things, the reality is that the Yankees and a few other rich teams are going to buy championships while the mid-major cities really can't compete.

—FRANK DEFORD, "Baseball's Sure Thing: Big Money Wins Big,"
National Public Radio, April 7, 2010

There's hope all over the baseball landscape, where the small-market "Davids" now know they can compete with and slay the large-market "Goliaths" and it's all because Selig succeeded in selling his previously-reluctant (and self-interested) owners on revenue sharing.

—BILL MADDEN, "Four Major Questions," *New York Daily News*, April 1, 2007

The basic idea behind the revenue-sharing system is easily understood:

1) Rich teams give poor teams money that
2) poor teams use to improve so that
3) baseball's competitive balance improves.

It's simplicity itself, and sometimes it does work.

The first part is a mandated no-brainer, as bigger-market ball clubs now chip in over $400 million per year for the MLB's annual revenue-sharing pool every year.

It's not hard to see how the second part can work out, too. Some lower-revenue ball clubs have, indeed, used revenue-sharing checks to bolster both their payrolls and winning ways:

- The Athletics have used revenue-sharing money to become one of the most winning franchises in the new millennium. Without outside help accounting for anywhere to one-half to one-third of his payrolls, Billy Beane would've probably lacked the resources to produce winners since 2000.

- The Twins, similarly, have utilized annual payments to establish themselves as a low-budget/high-win total organization capable of signing stars like Torii Hunter, among others.
- In a year like 2006, nine of the 16 revenue-sharing recipients boasted winning records.

So far, so good. There were well-meaning franchises that spent their revenue-sharing money in service of well-played baseball. There were some well-intentioned, well-run teams out there.

Unfortunately for competitive balance, those weren't the only teams involved. In addition, there were teams run by executives like the notorious Kevin McClatchy of the Pittsburgh Pirates.

The Pirates had a remarkable ability to lose both games and fans during McClatchy's early ownership tenure, perennially finishing with league worsts in both wins and attendance. Not surprisingly, they were among the cheapest of ball clubs, too, averaging a $20.3 million payroll that typically ranked 27th in the Majors from 1996 to 2000.

Things seemed to change in the 2001 to 2003 period, though, as additional revenue-sharing dollars and a spiffy new venue bolstered the team's bottom line.

At first, McClatchy tried to do the right thing by investing his newfound wealth in the ball club. His payroll jumped from $31.9 million in 2000 to $52.7 million and $54.5 million shortly afterward. For a time, Pittsburgh approached a mid-level salary structure.

As it turned out, though, the problem wasn't in the spending but in the spenders. McClatchy and his front office chose to spend their newfound wealth on players like the light-hitting Jason Kendall, the soft-tossing Jeff Suppan, and various other nonentities. When the club signed a free agent to a contract that funded both a yacht and a rotten attitude, a local columnist wrote, "Derek Bell is the ultimate Pirate—he lives on a boat and steals money."

With Bell and company in tow, McClatchy merely transformed cheap 90-loss teams into *expensive* 90-loss teams. Having realized that he lacked both IQ points and big-money returns, he surrendered.

Even as McClatchy's revenue-sharing payments multiplied in the years since 2004, he reverted back to the skimpy payrolls that put them among the bottom few clubs in baseball. He even tolerated Dave Littlefield, the clueless general manager who averaged 92 losses per year in his six years on the job. Such is life when "a safety net" is treated as a hammock.

McClatchy's uninspired nonactions may have had terrible consequences for Pittsburgh's dispirited followers but they weren't irrational within the context of the revenue-sharing system. On the contrary, it would've been irrational for anyone to work hard for easy money.

Unfortunately, there were other MLB owners who fell into the perverse incentives created by the revenue-sharing system. Bosses in Kansas City, Tampa Bay, and Milwaukee were so well compensated that they didn't feel motivated to revamp their franchises from top to bottom. Even as revenue sharing lifted well-run teams like the Athletics to new heights, it also allowed badly run clubs to stagnate in third and fourth place; the system's overall effect on competitive balance has been, at best, mixed.

The solution to the revenue-sharing problem may be in introducing consequences to owners. A reformed system may link financial help to regular-season records. If the owners of the Athletics, Twins, and other smaller-market teams continue fielding winners over time, they might be rewarded with escalating bonuses even as laggards are punished through dwindling payments. If a revenue-recipient team cannot produce a winning season within a generous time frame of five years or so, its support can get cut more and more, right up to the point where McClatchy types are induced to sell out to newcomers capable of restarting the revenue-sharing clocks and, in time, making their franchises far more competitive. The exact workings of a reformed system wouldn't matter much just so long as it establishes a new connection between shared revenues and effective spending.

Introducing the reforms won't be easy, of course; today, after more than a decade in the current revenue-sharing system, some bosses treat big-money transfers as inalienable rights rather than unearned luxuries. They must be weakened before baseball becomes stronger.

MYTH #72

"... Levels the Playing Field"

The last two CBAs have leveled the field.

—TOM VERDUCCI, "Blue Skies Everywhere,"
Sports Illustrated, February 26, 2007

We are trying to level the playing field. We have made enormous progress.

—MIKE SILVERMAN, "Commissioner Happy with the 'Golden Era,'"
Boston Herald, July 12, 2006, quoting Commissioner Bud Selig

In theory, the revenue-sharing system levels the financial playing field. In concrete terms, ball clubs maximize profits. The concrete won.

On the one hand, there's no doubt that the revenue-sharing system has motivated bigger-market franchises due to "payroll taxes." Certain threshold levels trigger penalties that can reach into the tens of millions, and the penalty-inducing levels have been treated as de facto salary caps by teams like the Cubs and Red Sox. Even the Yankees seem to cut back on potential free agent spending because they shied away from the penalties that would come along with hefty payrolls.

Such downward pressure on salaries might be expected to reduce the gap between the rich and the others, but the system also motivated smaller-market teams to reduce spending. Because revenue-sharing payments to teams like the Pirates, Rays, and Royals came without stringent requirements, the teams had license to minimize payrolls and, in that way, maximize profits.

The downward spending trends affecting both big-market teams and smaller-market teams have meant that the revenue-sharing system has had little, if any, net effect on salary structure.

The following chart includes the four most expensive team payrolls versus the four least expensive payrolls, along with the teams' percentage disparity from the overall Major League average, for the years 2001 and 2005 (the last year before widespread revenue sharing and one of the first years afterward):

2001 PAYROLLS' DISPARITY FROM MLB AVERAGE				
Most expensive payrolls	$109.8 million	$109.6 M	$109 M	$93.2 M
Disparity from Major League average	73%	72%	71%	47%
Least expensive payrolls	$35.5 million	$34.8 M	$33.8 M	$24.4 M
Disparity from Major League average	−44%	−45%	−47%	−62%

2005 PAYROLLS' DISPARITY FROM MLB AVERAGE				
Most expensive payrolls	$208.3 million	$123.5 M	$101.3 M	$97.7 M
Disparity from Major League average	184%	68%	38%	33%
Least expensive payrolls	$39.9 million	$38.1 M	$36.9 M	$29.7 M
Disparity from Major League average	−46%	−48%	−50%	−59%

The introduction of revenue sharing actually increased the disparities, whether those disparities were measured in absolute or relative terms. The system didn't level the playing field but left the rich rich and the poor poor.

Through the Parks

"The New Ballparks Are Expensive"

*When a profit is made the millionaires get to keep it
but when they need to fleece the tax coffers . . .*

—GARY THORNE, "Corporate Greed Often Wrapped in Ballpark
Packaging," *USA Today*, September 22, 2006

Sports teams fleece the taxpayer again.

—MATT WELCH, "If You Build It, They Will Leave," *Reason*, January 2004

With recent years seeing the introduction of new ballparks in New York, Minneapolis, and Miami, baseball is quietly nearing the end of a remarkable cycle. By the time the current round of venues debut, the majority of Major League teams will be playing in venues built or substantially rebuilt since 1989.

The new buildings have been called many things. Civic leaders called them important investments in city transit and parking. They were. Fans called them upgrades in design, comfort, and safety. Also true. Meanwhile, some commentators also called the new buildings expensive government rip-offs. This part wasn't true.

To be sure, baseball owners asked for subsidies in getting the new foul lines lined, light towers lit, and infields fielded. City and state taxpayers ponied up about $306 million for each of the new ballparks (about two-thirds of the average building's cost).

171

Now a couple hundred million sounds like a lot of money to those who did-n't invest in early Microsoft stock, but the sums deserve context.

For starters, those who declared "this ballpark cost the city $300 million" or so invariably referred to a final, unadjusted amount. However, the public expenses could be paid out in relatively small payments over a long term, much like private home mortgages could be paid down over decades. What was casually described as a nine-figure cost could be amortized into far smaller sums on a per-year basis, and even at their face values the payments were negligible amounts in relation to municipal budgets that were often measured by the hundreds of millions.

The annual expenses were so light, in fact, that they could easily be offset by relatively painless new taxes. When Seattle and Washington State made a $393 million contribution toward Safeco Field in 1999, for example, the record-setting sum was fully funded by one dime in taxes for every $100 worth of nonessential purchases in five surrounding counties. Similar stories abounded. The tax money put into Baltimore's beloved Camden Yards worked out to roughly $14 per state household per year, which was less than the average fam-ily's annual spending on chewing gum.

The new ballpark taxes were both relatively light and avoidable, since many of the fees were focused on upscale hotels or on "sin" items like cigarettes. In other words, the burdens, slight as they were, mostly fell on the wealthy or the unhealthy.

The cost to home cities went down still further because they were awarded with All-Star Games, events which could infuse more than $65 million into area economies. Many cities also saved millions by nullifying the maintenance fees needed for the decrepit buildings that were replaced.

When pressed, even the harshest critics might concede that these were pretty good deals for the cities. Still, they might protest, it was offensive for well-off owners to demand a single dollar in taxpayer revenues. The million-aire owners were supposedly being rewarded for *not* moving away, like some farmers got cash for not growing crops or some welfare recipients received handouts for sitting on street corners.

That was the perception, but the reality has been something different. The new tenant teams gave back a lot.

The public-private partnerships varied, but many cities received iron-clad deals guaranteeing MLB for generations to come plus chunks of revenue streams in concessions and advertisements. Like all businessmen, the owners hoped to gain from their deals but they also invested an average of over $100 million in the new ballparks while shouldering the risk of future operating deficits and franchise sale losses.

It's always been the "business of baseball" and never been the "hobby of baseball," so of course the new ballparks cost money. That was no surprise. The surprise was in the building boom's affordable costs.

MYTH #74

"The Owners Use Blackmail"

The history of the stadium game is the story of how, by slowly refining their blackmail skills, sports owners learned how to turn their industry from one based on selling tickets to one based on extracting public subsidies.

—DAVE ZIRIN, *Bad Sports*, 2010

"They're trying to blackmail us," [Florida State Senate president Tom] Lee said [of the Marlins ownership]. . . "I feel like they're trying to put a gun to our head."

"Marlins Want $60 Million in State Money," Associated Press, January 20, 2005

There seems to be a signature feature for nearly every phase of the baseball season. Sunshine marks spring training, summertime heat accompanies the mid-season, autumnal chill greets the playoffs, and the off-season sees "blackmail" accusations in ballpark financing.

That last is unwelcomed but it's a perennial. Every time a Major League club negotiates a hometown contribution, it seems that the fans get the same earful regarding big league "blackmail" and "extortion." One headline from *USA Today* described the development in language suitable for outlaws-at-large ("Stadium Blackmail Escalates, Touching at Least 20 States").

It might be a wee vitriolic, calling someone a blackmailer or an extortionist. The *Merriam-Webster's Dictionary* defines blackmail as a noun signifying "extortion or coercion by threats especially of public exposure or criminal prosecution." Extortion is "the crime of obtaining money or some other thing of value by the abuse of one's office or authority."

Those definitions didn't bear any obvious connection to ballpark negotiations. No team executive has ever pulled a knife on a city councilman, for example. No big-city mayors have been bound and gagged in abandoned warehouses. Partisans write editorials rather than ransom notes.

In actuality, ball clubs are similar to other businesses that deal with city halls. The two sides run through several offers and counteroffers until, through some series of twists and turns, eventually they find resolutions that politicians can sell to their voters and executives can sell to their shareholders; the processes apply whether the Mets ask for ballpark financing or MetLife Insurance requests zoning revisions. A nationally known ball club can attract far more publicity than another faceless corporation, that's all.

Leaving aside their vivid language and propensity toward exaggeration, pundits may have believed that the clubs were doing something inherently unethical or unfair in obtaining their new ballparks. Team owners seemed to wield so much power that they make demands, not requests.

In fact, baseball teams have never had the leverage necessary to drive hard bargains.

The relocation threats were mostly bluffs, because the teams chiefly depended on the local revenues to be gained in the richest, most heavily populated metro areas in the country. They settled into the markets long ago, so relocations into secondary markets like Portland, Oregon, would only cause revenue shortfalls. First-tier markets like Denver, Colorado, and St. Petersburg, Florida, did emerge in the 1980s but it was always in the interests of the Majors to establish new markets not through disruptive relocations, but orderly growth; only expansion teams could provide nine-figure checks to the established owners.

From time to time, team owners threatened to leave—they may have *wanted* to leave—but they had no viable destinations. Even if a stray owner was dumb enough to try, they wouldn't have overcome an owners' fraternity armed with both the financial incentives and antitrust powers needed to knock them back into line. Only in their dreams could individual owners blackmail anyone, and it was a major reason every single Major League team stayed in place for the three decades following 1972.

There were no facts, only hidden agendas, behind the blackmail hoax. Team owners talked up relocation possibilities because even empty threats could add momentum to ballpark negotiations that could've otherwise dragged on for years and years. After cobbling the deals together, city politicians gladly took credit for overcoming relocation threats. Many sportswriters actually believed in the "rip-offs," and even those who knew better were ever willing to stoke class resentments against ever-unlovable team owners.

Whatever its uses, the blackmail notion was always rhetorical, never realistic. Major League teams didn't walk away because they couldn't walk away.

MYTH #75

Ballparks & Stadiums and Apples & Oranges

When it comes to sports venue financing, commentators always make the casual assumption that ballparks are more or less the same as football stadiums. "One way or another, a rich guy asks for the cash to build a big athletic thingamajig where a lot of people cheer and yell and it all winds up in the same newspaper sports section, right?"

However, baseball and football business practices can be as vastly different as a single and a screen pass.

The first big difference is in the per capita usage of the venues. While the typical baseball team averages upward of 2.45 million spectators per year, NFL teams average little more than 541,000 in total regular season attendance. Concerts and other one-off events can supplement a building's main purpose, but otherwise a football venue sees about 22 percent of the total patron usage of a MLB park.

The disparity between ballpark/stadium demographics is even more one-sided. Because so many seats are available, baseball tickets can be distributed among the general public. Everyone from pensioners to financiers find realistic opportunities to attend the venues that their taxes helped build.

Football tickets, on the other hand, are scarce enough to be grabbed by relatively tiny fan bases, and that is why decades-long waiting lists can pop up in a relatively small town like Green Bay, Wisconsin, or in a relatively remote college outpost like Lincoln, Nebraska. An estimated 95 percent of self-described NFL fans have *never* seen a live game, so their stadium taxes are funneled into buildings that mostly exist as open-air television studios.

Then there are the construction costs to consider. Since ball clubs play more than 80 home games per year, they can get by with relatively intimate venues averaging about 46,000 in seating capacity. NFL clubs play only eight home games per year, however, so they can only maximize revenues with buildings seating 67,000 or more. This means that the practical difference between a baseball building and a football stadium is the difference between a relatively modest facility and a concrete giganto-plex with nearly twice the real estate footprint. If you've ever wondered why a new football stadium in Cincinnati or Chicago can cost $100 million more than a top-of-the-line baseball facility within the same metro area, that's the reason.

The bottom line is that ballparks seat far more spectators, serve a more widespread clientele, and spare the public tens of millions in taxes. There is a distinction between apples and oranges and an even bigger distinction between ballparks and football stadiums.

MYTH #76

"The Financing Short-Changes Spending on Schools, Roads, and Other Good Things"

Once again a community that needs better housing, better schools, and better hospitals is given a better stadium.

—NORMAN CHAD, "Cash Cow Gets New Barn," *Washington Post*, July 7, 2008

"How anyone could walk through the public schools of Washington," former player Jim Bouton wonders, "and then say that paying for a new professional baseball stadium should be that city's priority, amazes me."

—STEVE TREDER, "THT interview: Jim Bouton," *The Hardball Times*, January 10, 2006

Baseball. It's among the most venerated elements of Americana. What can compare in its hold on the heart of our great nation? The red, white, and blue of Old Glory, without a doubt. Motherhood, certainly. Apple pie. Tom Hanks. It's a short list.

Americans love baseball. They would do nearly anything for baseball.

Well, they would do *nearly* anything.

One thing that we won't do is shift governmental funding from worthwhile social services to ballpark construction. Robbing Peter to pay Paul rarely makes a lot of sense but it makes no sense at all if Peter's money is dedicated to schools and safe streets while Paul's money is earmarked for a sport, however glorious that sport may be.

This is the reason why it's never done. Every single time that a government subsidizes a new ballpark it uses brand-new revenues raised for that express purpose. No existing funding is cut. If dedicated ballpark taxes or debts aren't approved, the money wouldn't be spent.

Social services don't lose when baseball wins. No one loves the game that much.

MYTH #77

The Greatest Comebacks of All Time

*There are many examples of new ballparks causing a spike
in attendance only to see the crowds dwindle when the novelty
wears off and the home team sputters.*

—Ron Kroichick, "Giant in Many Ways," *San Francisco Chronicle*, **July 22, 2007**

*The vast money generated at the new stadiums fooled these teams into
thinking they suddenly were running their teams well when they actually
were just benefiting from temporary corporate welfare.*

**—Jim Caple, "Continued Losing Main Reason for Empty Parks,"
ESPN.com, May 20, 2003**

When fans think of baseball turnarounds there is no shortage of exemplars.

There were the 1964 Cardinals, coming from 11 games back to win the World Series. There were the 1969 Mets, who overcame a history of franchise failure to win a miracle championship. No one will forget that the 1978 Yankees were 14 games back before they defeated the hapless Red Sox.

Those upsets featured unforgettable baseball players, teams, and pennant races, but they weren't the greatest comebacks of all time. No, the greatest turnarounds have come within the last 20 years or so, and they were defined by a new generation of improved teams, new playoff runs, and new attendance booms.

The new energy came from all-new ballparks that made it onto the Major League scene. Some 16 teams built baseball-only venues for themselves between 1989 and 2006, with a lucky 13 playing five or more seasons in their new digs by the conclusion of the 2006 season.

The first effect came in the standings. In their first five full years in the new venues, five new tenants made improvements averaging 14 wins per season, three others made negligible changes in their records, and four others saw declines averaging five games per season. Overall, five additional wins per year were produced for tenant ball clubs.

The new buildings also saw increased on-field successes. The teams were bumped from a pre-ballpark average of 80 wins to a post-park level of 85 wins, so teams that had enjoyed winning seasons at a 45 percent rate went up to a 66 percent rate. In a sport that values statistical thresholds, the new venues gave clubs enough momentum to move from net losers to net winners.

The new ball boosts were all the more important for the fact that they presented tipping points for postseason clubs. The tenant teams made the playoffs at a 22 percent rate in the five years prior to the debuts of their new ballparks, but established a 40 percent success rate at their new addresses. The pre-move clubs totaled 12 division titles, two league championships, and one World Series championship, while the post-move clubs ended up with 17 divisions, six pennants, and two world titles. Four of the ball clubs made the playoffs for the first time in a decade or more.

The new venues saw a new vitality in their box offices. The teams in question saw average per-game attendance go up from about 24,500 fans to 35,000, an overall increase of about 40 percent per game. Over the course of a single season, a new ballpark could be expected to boost average attendance by more than 850,000 spectators, and over five years the typical ball club could welcome an additional 4.25 million.

To put the magnitude of those changes into perspective, the 1990s and new-millennium ballparks averaged annual attendance gains greater than the *overall* attendance for 1970s-era teams like the Giants, Athletics, and Padres. Even after the Majors set new attendance records in the late 1980s, teams still reached new levels of popularity.

To paraphrase a movie line, "If you build it, they will come."

If the new ballparks had undeniable impacts on wins, winning seasons, postseason appearances, and gate counts, it was possible to overstate the effects. As the novelty in the new ballparks wore off over the years, winning ways became increasingly important to the fans.

With that being said, however, the buildings also presented fundamental, lasting strengths. As their millions of approving guests have affirmed, the new ballparks represented upgrades in everything from transportation and parking to concessions and bathrooms. By presenting better value, the new tenant teams could hike average ticket prices by more than 40 percent and bolster revenues by an average of $17 million or more per year.

The increased revenues presented increased incentives to win. While teams like the Indians and Giants were assembling contenders before they headed into new confines, their richer rewards gave the clubs every reason to keep up the good work.

The enhanced incentives didn't always produce good management results, of course. Teams like the Pittsburgh Pirates maintained a familiar state of disarray at their new ballpark but even those franchises could look for long-term benefits in their new ballparks. On the happy day when their current owners pass from the scene new franchise owners can come in with greater potential rewards. That hope is built into the bricks and mortar; it's not temporary.

MYTH #78

"Ballparks Are Economic Investments"

There's an old saying that "a fool knows the price of everything and the value of nothing." Whoever came up with that one must've spent a lot of time with the critics of new ballparks.

Several studies, including those conducted by Professor Robert Baade, indicated that the consumer spending associated with the venues was simply shifted from other spots in the same metro area. That's to say, local residents spent less disposable money on various restaurants or movie houses in order to spend in the new ballparks and their environs. There seemed to be a "substitution effect" at work, one that ensured that the new buildings provided little, if any, net addition to the municipal tax bases.

Because the ballparks didn't inject massive amounts of new spending into a local economy, many critics decided that they were unworthy endeavors. Along those lines, they penned gloomy tomes carrying titles like *Major League Losers* and *Field of Schemes*.

This would've made sense if ballparks were to be defined exclusively as economic investments but this has never been applicable. In fact, the venues are properly measured not in finances but in quality of life; in this sense municipal ballparks are properly compared with national parks.

The new ballparks present social value first through their sheer attendance numbers. With tenant teams attracting more than 30,000 spectators per game and 2.5 million spectators per year, the new buildings put the "mass" into "mass entertainment." Such communal experiences always had a welcomed effect but they are particularly valuable in a highly fractured era, as urban sprawl has only increased our physical separations even as ever-increasing job turnover, class inequality, and divorce rates have worked to remove the traditional moorings of work and family. Such alienation cannot be directly mitigated by digital-only contacts like texting, twittering, twiddling, and more, so it's easy to feel that now, more than ever, we're on our own. One sociologist said that, today, we're "bowling alone."

To find huge baseball crowds making a choice to come together on a common ground, though, the effect can be wondrous. One can experience that rarest of feelings in a ballpark, a feeling that we're joined in something bigger. Tens of thousands find common ground. Civic life is more livable within the walls. There's a return to the ancient belief that community spirit is most vital when it is channeled into immediate, face-to-face gatherings.

The cohesion within the parks may be difficult to articulate in exact ways but this much is indisputable: it meets a need unmet when the same number of individuals scatter among 1,000 diners, multiplexes, and, yes, bowling alleys.

The ballparks had such powers that, frequently, they could be felt far beyond city limits.

Even for those who've never set foot in the parks, cities like St. Louis and Philadelphia have been symbolized by the new Busch Stadium and Citizens Bank Park. Their distinctive architecture and surrounding vistas brought their hometowns alive to the popular imagination. At the risk of sacrilege, it's possible that, on a day-to-day basis, the ballparks are at least as relevant as the Gateway Arch or the Liberty Bell. Tourist attractions have visitors strolling about and snapping pictures but ballparks have local residents actually living their lives, rooting and hollering, interacting within a common identity. I mean, most Philadelphians have seen the Liberty Center far less often than they've seen their centerfields, and when residents travel they can most readily connect to their hometowns through the memories and emotions they once shared with their fellow fans, friends, and families. To appreciate the joys in such experiences, just try asking baseball fans about the times they share at ballparks. They might talk about forging ties with their parents or kids, bonding friendships, or feeling at home in their hometowns. Because an ineffable love for the game can be rooted in effable places, even long-gone buildings like Tiger Stadium and Shibe Park can be both well remembered and well chronicled. All this is rarely, if ever, included in the economic studies. Like strict materialists, the critics treat ballparks according to the strictly financial conventions applied to cement factories or ceramic tile distribution centers. Like confirmed baseball haters, they remained blind to the enriching effects within hometowns. In keeping with an old adage, they shout about prices and keep silent on values.

In Balance

"Someone Can Define Competitive Balance"

Many talk about competitive balance but not many know what it means.

The threshold importance of the issue is clear. Competitive balance is often taken as a moral matter because in the national pastime every worthy competitor should get a fair shot at getting ahead. If the game boils down to competing checkbook ledgers rather than competing lineups, a merit-based balance might give way to impersonal imbalance. Smaller-market teams would act as de facto feeder systems for the larger-market teams.

While the stakes are clear the issue's definition is unclear.

In competitive balance there's a temptation to misinterpret a "fair shot" as being equivalent to an "equal shot," for example. MLB's objective is to maximize fan interest through the range of markets, so its leadership basically wants smaller-market teams to maintain enough opportunity to keep their fans interested while still allowing bigger-market teams the competitive advantages needed to consistently draw in their fan bases. To be sure, Kansas City's continued cellar dwelling is a source of despair for Billy Butler's followers, but it's no great crisis for the sport as a whole, if only because the Kansas City metro area is about one-ninth the size of the New York City market. With no match in the financial and popular clout of these cities, there's no necessary need to match their competitive stances.

Starting off with that oft-unacknowledged reality, it's difficult to set out just how much competitive opportunity should be allocated throughout Major League markets.

High-level mathematics isn't very helpful in the task. The distribution of outcomes like first-place finishes and winning records can be gauged by Gini coefficients, Markov modeling, and several other math equations that would make a tenured statistician weep in frustration. More prosaic measures look at deviation in win percentages, ratio of top-to-bottom percentages, and win percentage ranges, but those numbers are scarcely more cogent. The most competitive/balanced possible situation would have even the smallest-payroll teams with a shot at a championship if they make even a few competent moves, but it's hard to apply an objective definition to "a few competent moves."

Folksy measures tend to get lost in generalities. Commissioner Bud Selig never tires of expressing competitive balance in terms of "hope and faith" but the phrase is more suited to churches than green cathedrals. How to measure what everyone's so hopeful and faithful about, whether certain franchises are feeling good enough or maybe too good? Many fans tend to measure failures and successes in terms of their local clubs, not the jumble presented by a 30-team collective. If the Dodgers consistently finished in third place, for example, L.A. fans would be downcast about competitive balance and, in the alternative, Mariners pennants would leave Seattle followers with good feelings about the sport's overall balance.

Since neither strict numbers nor platitudes are very useful in measuring competitive balance, a more broad-based measure might fill the breach. A stock market analyst named James Surowiecki has spoken of the "wisdom of the crowds" thesis, which anticipates that the diverse decisions of independent individuals can be aggregated into optimal results on the subject. In our present context Surowiecki's theory predicts that millions of independent baseball fans are capable of validating a sport's competitive balance through spinning turnstiles and robust ratings. They can make their own judgments on the chances for well-managed clubs throughout any number of markets.

As it happened, this is what happened. Today we know that baseball's competitive balance is great mostly because its public tells us so.

Previous chapters described the ways that baseball has exploded in popularity in the new millennium, and it's worth mentioning the universality of that popularity. Winning teams in the biggest markets in the country have shattered attendance and ratings records since 2000 but so have winning teams in considerably smaller markets like Milwaukee. Even middling performers in modest markets, including the 2006 Reds (80 regular season wins) and the 2005 Padres (82 wins), can still be assured of annual turnstile counts in excess of two million. This was a level of *Sports Illustrated* fan support that would've put them among MLB attendance leaders in the late 1970s, well after a cover story trumpeted "The Baseball Boom."

In the extraordinary attendance numbers we've seen the "wisdom of the crowds" affirm something of importance.

MYTH #80

"The NFL Has Better Competitive Balance" (Pt. 1)

*While the NFL and the NBA have achieved genuine parity, . . .
baseball keeps lagging behind.*

—MATT TAIBBI, "How I'd Save Baseball," *Men's Journal*, April 1, 2010

*According to my dictionary, parity means: The quality or state of being
equal or equivalent. Sorry, that doesn't fit MLB. It comes very close
to fitting the National Football League. . . .*

—BOB SMIZIK, "Parity Is a Dream, Not a Reality," *Pittsburgh
Post-Gazette*, October 22, 2006

Abraham Lincoln sometimes told jokes in order to make a point about one issue or another. According to lore he would sometimes ask, "If you call a dog's tail a leg, then how many legs would a dog have?" More often than not his companion would answer, "Five," to which the president would counter, "No, the answer is four, because calling a tail a leg doesn't make it so."

Honest Abe would've disliked the NFL.

The NFL is never shy about touting the supposed balance in its competition, in the fact that nearly any team can win "on any given Sunday." In reality, Major League Baseball has a far greater parity and by multiple measures.

Comparative parity can be established in the variation in its team winning percentages, for example. In the ten seasons from 1997 through 2006, an average of 2.6 MLB teams per year were good enough to finish with winning percentages above .600, while an average of 2.1 teams per year were woeful enough to finish with winning percentages below .400. This is to say that, in a typical year, 25 of 30 Major League clubs could be expected to finish within a relatively narrow band above or below the break-even (.500) level.

The typical NFL season in the 1997 to 2006 period was far more tilted. An average of 10.2 football teams per year finished with .600 or greater winning percentages, while an average of 10.8 clubs per year finished with .400 or lesser win rates. While 83 percent of Major League clubs were bunched together in a typical year, a mere 30 percent of NFL teams were that close to the middle.

The disparity within the sports also showed up through in-season performances. Even the most extreme baseball mismatches of the 1997 to 2006 decade weren't completely predictable; in games featuring teams among the four worst regular season finishers versus the four best teams of the same year, the lesser ball clubs won at about a .340 clip. In football, by contrast, a similar matchup between the league worst and league best yielded a microscopic winning percentage of .027. (The lesser teams won only three of 111 matchups.)

It's much the same "unpredictable baseball/predictable football" story when it came to home contests. In the Majors, teams sustained a 53 percent edge through winning percentage but NFL teams' home field advantage was about 70 percent per year. Franchises like the Broncos or Patriots have gone through consecutive years without a home loss.

Football defenders might assert that none of that really matters; many seem to believe that the NFL mixes up the competitive environment from year to year so that few teams will dominate or be dominated over the long term. The evidence is to the contrary.

The NFL featured more than its share of both bullies and bullied. Four franchises sustained .600 or better winning percentages while another three franchises were well below .400. At the lowest extreme the Cleveland Browns posted a .313 winning percentage that was only .313 better than what they would've posted if they had only suited up a Brownie troop.

Over the course of the 1997 to 2006 period, however, only a pair of baseball franchises (the Braves and Yankees) managed to sustain winning records of .600 or better while a single franchise (the Devil Rays) struggled with an overall record under .400. All three franchises were barely above or below the thresholds.

It turns out that baseball had more unpredictable results in its everyday competition, most lopsided matchups, home games, and long-term win/loss records. Dogs don't have five legs and the NFL doesn't have superior competitive balance.

MYTH #81

"The NFL Has Better Competitive Balance" (Pt. 2)

Yes, as sure as the flowers are blooming again, every team has a chance. Whereas that is true in the NFL, in baseball it's understood from the start that some competitors just don't have a prayer.

—FRANK DEFORD, "Baseball's Sure Thing: Big Money Wins Big," National Public Radio, April 7, 2010

It would really be nice to see Major League Baseball reach the same level of competitiveness as the NFL.

—J. MILLER, "Competitive Balance," *Baseball Digest*, August 17, 2010

If the NFL is the league of "any given Sunday," then the numbers say that MLB is the league of "any given Sunday, Monday, Tuesday, Wednesday, Thursday, Friday, and Saturday." The football-parity notion seems to be sustained not on metrics but on misperceptions about football's real attraction.

Most baseball fans feel no compulsion to "make it interesting" by putting money on the line. Pete Rose aside, they most often watch because they love the game for its own sake. Just for the sport of it, one might say.

Football is very different. Gambling on that sport takes an estimated 70 percent of Vegas sports action to baseball's piddling 5 percent, and it's hard to imagine what would remain of football if a magic wand suddenly eliminated office pools, bookies, casinos, and the like. It might not be much.

It's important to remember that bettors don't have a stake in the final game outcomes that are measured by "competitive balance." To the multitudes who monitor point spreads, it doesn't matter that a handful of teams will win most all their games. To those who put money on over/under totals or prop bets, it doesn't matter that a first-place team is all but certain to clobber a fourth-place team. Still less important is the fact that a number of teams are either terrific or terrible for years on end.

Since football is based on gambling, and many gambling outcomes are indeed unpredictable, many assume that the sport itself is unpredictable. This is to mistake bets for balance.

Playing Monopoly

"Major League Baseball Is a Cartel"

*Throughout its history Major League Baseball has monopolized the market,
preventing upstart competitors from getting off the ground.
In many ways Major League Baseball is the only true monopoly in the
United States and has been since its inception.*

—PETER BENDIX, "The History of Baseball's Antitrust Exemption,"
Beyond the Box Score, December 3, 2008

*Baseball may be our national pastime but it's a totalitarian state.
The owners are basically dictators and there's an antitrust exemption
that shields them from market forces.*

—ERIC NEEL, "*Fantasyland* Author Q&A," ESPN.com, April 6, 2006

Gene Mauch once said that, like malaria, baseball sometimes goes away for a
while but keeps coming back. The same goes for references to its so-called
monopoly.

The constant commentary is probably based on the fact that, in the strictest
legal sense, Major League Baseball isn't treated as just another business engaged
in interstate commerce. A 1922 Supreme Court decision held that most federal
antitrust laws didn't apply to MLB.

It's all very fascinating except for the fact that a monopoly doesn't function
through an ancient lawsuit but in contemporary business practice. It exists when
a producer restrains trade in an important economic asset, only to jack up prices

and generally act out as an unaccountable, fat-dumb-and-happy monolith. In shorthand a monopoly requires:

1) a stranglehold over a vital service or product that provides
2) the overwhelming market leverage that eventually leads to
3) managerial stagnation.

This is how monopoly is played in the real world, but it's far removed from baseball.

First, the contemporary Major Leagues are in the "baseball" business in only the narrowest sense of the term. In practice, the game operates within a larger entertainment industry that bustles with hundreds of substitute options in television, movies, the Internet, live theater, and so on. This is to say, baseball has never had the kind of singular market position comparable to the Organization of Petroleum-Exporting Countries' stranglehold on petroleum or a local utility's grip on flowing water. If fans one day decide that the game doesn't provide quality entertainment at affordable prices, they can always defect to the many other entertainment options, and no dusty Supreme Court case could ever slow the exodus.

In addition, MLB is missing a cartel's typical stagnation/lack of innovation. In barely over one decade, from the early 1990s to the new millennium, teams implemented new programs in everything from advanced rehabilitation to sports psychology. The pastime also started up the most advanced sports-league site in the world, MLB.com, and then used it as a platform for online broadcasts, ticket sales, and stats-on-demand. In 2009 the MLB Network made the biggest cable channel debut in American history.

Everywhere one looked, what was once the most hidebound of sports felt the need to introduce more fan-friendly improvements. It's safe to say that the game has never been more entrepreneurial. Does all this make baseball a complete, 100 percent realm of free marketeering?

Yes.

No. I jest.

Major League owners do collude to direct franchise sales, limit the number of franchises, cooperate to share revenue, and allocate draft picks. Such competition-crimping features are also found in the NFL and the NBA.

Even among team sports, however, baseball is relatively freewheeling. The Majors feature the least restrictive revenue-sharing system among the "big three" sports, along with the most unfettered free agency rules. Individual club owners are given wide latitude to negotiate their own media and marketing deals and, in this, they're competitors as much as they're partners.

Contrast all of this to the NFL, which maintains a narrow band of maximum and minimum payrolls, nationalizes its media and merchandizing deals, shares virtually all revenues, and dictates payroll spending according to red tape that would make corporate lawyers weep in befuddlement. A formal monopoly isn't written out in so many words, but then again, there's no need for such formality; owners have already implemented central planning in a way that has largely gone out of style since the Soviet Union gave up.

It's a strange outcome. It's the Major Leagues, that much-derided "monopoly," that's a shining example of free market capitalism.

MYTH #83

"The Antitrust Status Hurts the Fans"

[Owners] are . . . would-be monopolists looking to leverage their market power to the greatest . . . advantage. Consumers and baseball fans are merely pawns in this long-term struggle.

—STEVEN PEARLSTEIN, "Next on Baseball Agenda: Fix the Nats's TV Problem," *Washington Post*, May 5, 2006

If baseball's exemption were lifted, teams would stop holding cities hostage.

—ALLEN BARRA, "In Antitrust We Trust," *Salon*, May 19, 2000

Today's Major League Baseball is the opposite of a working monopoly. In its combination of free market competition and internal diversity, baseball actually utilizes the most competitive sports model in the country.

Even so, economists like Andrew Zimbalist concentrate on the game's antitrust status, claiming that it still restricts fan choices and prices. While pro football or basketball teams have an almost unfettered leeway to relocate themselves, MLB franchises employ exclusive rights to their respective markets.

Baseball's territorial rights do create local monopolies in the sense that MLB teams cannot easily move away to compete in new markets. Some have speculated that New York City, for instance, has enough fans to support as many as four MLB teams and the economies of greater Los Angeles and Chicago could probably sustain additional teams as well. Without territoriality, the bigger markets might gain a greater supply of baseball while their fans would see increased competition among the teams. Theoretically, fan bases would benefit from a repeal of the antitrust exemption. Theoretically.

In the real world, repeal of the territoriality concept would destroy baseball's unparalleled stability and thereby hurt its nationwide fan base.

Consider that seven NFL teams and eleven NBA teams relocated in the years between 1972 and 2005. Over the same period, zero MLB teams relocated. This is because only baseball had the internal control represented by "territoriality."

To see how the system worked in practice, take the example of Bob Lurie, the Giants owner who wanted to move his franchise from San Francisco to St. Petersburg, Florida, in 1992. If he was operating in pro football or basketball Lurie would've required little more than the U-Haul trucks to skedaddle eastward, but baseball's territoriality powers required that Lurie secure the approval of his fellow baseball owners. They vetoed the Giants move, mostly because they saw the imminent financial harm in the game's abandoning a well-established market like San Francisco while simultaneously forgoing future expansion-team fees from St. Pete.

The outside owners had less-than-zero financial motive to approve franchise relocations, in truth. Partnership groups buy Major League franchises according to the value of their club's territorial rights, among other factors, and any managing general partner who undermined territoriality would've probably violated a fiduciary duty to maximize economic value among his fellow investors. Even when a particular move didn't compromise a particular market, the precedent in a relocation would tend to undermine most markets.

In this way, a managing general partner who freely allows franchise relocation would almost certainly open himself up to ugly, drawn-out lawsuits. It would be as if he volunteered for an unnecessary dentist appointment costing about $10 million.

Baseball, unlike football and basketball, remained sane and stable because self-interest so strongly discourages franchise relocations. To see territoriality's importance, imagine a baseball world without it. Smaller-market teams like Pittsburgh, Cincinnati, and Milwaukee (along with goodness knows how many Minor League clubs) would displace themselves. A handful of megamarkets would gain new teams but the game would also hollow out its age-long presence in smaller cities and rural regions throughout the country. It wouldn't be long before a "national" pastime transformed into a "big city" pastime.

Anyone who would see this as a good thing for the fans, . . . well, they should help repeal the antitrust exemption. For those who disagree, the game is fine.

The Office

"It's Possible for the Commissioner's Office to Be Independent"

MLB needs to hire a person . . . with the executive and promotional skills to be commissioner. An independent commissioner to move the sport forward.

—GARY NORRIS GRAY, "The MLB Fraud," BlackAthlete.net, February 7, 2012

What baseball needs is a new leader who provides an unassailable presence on both sides of the labor fence and who also inspires confidence from fans.

—STEPHEN CANNELLA, ALBERT CHEN, DANIEL G. HABIB, and TOM VERDUCCI, "And While We're At It . . .," *Sports Illustrated*, August 5, 2002

Imagine you're offered a job.

You'll have the trappings of power. You'll make many millions per year in a suite high atop a Manhattan skyscraper and your press releases will be dutifully conveyed by television networks. Your signature will be stamped on every baseball used in every Major League game. Front-row seats will be comped. Billy Crystal will be nice to you.

There's a downside, however.

Despite the perks, the job is still, well, a job. You'll answer to a boss. Actually, you'll answer to a whole bunch of bosses, a collection of millionaires and billionaires who maintain the power to hire you, fire you, and otherwise lord over your professional existence. You must make the bosses happy, and—

this is the tricky part—you must pretend that you're in charge. Publicly, at least, you will pretend to call the shots.

That was what it was like for MLB commissioners from the 1940s to the 1980s. In their public image, they were leaders pursuing independent visions. In their private reality, they were followers pursuing the agendas of others.

The notion of an independent commissioner was something of a creation myth, one that went all the way back to the office's origins. In 1920, when the game was still reeling from the Black Sox gambling scandal, team owners were panicked by the game's declining credibility and revenue. They were so scared, in fact, that they gave a judge named Kenesaw Mountain Landis the bulletproof contract he demanded to take on the scandal; Landis couldn't be fired, couldn't see salary cuts, and couldn't be publicly criticized by the owners.

As a result of a one-time-only crisis, Landis assumed one-time-only power that rendered him "the only authentic American dictator in history." Long before Landis's life/tenure finally expired in 1944, however, the owners sorely regretted the installation of their imperious leader. Determined never to repeat their mistake, they treated the post-Landis commissioners as little more than hired hands.

It's true that, for the sake of appearances, the post-Landis commissioners maintained some figurehead duties. They had the autonomy to deal with administrative matters like player fines and acted as go-betweens with television networks and corporate sponsors. They were always free to consult, advise, persuade, cajole, and beg the owners on issues ranging from labor negotiations to franchise relocations. Like the Queen of England or the Wizard of Oz, the Commissioner of Major League Baseball retained a fancy title and scads of publicity.

When it came to bedrock financial decisions related to labor relations and revenue splits, however, the real bosses reserved de facto rights. Apparently the team owners believed that multimillion-dollar investments bought them free rein in their industry's most important investments.

In some isolated cases it appeared that the post-Landis commissioners were free to bite the hands that fed them, but those appearances were deceiving. In the 1970s, for instance, Commissioner Bowie Kuhn issued temporary suspensions for owners like Ted Turner and George Steinbrenner but Kuhn could only act because the owners involved were such pariahs that their fellow owners declined to invoke their prerogatives.

Isolated incidents aside, few commissioners even attempted to impose themselves on owners. The one real exception was Commissioner Fay Vincent, but his unsupported power plays only left him isolated, then unemployed. After his 1992 ouster Vincent wrote an autobiography entitled *The Last Commissioner*. A more appropriate epitaph would've been *The Last Guy to Figure Out That Those Who Pay the Piper Call the Tune*.

If the toothless status of commissioners has always been obvious to those within the halls of power, the "independent" facade wasn't without its benefits.

The hypocrisy did have a certain utility in connection to baseball's antitrust status, for example; at moments when angry politicians made noises about industry regulation, guys like Happy Chandler or Ford Frick would piously claim that they were acting as "trustees of a public trust." No one but the plutocrats had ever chosen commissioners to be the trustees of anything, of course, but there were moments when an above-the-fray image helped calm the waters.

In addition, owners sometimes found it useful to present their functionary as an honest broker during contentious dealings with the player union. The pompous Kuhn, for instance, would repeatedly insist that his owner-paid salary was irrelevant to his working as an impartial broker in labor negotiations. This didn't pass the laugh test among labor leaders, of course, but the self-proclaimed "conscience of the game" sometimes gained stature among the more gullible sportswriters.

Over time, though, even those tissue-thin veils of independence all but vanished. Landis came to be remembered as the retrograde authoritarian he was, and in the 1960s and 1970s, the owner cabal found a curb not in a paid employee but in a resurgent union. If that wasn't enough to kill the "independent commissioner" image, Mr. Allen H. Selig came into office.

Selig had an uncommon appreciation for real power shifts because, as the general partner for the Milwaukee Brewers from 1970 until 2005, he directed the management committees that frequently maneuvered around four commissioners. When Vincent tried to head off a labor confrontation in the early 1990s, Selig played a key role in deposing Vincent and then installed himself directly into the commissioner's office.

Having pushed around more than his share of over-ambitious figureheads, Selig dispensed with displays of "independence." Most often, he worked the phones and rubbed elbows to find out what the owners thought about the issue of the day, and then, as a "leader by consensus," he suggested that they implement their own ideas.

If everyone acknowledges that Selig isn't an independent commissioner, they can acknowledge his effectiveness as a dependent commissioner. Since he was so subordinate toward the owners, he gained their trust. Having forgone the pretense of impartiality, he maintained clear-cut communications with the players' union. With owner support and union pragmatism, Selig put a halt to the shuffle through the commissioner's office while presiding over nearly two decades of labor peace.

In this light, Bud Selig's tenure may be remembered as the workable epilogue to an unworkable idea. In the way he entered office, he reminded us that the post-Landis commissioners have never been independent. Since then he proved that there's no need to pretend anymore.

MYTH #85

"We Need a Fans' Commissioner"

The commissioner has to be a fan first.

—BARRY WITTENSTEIN, "Q&A with Baseball Legend Joe Garagiola," SNY.TV, March 17, 2007

Baseball needs a commissioner who has only the welfare of the game in mind, who works to protect the interest of the fans.

—FAY VINCENT, *The Last Commissioner*, 2002

The bad news is that Bud Selig, commissioner of baseball, doesn't truly represent the best interests of the players and fans. The good news is that we don't need Bud Selig to represent the best interests of the players or the fans.

Like any other highly placed business executive, Selig places a primary priority on his bosses' profits. Selig can surely appreciate the fact that happy customers can generate those profits for the medium and long terms, but only Selig's immediate superiors have the power to fire the commissioner through a direct, short-term action. If the commissioner intends to retain his job, he must cater to the views of the team owners, first and foremost.

Thankfully outsiders have their own power bases. Fans possess leverage through their proven ability to inflict nine-figure revenue losses, as in the aftermath of the 1994–1995 strike. The players are likewise well positioned, through one of the strongest unions in the nation. Some say the Major League Baseball Players Association (MLBPA) is *the* strongest union in the nation.

With such real-world power, fans and players need not muse about a "fan's commissioner." If and when the people decide to act out again, they'll command undivided attention within the corner office.

MYTH #86

"We Need a Visionary in the Commissioner's Office"

The game we love and cherish needs . . . a commissioner with vision, and a conviction to match.

—"Baseball Could Use Costas as Commissioner,"
New York Times, October 5, 2003

If the owners had any interest at all in reforming the sport or helping baseball to regain the primacy it once held on the American sporting scene, they would long since have hired someone with vision, organizational ability, and impeccable integrity.

—JACK TODD, "Selig Is a Total Disaster," Montreal Gazette, July 19, 2002

When you take a good, hard look at Bud Selig stammering before Congress or in some news conference, it's tempting to get ticked off.

It's not only the expectation that a commissioner should strike a more impressive figure. Many can overlook Selig's collection of rumpled suits and repertoire of frowns, scowls, and sighs. It's not strictly necessary for baseball's commissioner to bring the slickness that Roger Goodell lends to the NFL or the gravitas David Stern brings to the NBA.

No, more of the frustration is rooted in Selig's sorry track record as an owner and executive. This was the owner who ran the Milwaukee Brewers into years of mediocrity and worse. This was the boy who cried wolf on competitive balance. This was the heavy who issued the phony franchise death threats known as "contraction." He called himself a "temporary" commissioner . . . for six years.

Like Mr. Magoo, Bud Selig displayed a lack of vision. Yet, like Mr. Magoo, things always seem to work out for him in the end.

There were more than a few positives to even out the "Bud Light" side of the ledger, however. Selig helped introduce interleague scheduling in the mid-1990s, a box office bonanza that shows no signs of slowing down after its first decade. By establishing the wild card system, he helped boost September gate figures by about 15 percent while more than doubling postseason attendance. In the debut of four expansion teams, Selig brought in markets that typically contribute more than 7 million fans per year.

It's tempting to think that Selig's combination of an unimpressive background and impressive success has been somehow unprecedented, but history says otherwise. In fact, baseball has always persevered in spite of its commissioners.

KENESAW MOUNTAIN LANDIS (1920–1944): AMERICAN CZAR

Background: Landis was a Chicago-based lawyer who had enough political connections to be named to a judgeship in 1905. Once on the bench he handed down several outlandish verdicts against antiwar protesters and labor activists, then came into national prominence during the Federal League dispute. When a rival organization's lawsuit challenged Major League business practices in 1915, Landis refused to hand over any judgment for eleven months in an unconscionable delay, which, predictably, forced the Federal League's surrender. Soon afterward grateful MLB owners repaid Landis with a lucrative job offer.

One Chicago journalist described Landis as the most arbitrary jurist he had ever seen, and when someone from Chicago thinks you're an arbitrary jurist, you're an arbitrary jurist.

Résumé: Once in office, Landis answered to no one, and baseball's "czar," like czars of the Russian variety, was wary of ingenuity and freedom. He either delayed or blocked everything from prospect development and radio broadcasting to racial integration and free agency. Landis opposed the placement of electrical lighting within ballparks, believe it or not, and it's a small mercy that he never had veto power over the electric bulb itself.

Landis was also a phony on a personal level, as he advocated morality and alcohol prohibition in public while engaging in profane racism and drinking behind closed doors. Even the spelling in his name was false; there's a Kennesaw Mountain in Georgia but a Kenesaw Mountain nowhere. This was a man who was wrong every time he wrote his own name!

Result: Four new attendance records in the 1920s.

HAPPY CHANDLER (1945–1951): BLUEGRASS JACKASS

Background: A Kentucky politician, Chandler was a compromise choice after six other candidates couldn't muster the support necessary to succeed Landis, the commissioner for life whose job/life ended in 1944.

Résumé: Years after Jackie Robinson passed away, Chandler bragged that he had supported Robinson's pivotal desegregation effort all the way. In reality, Robinson was signed before Chandler came into office, and the definitive Robbie biographer, Jules Tygiel, described the commissioner as "a bit player" in the desegregation struggle.

Apart from that episode, Chandler was notorious for capricious fines and for completely botching the pastime's first network television agreement—after he sold off MLB television rights, the buyer quickly resold them at four times the price. That debacle, along with loud and unprompted renditions of "My Old Kentucky Home," were the primary reasons Chandler was known as "the Bluegrass Jackass."

Result: Four attendance records from 1945 to 1948.

FORD FRICK (1951–1965): EMPTY SUIT

Background: A ghostwriter, Frick was president of the National League.

Résumé: Frick is probably best remembered for his disparaging of Roger Maris's home run record in 1961. If he's remembered for anything else, it may have been his habit of consistently dodging controversies by claiming, "That is a league affair," which led one reporter to say that "an empty cab pulled up to the curb and out stepped Ford Frick."

Result: A new attendance record in 1962.

SPIKE ECKERT (1965–1968): UNKNOWN SOLDIER

Background: A retired U.S. Air Force officer with no background in business or labor relations, Eckert was unfamiliar with baseball, too. At the time he was voted into office, he hadn't seen a live game in ten years and once expressed sincere surprise that the Dodgers had once played in Brooklyn.

Résumé: Eckert allowed baseball to play through the 1968 season without a pause for the shattering assassination of Senator Robert F. Kennedy and was also ridiculed for his colorless demeanor and public speaking gaffes.

By the time the owners ushered him out the door, there was a widespread rumor that Eckert was only hired because the owners had confused him with another high-ranking military man (the similarly named Gene Zuckert).

Result: New attendance records in 1965 and 1966.

BOWIE KUHN (1969–1984): MR. WRONG

Background: Like other commissioners, Kuhn held a degree from a famous college. As to whether this was an unfortunate coincidence or an indictment of Ivy League tuitions, opinions vary.

Résumé: Kuhn was the functionary who defended restrictive contracts against Curt Flood's pioneering legal challenges. When Flood wrote that "I do not feel that I am a piece of property to be bought and sold irrespective of my wishes," Kuhn was kind enough to admit that Flood was, indeed, a human being but said, "I cannot see the applicability to the situation at hand." Flood did see the applicability to the situation at hand, as did the neutral arbitrator who opened the door to a free agency system. Kuhn then fired the arbitrator, continually claimed that free agency threatened baseball's very existence, spearheaded the pointless 1981 strike, and got himself fired for his troubles.

Kuhn had a Landis-like knack for jumping on the wrong side of issues. The commissioner deemed Jim Bouton's *Ball Four* memoir "detrimental to baseball," attempted to segregate Negro Leaguers into a separate wing in the Hall of Fame, snubbed Hank Aaron on the occasion of his record-breaking 715th home run, showed up in short sleeves for a chilly World Series night game, banned the beloved Willie Mays due to his community relations work for casinos, once said promotional giveaway days were "prostituting" baseball, and consistently lost at tic-tac-toe.

Only that last one was a joke.

Result: Nine attendance records from 1969 to 1983.

(Afterward, *Ball Four* became one of the most respected baseball books of all time, Cooperstown integrated, Aaron was saluted, people kept wearing coats, Mickey and Willie were reinstated, and the giveaways continued).

PETER UEBERROTH (1984–1989): CRUEL AND UNUSUAL

Background: Ueberroth was a travel agent before becoming an organizer for the crass-but-cashful 1984 Summer Olympics. His looks were sometimes compared to those of Robert Redford, presumably by those who disliked Robert Redford.

Résumé: Ueberroth's sarcastic, bullying style was frequently deployed to make owners limit bidding on free agent player contracts but when his "dumb and stupid" owners were goaded into outright market rigging, the Players Association eventually won a $280 million settlement. Many believe that the collusion poisoned labor relations to the point where the 1994 strike became highly likely, perhaps inevitable.

Result: Five straight attendance records from 1985 to 1989.

BART GIAMATTI (1989): GRADE: INCOMPLETE

Background: Giamatti was a college dean before being appointed NL president. He passed away after less than a year in the commissioner's office, with his tenure being dominated by the Pete Rose controversy.

In some respects, Giamatti was the John F. Kennedy of baseball: a well-liked, bright guy who died before his time and before a lot of trouble went down. Granted, the 1994 labor strike wasn't as bad as Vietnam, so the comparison is incomplete.

FAY VINCENT (1989–1992): AUTHOR OF *WHAT? WHERE? HOWE?*

Background: Vincent, Giamatti's assistant, was the default choice to quickly replace the late commissioner.

Résumé: Vincent was known for his stumbling on various issues. He didn't seem to know what to do in the George Steinbrenner blackmail investigation, the geographical alignment of league divisions, and the drug suspension of Steve Howe. In 1992 after clashing with the owners over divisional realignment, Vincent resigned just after a no-confidence vote and just before a firing.

Result: Attendance records in 1989 and 1991.

There you have it. Even before Bud Selig, baseball survived, in succession, the keeper of a kangaroo court, a bit player, a nonentity, a grown man named Spike, a dim bulb, and three other guys. If our national pastime required visionary commissioners, America would've taken up cricket a long time ago.

Laboring

"The Players Union Is Radical"

The union, which never met an intractable position it didn't like . . .

—STEVE KETTMANN, "The Players Are Loaded,"
New Republic Online, June 7, 2002

There's nothing righteous about the baseball labor movement anymore.

—HARVEY ARATON, "Free-Agent Shoppers Dwindling,"
New York Times, December 4, 2001

The face-off between ballplayers and team owners is almost as long-lasting as the competition between pitchers and hitters.

When the "professional" part of "professional baseball" first came about in the 1870s, athletes had the freedom to receive salary bids from competing teams. The owners loathed how the "revolving" practice encouraged higher salaries, however, so they responded in the manner of robber barons—they rigged the system. In their particular case, they inserted "reserve clauses" into all player contracts.

The clauses established decades-long business practices that gave tradition a bad name. All pro players, from Babe Ruth on down, were subjected to "take-or-leave-it" contracts as enforced by blacklists, retaliatory trades, and punitive demotions. Even superstars could be subjected to big salary cuts based on nothing more than their bosses' grudges or greed. When teams sold off players in return for small fortunes, the teams collected 100 percent of the money while the players received 0 percent. As for injured players, they could be dumped at virtually any time, rejections made all the more painful by the absence of meaningful pensions.

Dr. Gerald Scully once estimated that in the reserve clause era, owners paid out only 10 percent or so of the revenues generated by their employees, but, incredibly enough, that wasn't the worst of it. To African Americans the owners paid nothing.

Prior to 1947 a comically misnamed "gentleman's agreement" within the ownership clique prevented the gainful employment of black athletes. Negro Leaguers like Josh Gibson and Oscar Charleston are now recognized among the greatest baseball players who have ever lived, but in their own time they were denied MLB roster spots in favor of white players with conspicuous arrest records, gambling habits, mental illnesses, and lesser athletic skills. Legendary African Americans were passed over in favor of a one-armed white player and a 15-year-old boy, even. Can you imagine such a sham in any other context? "Thank you for your job applications, Mr. Hendrix and Reverend King, but we already have a one-armed guitar player and a divinity student on the payroll. For this reason we will not require your services."

After decades of such treatment, most athletes became so cowed as to take their helpless status for granted, as if the reserve clause system was an internal feature rather than an outside fix. When a hardy few attempted to take on the racket the matters always ended in tears.

In 1938, for instance, a young punk named Joe DiMaggio attempted to hold out for a meager raise, but with no outside alternatives, he quickly returned with a whimpering apology. In the 1940s several stars attempted to flee for better wages in Mexico—Mexico was a land of opportunity in comparison to baseball's America—but blacklist threats brought the holdouts to heel. When a Yankee infielder was mixed up in a fistfight in 1957 he was banished to a seventh-place club. We can only guess how many would-be dissenters were silenced before they uttered a single word; it was as if the powers that be owned not just teams but also human beings.

The labor infamy, bad enough in itself, systematically harmed the fans, too. Growing cities were denied new franchises for nearly six decades, from the early 1900s to the early 1960s, and in the Major League towns community outreach consisted of little more than "GAME TODAY" signs tacked on ballpark exteriors. As late as the 1970s, the entire marketing department of the New York Yankees consisted of two full-time staffers and a couple of exhausted interns. Many owners filled their front offices with half-educated, half-drunk cronies. Talent development systems could be so stingy that clubs like the Senators and the Indians were stuck in second divisions for years, nay, decades on end.

The bleakness wasn't without its light moments, of course. One of the team magnates was a plastics manufacturer and someone once said that he knew players about as well as players knew plastics manufacturers. Swimming was invented on the day when Calvin Griffith was confronted with a toll booth on a river, rumor had it. An anonymous source said that money was the last thing that the lords thought about, right before they fell asleep and started dreaming. Someone else said that it was impossible to predict what Phil Wrigley would do to the Cubs but that, whatever he did, it would be wrong.

The laughs could only do so much to distract from the tears, however. On the few occasions paleo-baseball reformed itself, it was because external political pressures or lawsuit threats forced the reforms. Hall of Famer Bill Terry said it all when he said that "baseball must be a great game to survive the fools who run it. No business in the world has ever made more money with poorer management."

Terry might've added that the foolish were, simultaneously, shameless. Even as they chiseled players out of fair wages the owners claimed that they were mere "sportsmen." They said the pastime was racially segregated based on player performances rather than owner bigotries. Even as they ignored the public's need for change they paid lip service to the people's interests. Until woodworkers begin denouncing trees such statements will stand alone in the history of hypocrisy.

Then came the end of the world as baseball knew it. In the 1970s, for the first time since the 1870s, the ballplayers got back into the game through a labor pioneer named Marvin Miller.

By the time Miller took leadership of the Major League Baseball Players Association in 1966, he had already gained nationwide renown through work on the National War Labor Relations Board and the United Steelworkers of America. Miller declined a position as a college professor immediately before coming over to the MLBPA, instead acting as an educator among Major Leaguers. Yes, he insisted, federal law guaranteed rights to collective bargaining. No, a unified membership could reject unsafe working conditions that included unpadded outfield walls and uncovered drainage pipes. Yes, he taught, workers deserved basic insurance coverage and pensions. Most important, Miller educated the Players Association as to the illegality and absurdity of the reserve clause. After several legal suits and negotiations, the reserve clause era made way to a free agency system in time for the bicentennial, independence-minded summer of '76.

The moguls were not unmindful of Miller's leadership, not at all unmindful. Actually, they met Marvin Miller with a white-hot hostility not again seen until sportswriters encountered Barry Bonds. The low point came when pooh-bahs referred to Miller as an outsider and a misguided young man, words that would've stung but for the fact that Miller was a lifelong fan who took office at age 49.

As for Miller's unionists, the old boys expressed their contempt through well-tested gambits. The owners sometimes stonewalled and occasionally offered small payoffs. They alternated between threats and promises. They tried both bluster and the silent treatment. They posed as friends even as they sought to divide the players. They cried poor even as they shut their accounting books. The owners rarely engaged in private negotiations but frequently sent public warnings:

"The!"

"Game!"

"Will!"

"Die!"

"Free agency will destabilize everything!"

It didn't quite turn out that way, of course. The free agency system led not to death, but rebirth.

When free agent bidding led to rising player salaries, baseball men finally began acting like businessmen. They recouped rising costs with the increased revenues that came with new broadcast slates, revamped schedules, and more. In a 180-degree turnaround from the bad old days, front offices were staffed by executives smart and sober enough to make long-overdue reforms among scouts and coaches. When bewildered heirs/owners like Ruly Carpenter fled their exits, new-generation owners were allowed to institute reforms in more rapid and comprehensive fashion. The pastime destabilized its way into a new vitality and newly revitalized fan bases.

Despite all the years of inequity and inertia, it turned out that ideas matter and that the union's ideas mattered most of all. Their ideas carry on to this day. When some portray labor struggles as mere food fights, the union recalls how they abolished 19th-century feudalism in favor of 20th-century capitalism.

Where there's fretting that labor clashes will destroy the pastime's appeal, the union maintains a confidence that the game can always bounce back.

When some fear an intractable labor force, Miller's successors note that they're only defending free agency against repeated efforts to turn back the clock.

When some lament divisions between the players and the owners, activists see a partnership in which employees collect millions only because employers collect billions.

When some speak of . . .

No matter. What is spoken is far less important than what is done. It's the Players Association, the notoriously "radical" Players Association, that has dragged the national pastime into the American mainstream. When they prevail, baseball wins.

MYTH #88

The Union Label

Some people still refer to Marvin Miller and his successors, Don Fehr and Michael Weiner, as "union bosses." Some people are wrong. True union bosses go to extremes that have never been seen in baseball's labor leadership.

Outside unionists sometimes negotiate uniform wages for entire worker classes, thereby leaving underperforming workers with undeserved salaries. In contrast, the Major League Baseball Players Association gives team owners free rein to offer virtually any contract paying more than a minimum level, just as long as two or more organizations don't collude on lowball offers. Don Fehr once said, "You can pay anybody what you want, just as long as you don't conspire about it."

Bosses in the steel and auto industries still maintain a notorious reputation for imposing rigid work rules. In baseball the union does insist on outside mediation of fines and suspensions but otherwise allows management to run clubhouses as they see fit; if a team imposes a rational punishment, that is that.

Other labor movements can obtain unreasonable worker protections that obstruct healthy innovations within their businesses. The Players Association does hold fast to its bilateral contracts but has adjusted collective agreements for the sake of initiatives like drug testing.

Honchos in industrial-age unions can institute red tape and regulations that make it difficult to fire incompetent workers. In baseball, veterans who (unwisely) choose to play without guaranteed payouts and no-trade clauses can be released like last week's newspapers.

Another cliché has union leaders as blusterers who sometimes work through intimidation, whether that comes through legal or illegal methods. Baseball is different. The founding father of its union activism, Marvin Miller, never found himself within the same ballpark as a broken law. With his horn-rimmed glasses and tweedy suits, Miller intimidated only through the power of persuasion.

Leaders of the Players Association are typical "union bosses" in the sense that they often face antagonistic management, an unfriendly media, and a confused public. In other ways, they go their own ways.

At Peace

Every time [the owners] have gone head-to-head with the Players Association over the previous quarter century, they . . . somehow wound up looking like a bunch of chumps.

—HOWARD BRYANT, *Juicing the Game*, 2005

Charlie Brown once said, "You win some, you lose some," but he never met Major League team negotiators. For more than 20 years the owners attempted to impose draconian new rules on their players, only to lose every time.

The catalogue of failures was long and dismal. In 1972 the owners were forced to cede salary arbitration rights. In 1976 they tried to lock out free agency. In 1981 management lost its campaign to restrict free agent movement. In 1985 there was another unsuccessful assault on free agency. In 1989, ditto. The 1994–1995 battle was the lowest point of all, as management's bad-faith negotiations were shut down by a federal court ruling.

On the occasions the owners went to war they appeared to lose, lose, lose, lose, and LOSE. A comparison to the Wile E. Coyote-Roadrunner rivalry comes to mind.

For all that, though, the owners ultimately won. After all, the labor/ownership showdowns weren't about immediate, short-term goals as much as they were about money; the owners wanted more of it.

Back during the labor wars the owners believed that they would increase revenue by imposing downward pressure on player salaries but, contrary to their own beliefs, the efforts were both unnecessary and futile. As mentioned in the previous chapter, the competition injected into the baseball business in the 1970s and following years yielded the astonishing growth that they had long sought. To cite but two important measures, live attendance more than doubled while gross revenues grew more than 20 times over and team values increased by four-fold. The spinning turnstiles and cash geysers became so perennial as to become expected.

Over more than 30 years the Major League owners developed "foolproof" businesses on a very literal level. Kevin McClatchy of the Pittsburgh Pirates, for example, could be counted among the worst losers in pastime history but nonetheless found his franchise tripling in value over a mere 12 years. Frank McCourt of the Dodgers also found a windfall. His tenure featured a quite public divorce, nepotism, personal bankruptcy, and financial misdeeds up to and including the "looting" of team coffers, but his franchise value still increased by hundreds of millions of dollars in less than eight years. MLB owners, no matter how stupid or sleazy, couldn't miss out on outrageous returns, no more than they could jump into the Pacific Ocean and avoid moisture.

With such financial success at hand, owners lost their taste for brinkmanship. Since 1995 the owners have conducted four straight negotiations with a minimum of drama, then ratified them by cumulative votes of 119–1. Contests between lions and lamb chops have been more eventful and the most recent bilateral agreement, passed in 2011, ensures owner/union cooperation for 21 consecutive years and the foreseeable future. Evidently the moguls were content to merely hold on to the financial victories they had already won.

It was without a grand declaration—without a declaration of any sort—that the owners finally established a cease-fire in the labor wars. Finally, after many battles and many losses, the game found a labor peace.

And in Conclusion

MYTH #90

The Good News in the Bad News

It'd be reassuring to believe that people are drawn to baseball only because they want to cheer. Chief Justice Earl Warren once said, "I always turn first to the sports pages, which record people's accomplishments. The front page has nothing but failures." Such sunny thinking surely motivated Chris Chambliss when he said, "If you're not having fun in baseball, you miss the whole point of everything."

Reassuring words from a great judge and a good hitter. They had a validity. Within the pastime many seek teamwork involved in on-field athletics but, even more importantly, the kind of teamwork that might involve family, friends, neighbors, fellow residents, and fellow citizens. Someone once described baseball as America's longest-lasting conversation, and anything that can bring it so together must be beautiful.

For all those positives, negativity also has a hold on the sport. When baseball disappointments come along, as they so often come along, they represent opportunities to vent frustrations. Booing has its own catharsis and that may be a reason why team rivalries can involve so much contention or why live contests can feature so many heckles. Pete Toms once wrote that the only thing that fans love more than baseball is complaining about baseball.

The complaining may be particularly sharp when the present is compared to the past. Many fans start off with close associations between their game and their childhoods, as a function interweaving summertime vacations, memorable outings, pickup games, and role models. A "kid's game" may never be completely outgrown. A "childhood ~ baseball" equivalence can endure and that connection can have its own downside. Because childhood most often fades into adulthood, with complications and challenges, fans might imagine that childhood's favorite leisure also transitions into new complications over the years. Even more, fans can imagine an institution that's constantly falling behind, declining, slipping. Such views may not slight the realities of the present as much as they flatter the imagined past, but such are the uses of nostalgia.

If it's easy for everyday fans to think that baseball was better back in the good old days, the instinct may be even more understandable among the mass media. Pastime pessimism and the media have always gone together like a 6-4-3 double play, in large part because it's their job to fill up 24/7 broadcasts, daily newsprint, and infinite cyberspace. Intriguing sports stories are incomplete without twists and turns, so they must feature both successes and failures. A media story stating that an institution is as strong as ever, well, that would be worse than false—it would be boring. Don't ever expect headlines reading "As It Turns Out, Baseball Is A-OK!," "Everyone Hail These Sometimes Perplexing but Highly Functional Workings!," or "We Were Wrong When We Said that the Sky Was Falling!" Far more marketable are the airing of grievances relating to so-called labor disasters, slipping youth involvement, and declines in the talent pool as the parade of horribles goes on.

There's a noticeable lack of evidence, context, or even sense in most of these recycled narratives; even the most skeptical commentators, when cornered, might admit as much, but that's largely beside the point. Controversies goose interest, bolster ratings, make reputations, and fatten bank accounts. They're better than the truth.

Big cultural expectations are another reason why baseball's always been such a favorite target for commentators.

There is a higher standard for the national pastime, one over and above the standard applied to pro football or basketball. Rare indeed are ruminations about the ways NFL training camps epitomize the cyclical nature of life or the symbolic import of basketball dunks. The sports are mostly consumed as infotainments, as spectacles for the here and now. This helps explain why there is no great fracas over the endemic corruption within their NCAA feeder systems or over the chronic criminality chronicled in books like *Pros and Cons* and *Out of Bounds*. Basketball and football do have significant followings, of course, but no one claims that they're capital-M meaningful and they're in no way romanticized or sanctified, venerated or consecrated. There's only one American sport that attracts such a level of respect.

Reggie Jackson once said that he never minded booing from the grand-stands because "fans don't boo nobodies." The good news in the bad news is in the way that angry attacks actually validate baseball's valued place in our national life. The criticisms only place the sport's enduring hold into stark relief.

In recent years the trumped-up steroids issue within clubhouses may have received more attention than very real, trillion-dollar health care bills within Congress. It's not uncommon for Americans to know more about their pitchers and hitters than about congressmen and senators, for wins and losses on the diamond to be analyzed with an attention that might be more fitting for issues of war and peace.

Baseball matters, all right. If the pastime was in less than solid shape, there would be no howls of outrage; its demise, or decline, would be a relatively quiet affair. The nation would simply move on to something else, just as it did when boxing, horse racing, and other sports transitioned from relative ubiquity to obscurity. In baseball that's never happened.

Here's hoping that today's glory days last for years to come. Here's hoping that baseball plays through this season and all seasons.

Extras

MYTH #91

The Urban Legend

During his 1920s and 1930s heyday with the New York Yankees, Babe Ruth presented the most super of superlatives.

Ruth was the best player on a flagship team within the biggest city and the preeminent sport. It's true that no one has ever hit longer home runs, displayed more charisma, or attracted bigger crowds. The Babe also left behind a number of enduring but not-quite-true anecdotes. It's still said that he was fat. That his numbers were probably inflated by the fact that he didn't play against Negro Leaguers but did target a short outfield porch. He once promised a homer for a sick kid in the hospital. People called him "The Sultan of Swat" and blamed him for "the Curse of the Bambino."

Most of these claims, plus others, range from semi-true to flat-out wrong. Here are some Ruth truths:

A WEIGHTY ISSUE

Casting a tub 'o goo like John Goodman in a 1992 Babe Ruth biopic was a big insult to the Bambino's athleticism. From the looks of him, the on-screen Goodman was well north of 300 pounds, most of it consisting of cheeseburgers and ice cream, but his real-life counterpart was far less stocky and soft.

The 6'2" Ruth reported to the spring training camps of the 1920s and 1930s tipping the scales at anywhere from 215 to about 235 pounds, but a fairly massive upper chest tapered off to a 40-inch waist and surprisingly slender legs. Even at his heaviest official playing weight, at around age 40, the Babe was

215

lighter than new-millennium athletes like Jim Thome and Pablo Sandoval.

Far from being flabby, the Babe was notably more muscular than the average pro athlete of his time, mostly because he was one of the rare stars with the resources needed to hire a personal trainer and exercise throughout the off-season months. It didn't exactly jibe with his effortless reputation, but associates knew that the Bambino could work and sweat as much as anyone.

The most convincing proof of Ruth's athleticism was in the way he stood out as one of the most durable ballplayers of his era. There's no way that a genuine fat man could've outplayed *and* outlasted all but a few contemporaries over the course of a 22-year career.

Despite the well-documented conditioning and its results, Babe Ruth was still considered a heavy hitter. So to speak. He was widely known for being wide. So to speak. People said that he spent a lot of time in front of a plate and not just home plate. All right, no more fat jokes.

The weighty perception may have owed much to the fact that Ruth did master the arts of both playing well and living large, with witnesses recounting occasions when he drank beer by the pitcher and ate spare ribs by the rack. It's said that he once ate a dozen hot dogs and an apple in one sitting, came down with a painful stomachache, and then blamed the apple. Such extreme eating would've bloated an ordinary individual but Ruth was blessed with a turbocharged metabolism that allowed him to run around for up to 20 hours per day; evidently the Babe burned off sufficient calories to neutralize the gluttony.

There was no denying that Ruth's appearance could also deceive. He was born with a moon-shaped face and, like Roger Clemens, never quite lost a double-chin look, no matter how hard he worked out. Ruth's above-average height and completely oversize achievements doubtless contributed to a heavyweight reputation, as did a post-retirement life when youthful stoutness expanded outward.

CURSE THAT

Babe Ruth loved Boston.

It was the city where the Red Sox fulfilled his big league dreams. It was the home where the masses cheered his first homer titles and celebrated his first championships. He met his wife there, partied there, joined the Knights of

Columbus there. When he heard that his contract had been sold off to New York, the Babe was quoted saying, "My heart's in Boston."

This was a man who also made regular, unpublicized visits to orphanages with wheelbarrows full of free bats, balls, and gloves. He was far too generous to curse any town, least of all his adopted hometown.

To be sure, Boston and the Sox saw more than their share of losses for more than 80 years after the Babe's departure, but the Ruth-less results could be traced directly to know-nothing executives and no-account players. The so-called Curse of the Bambino was the equivalent of a badly managed computer company firing a young Steve Jobs, then blaming their fate on a "Curse of the Steverino."

"THE HOUSE BUILT *FOR* RUTH"

In a certain, little-noticed way, the new Yankee Stadium was custom designed for Babe Ruth. From the time of its 1923 debut, the Bronx ballpark was laid out in such a way that late-afternoon shadows fell on the Babe's customary position in right field. This ensured that he would stay nice and cool while the stadium's left fielders roamed one of the harshest sun fields in the Majors.

That was about the only way that "The House that Ruth Built" was "The House Built *for* Ruth," however. When Harvey Frommer wrote that the dimensions were "tailored for Ruth's left-handed power," he was repeating a misconception.

In Ruth's playing days the right-field line was a mere 307 feet from home plate, yes, but that cozy distance dropped away to 399 feet in right-center and 408 feet in dead center.

The friendly "Ruthville" section next to the foul line quickly made way to a hostile "Death Valley" gap in such a way that, on balance, the old stadium's dimensions were very challenging for a left-handed hitter.

Ruth wasn't helped but hurt by his home turf, and author Bill Jenkinson recently asked how much he was hurt. In an exhaustive study of Ruth's homers from 1923 to 1934, the historian found that the Bambino hit 56 center field or left/center homers on the road but only one such shot in the old stadium. If that was true then Ruth was consciously going with a more natural, all-fields approach on the road but a more extreme, dead-pull approach in the Bronx. If, hypothetically, he was free to launch those center/left-center drives all the time—if the Yankee Stadium outfield was ordinary—Ruth would've hit 50 more career homers. He would be the career home run king to this day.

BLACK BALL

When Ruth's career homer total was challenged in past years, the debate over a potential asterisk sometimes strayed into a debate over Ruth's unfair advantages. The Babe never played in an official game against the best black pitchers of his day, and if he had faced stars like Bullet Rogan and Satchel Paige, he might not have shined so brightly.

It's possible to make that call but it's more probable that Ruth was an equal-opportunity slugger.

Ruth did actually play against dark-skinned players on dozens of important occasions; his off-season tours across the United States and Cuba were racially integrated. The games may not have counted in the American League standings but the bragging rights surely mattered to the players and audiences involved, and on those occasions Ruth was still Ruthian.

In 60 documented at-bats against the Negro Leaguers of the 1920s and 1930s the Babe put up a 1.000+ slugging percentage with 11 homers. During a ten-game visit to Cuba in 1920 he went 11 for 32. On the one occasion Ruth faced Paige, in 1938, the 43-year-old Bambino swatted another long ball.

The same Negro Leaguers who routinely beat all-white barnstorming teams were awed by the star power. Judy Johnson, a Hall of Famer who participated in the integrated games, said, "We could never seem to get him out, no matter what we did."

THE BABE AND THE KID

There's an old story that says that Babe Ruth once promised a sick little boy he would hit a home run just for him. The reality was even better.

When an 11-year-old named Johnny Sylvester fell from a horse in 1926, his family asked the famed Mr. Ruth to convey get-well wishes to the hospital. The Babe happily obliged with a signed baseball and a note promising, "I'll hit a home run for you in Wednesday's game."

Ruth did knock a home run in "Wednesday's game"—Game Four of the 1926 World Series—and added another two long balls. It was the first time anyone had ever knocked three homers in a postseason game, thus proving that the Bambino could do nothing in a small way.

BABE RUTH AND BABY RUTH

Imagine this scenario: you're a lawyer, the year is 1921, and your employer is the Curtiss Candy Company.

Curtiss needs a new name for a chocolate, caramel, nougat, and peanut concoction that it's preparing for the consumer market. The candymaker has decided to associate their product with the most exciting athlete in the country but wants to avoid the expense of an official endorsement.

You, the Curtiss lawyer, come up with a cagey solution, claiming that Curtiss doesn't require an endorsement. This is because the Baby Ruth bar is being named after . . . Ruth Cleveland.

Ruth Cleveland?

Ruth Cleveland, the infant born to President Grover Cleveland and wife back in 1891.

You ignore the fact that Miss Ruth had sadly died in 1904, 16 years before. You ignore the more-than-slight resemblance between the names Baby Ruth and Babe Ruth. You somehow hoodwink a judge, too, thus denying the Bambino some sweet royalty checks.

Then, as a topper—the metaphorical peanuts atop the metaphorical chocolate—within a few years you successfully sue Ruth for introducing his own candy bar. You claim that Ruth's candy would be confused with your company's product, the one that supposedly has nothing to do with Babe Ruth.

Presumably, you do this while keeping a straight face. All of this makes you a very successful, if dishonest, attorney but if little Ruth Cleveland inspired that candy bar then I invented Snickers.

THE SULTANATE

The breathless newspaper accounts of the 1920s and 1930s habitually tagged Babe Ruth as "the Sultan of Swat," "the Caliph of Clout," "the Behemoth of Bust," "the Prince of Pounders," "The King of Clout," "The Wizard of Whack," et cetera. There were a dozen variations of those alliterative gimmicks, but the nicknames only existed in newsprint.

When the 19-year-old George Herman Ruth Jr. debuted in 1914, his teammates dubbed him "Babe" because he was "a babe in the woods." Later, the

Italian-language version of the nickname, "Bambino," gained popularity so, for variety's sake, some friends took to calling him "Bam" or "the Big Bam." All along, childhood acquaintances called him "Jidge," which was a variation of his birth name.

That was it, though. Outside of the funny papers, no one ever called him "Sultan" or "Caliph." Given their keen disinterest in Middle Eastern politics, it's highly doubtful that Ruth and his friends knew about caliphs.[*]

THE PINSTRIPERY

Robert Creamer's *Babe* biography contains a passage explaining how the iconic Yankee uniform was inspired by its most iconic player: "Because of Ruth's bulk, [team owner] Jacob Ruppert decided to dress the Yankees in their now-traditional pinstripe uniform. The natty, clothes-conscious Ruppert felt the new uniform would make Ruth look trimmer."

The notion was subsequently picked up by Richard Ben Cramer and others but there are at least three problems with it:

1) The pinstripes first appeared on Yankee uniforms in 1912 and became permanent fixtures in 1915, five seasons before Ruth's contract was sold to New York.
2) As noted above, Ruth wasn't very rotund during his playing career.
3) Pinstripes don't make the fat look thin, as David Wells might attest.

"THE UNCALLED SHOT"

This much is undisputed: on October 1, 1932, the New York Yankees were visiting the Chicago Cubs for the third game of the World Series. The two teams were knotted at 4-4 with one out and the bases empty in the fifth inning as Babe Ruth came up against Cub starter Charley Root. He worked a 2-2 count as players in the Cubs dugout hooted and hollered and then . . . something happened. The Ruth/Root showdown became one of the most disputed at-bats in baseball history.

---

[*]A caliph is one who rules over a kingdom according to Islamic laws. The Babe was raised as a Catholic but wasn't religious in any sense; when a teammate was asked the identity of Babe Ruth's role model, the teammate answered "Babe Ruth."

Some spectators said that, immediately after the 2-2 pitch, Ruth merely gestured to the dugout or Root while saying something to the effect of "one strike left" or "it only takes one pitch to hit it out." Others said that, to the contrary, the Babe deliberately pointed beyond the mound and out to center field, as if to mark the direction where he intended to blast a ball out of Wrigley Field. To the latter group, Babe's booming homer on Root's next pitch meant that he had called his own shot.

The conflicting eyewitness accounts gave little help in resolving the matter. Cubs opponents like Gabby Hartnett and Charlie Grimm all maintained that the gesture was intended for the dugout or pitching mound, while Yankees teammates like Joe Sewell and Bill Dickey backed the called-shot view. It came down to Ruth's opponents sticking to the more prosaic version while his friends held up the heroic story.

Apart from the standard "he said/he said" exchanges, other accounts tend to cast doubt on the called-shot view.

The Yankees were not unanimous in backing Ruth, for instance. Frank Crosetti and straight-shooting manager Joe McCarthy both denied that the Babe ever pointed out to center. Only an on-site newspaper reported the called-shot story at the time and in a postgame interview Ruth refused to say that he had called anything. ("Why don't you read the papers? It's all there.") It was only afterward that both the media and the Bam picked up on the tale.

Common sense tells you that if a called-shot gesture did happen, it would've kicked up a "Man Walks on the Moon!"–type sensation. All the Yankees involved would've been eager to affirm it on the spot. The fact that such things didn't happen strongly indicated that the called shot never happened.

If the aforementioned isn't enough to cast a dark shadow of a doubt on the called-shot story, put yourself in Charlie Root's cleats. If, hypothetically, the Chicago pitcher had seen Ruth call a home run to center field, he would've taken it as a grave insult that merited an equally insulting response. Root finished among league leaders in hit batsmen in the several seasons before the 1932 World Series, so he surely had few moral qualms in responding to a called shot with a well-placed beanball. The fact that Root responded to the Ruth gesture not with a beanball but a hittable pitch indicated that the Babe didn't provoke anything calling for retaliation. He must not have called the called shot.

TRAIN IN VAIN

The Babe grew up as a Baltimore street kid and never did lose a childlike sense of adventure. After hitting a home run he often skipped and saluted and laughed on the base paths. During poker games he never folded his hands, at parties he sometimes demonstrated sliding methods by sliding across marble floors, and he gave out tips as if handing over so many pieces of paper. It's said that when he appeared at a 1921 ceremony with Generalissimo Ferdinand Foch, former supreme commander of the Allied armies, the Babe took one look at the generalissimo's many medals and breezily remarked, "So you were in the war."

There was an amiable wildness in Ruth but no real malice; apart from a handful of fistfights on the diamond, he rarely found himself in violent situations. There was certainly no evidence that Ruth ever dangled his Yankee manager, Miller Huggins, off the railing of a speeding railroad car. No eyewitnesses ever saw him do any such thing and the only player to openly vouch for the story was a short-term Yankee who was once accused of stealing the Babe's wristwatch.

To the extent that the train tale had any truth to it, it was probably based on the Yankees's wild railroad trip back from St. Louis after the 1928 World Series. It seems that the Babe, dressed in nothing more than custom-tailored silk underwear, made his way through his triumphant teammates in several rail cars, drinking and dancing, striking up group sing-alongs, enlisting Lou Gehrig to lead a winding conga line. Ruth had discovered a certain technique for ripping dress shirts in such a way that most of the newly crowned champions were naked from the waist up. It was a heckuva scene, apparently.

Even then, in that tumult, Ruth didn't dangle Huggins.

Witnesses saw Ruth attempt to shove the jockey-size manager into one of the rail car's overhead compartments. The next morning, it was reported that Hug's dentures were missing and—no one knows how, exactly—the manager's tiny dog had a hangover. No arrests were made in The Case of the Drunken Chihuahua but there was one prime suspect.

MANAGEMENT

Claire Hodgson Ruth often said that one of the great regrets in her late husband's life was in the fact that he never got a chance to work as a manager. She painted a portrait of a forsaken star, waiting for a phone call that never did come.

There was a pathos but little plausibility in that portrait. As a threshold matter, it's not clear why Ruth, who frequently quarreled with managers, would want to become a skipper in his own right; one executive asked why the Babe would want to manage others when he had trouble managing himself. In addition, Ruth apparently suffered from a dyslexia that left him incapable of recalling the names of his closest associates, let alone the dozens of tactical options and signs involved in on-field management.

Finally, even if Ruth had a manager's temperament and memory, it's unclear why he would want the job's rigors. Like most kids at heart, the Babe often passed up responsibility in favor of irresponsibility. When he saw food, he ate it. When he found alcohol, he drank it. When he grabbed cigars, he smoked 'em. When he met willing young ladies, he . . .

The point is that the Babe wasn't managerial material. He was less a leader of men than a follower of women.

"THE MOST COMPLETE BALLPLAYER OF ALL TIME"

For a hitter to dominate today's AL in the way that the Babe dominated seasons like 1920 or 1927, the modern-day guy would have to swat more than 360 homers on the year. Despite his sweeping, all-or-nothing swings, the Babe was an accomplished contact hitter as well, finishing up with a .342 batting average that still leaves him in the top 10 of all time, third highest among those who played most of their games in the post-1920 era. It's an average so high that he could've finished on a 0-for-350 slump and still retired as a career .300 hitter.

Ruth's pitching was nearly as incredible as his hitting. The Babe was a lights-out starter in his early career, putting up a stingy 2.28 earned run average in over 1,000 innings, stats comparable to Hall of Famers like Chief Bender and Rube Waddell, so he gave up superstardom in the rotation only because he achieved super-duper stardom in the lineup. In this way he was the ultimate—the one athlete who could out-hit the hitters and out-pitch the pitchers.

The Babe was both a great hitter and a great pitcher, but that didn't necessarily mean that he was the most complete player of all time. An all-around performer should excel in switch-hitting, fielding, and base running, too, but in those areas Ruth was far from excellent.

Blame it on his notoriously short attention span, but in five of 16 years when he played at least half a season as a position player the Babe's fielding percentages were lower than the league averages. Ruth's putout and assist numbers were also below average, which led one historian to rate him as a "C–" with the leather.

Another personal shortcoming, recklessness, might've been responsible for Ruth's inept base running. While a superb player like Tim Raines might expect to steal bases with an 80 percent success rate, Ruth stole at a 51 percent rate that still ranks as one of the worst ever for those who have made at least 100 career attempts.

When columnists like Robert Lipsyte make the "complete" claim, they may disregard the Babe's fielding and running, or perhaps they disregard Mickey Mantle.

Mantle never pitched and no one has ever matched Ruth's lefty power, but the Mick was a switch-hitter who rated among the top ten hitters of all time from either side of the plate while simultaneously putting in multiple top ten showings in terms of putouts and stolen bases. The Bambino could do so much, but the Mick could do even more.

BREAKABLE

Ruth was remarkably offhand about his 50-plus records, but when pressed, he said he was most proud of his 29-2/3 consecutive shutout innings in World Series play. Ruth surely took pride in the fact that he participated in the most team wins of the 1920s, too.

Ruth's 60 single-season home runs weren't among his favorite records, though. As the cliché would have it, records are made to be broken, and Ruth was well aware that the 58-homer level was reached by both Jimmie Foxx and Hank Greenberg during the 154-game regular seasons of the 1930s.

The 60-homer level held up against assaults into the 1940s and 1950s, too, but the 1961 season presented unique record-breaking opportunities through the introduction of a 162-game schedule and the debut of dozens of rookie pitchers on expansion teams. Roger Maris had never won a homer title prior to 1961, so his record-breaking role was a surprise, but it was unsurprising that *someone* would reach Ruth.

TAKE A PICTURE

In some ways, Babe Ruth and Lou Gehrig were good friends. In other ways, they were strangers.

The Babe and Lou led intertwined lives. They grew up in working-class German American households and excelled in both left-handed pitching and hitting as teenagers before they became the number 3 and number 4 batters in the Yankees lineups of the 1920s, where they established themselves as the two greatest sluggers of their era. The duo also shared an agent and partnered for off-season barnstorming tours. Ruth sometimes joined Gehrig's family for old-country meals and the Babe's daughter, Dorothy, once developed a grade-school crush on Gehrig. In the decade beginning in 1923 the two probably spent thousands of hours in shared company.

For all that, the Babe and Lou were very different. One could be glib and overbearing while the other was usually quiet and polite. On one side was a taste for big bands and on the other was a preference for philharmonics. According to their respective biographers, Ruth got into near-annual car accidents while Gehrig often rode the subway. Possibly there were times when Ruth resented Gehrig's sterling reputation as much as Gehrig resented Ruth's riches.

Sometime in 1934, the two engaged in some kind of argument and rarely, if ever, spoke to each other in the ensuing five years.

Then, on the occasion of Gehrig's retirement in 1939, the Yanks held a gala on-field event that included former teammates; the Babe stood at Gehrig's side during the "luckiest man" farewell and then rushed to embrace the man of the hour. The Ruth/Gehrig photograph from that moment may be the most misunderstood image in baseball history.

In the picture Ruth wrapped his beefy arms around Gehrig, who smiled but kept his own hands at his sides. Observers like Bill Dickey took Gehrig's non-response to mean that Lou was uncaring toward Ruth, but the facts were more unfortunate.

Gehrig didn't embrace Ruth because he was incapable of an embrace. The amyotrophic lateral sclerosis (ALS) disease that had forced Gehrig into retirement had already begun killing him. Lou was too weak to hold aloft the gifts he had received minutes before, and with the July heat and the emotional strain, he may not have been far from a physical collapse. Summoning the strength to return Ruth's bear hug was out of the question.

What the Gehrig-Ruth photograph represented, instead, was the beginning of a final reconciliation. Over the next two years Ruth made frequent visits to the Gehrig household in Delafield Avenue, the Bronx, and, in the account of Eleanor Gehrig, the two didn't discuss death and illness but the lives and successes that they had co-authored. When illness rendered Lou unable to hear, talk, or breathe, only then was Ruth persuaded to leave; he was among the last people to see Gehrig alive.

On June 5, 1941, Lou Gehrig's body was laid in memoriam at the Church of the Divine Paternity at Central Park West and 76th Street. The Babe habitually avoided church services in general and memorial services in particular, but on that day he made an exception for his former teammate and business partner. Ruth came before the congregation, knelt before the coffin, and wept.

MYTH #92

The Silence before the "Shot Heard 'Round the World"

Ralph Branca's always been blamed.

When Branca came in as a relief pitcher for the Brooklyn Dodgers in the ninth inning of a 1951 playoff against the New York Giants, he was told to register the two outs needed to nail down a win. At minimum, he was expected to avoid giving up a three-run, game-winning home run to his first batter.

It was not to be. Branca's 0-1 pitch was quickly converted into Bobby Thomson's walk-off homer, the one now known as the "Shot Heard 'Round the World." To paraphrase the oft-repeated shouts of broadcaster Russ Hodges: "The Giants won the pennant! The Giants won the pennant! The Giants won the pennant!"

If blame had to be assigned to the one individual who didn't get the job done, then Branca had to be blamed. Even so, the pitcher didn't deserve the full burden of the 5-4 loss, much less a squandered season. To find the main culprit, you would've had to look past the mound and into the dugout, to Dodger manager Chuck Dressen.

Dressen's first mistake was about confidence. He had way, way too much of it.

Dressen established an early reputation as a preening, "me-first" type personality from his playing days, notwithstanding the fact that he was a pocket-size (5'5") infielder of no great distinction. Prior to his Brooklyn arrival in 1951, his managerial career produced 70 wins for every 162 games played. Dressen had never read a book in his life, even in school; lest anyone take that as a slander, keep in mind it was *Dressen* who said that Dressen had never read a book.

Notwithstanding his underwhelming athletic, managerial, and academic credentials, Dressen displayed an inexplicable exuberance as a skipper. He habitually took credit for team wins even as he blamed players for losses and, on at least one occasion, told his players to "stay close to 'em; I'll think of something." Dressen once attempted to overhaul Warren Spahn's mechanics, despite the fact that the future Hall of Famer was already notched several hundred wins by that point. (Spahn was too polite to remark that Dressen had never learned how to hit, much less pitch.)

In a career marked by overreaching, Dressen may have been at his delusional worst in 1951. The Giants had concluded 1950 on a 50-22 tear and actually outscored the Dodgers in the year's head-to-head contests, leading many beat writers to place New York as the odds-on favorite to take the National League pennant in 1951. When the Giants slumped in the early going, however, Dressen went public with his belief that his rivals were hopelessly behind. ("They're through. They'll never bother us again.") Sometime in mid-season Dressen reportedly told his players that a .500 record for the duration would be good enough to take the NL pennant. Just to drive home the point, he also told reporters that "the Giants is dead," one of the rare expressions that proved to be equally lacking in facts and grammar.

It was just like that time when Mike Scioscia waved away would-be contenders or when Charlie Manuel told his charges to give 50 percent . . . oh, wait. Such things never happened. No pro manager has ever been blithe enough to completely disrespect either the opposition or the need for full effort. Well, *with one exception*, no pro manager has ever . . .

Making matters worse, Dressen's arrogance was matched by a distinct tinge of incompetence. Even as the Dodgers played it safe with few lineup shuffles, Monte Irvin of the Giants believed that his manager's unconventional moves produced an additional five or six wins on the year. Irvin was almost certainly correct because Leo Durocher's club ended up matching the Dodgers in regular season victories despite scoring 74 fewer runs (781 to 855) and tallying more than 100 fewer hits (1,396 to 1,511). Making the Giants/Dodgers disparity more perplexing was the fact that Durocher was Dressen's boss only a few years before; perhaps Leo hid his managerial tactics inside a book.

Willful ignorance also came up time and again in Dressen's 1951 decisions. For example, the notoriously unethical Durocher set up a sign-stealing operation in the center field area of his home field; Dressen was oblivious. Allan Roth, the official statistician of the Dodgers, begged the manager to take a look at the numbers he had compiled on pitcher/batter matchups; Dressen ignored the reports. At one point Clem Labine asked to pitch from a stretch position; Dressen put him in the doghouse.

Having shed duties related to urgency, imagination, or awareness, Dressen had plenty of time to instill motivation. He did do that. Unfortunately for the Dodgers, he instilled all the motivation in the other side.

After sweeping a crucial August series several Dodgers felt free to openly taunt the Giants in their own clubhouse, knocking their bats against the room's flimsy doors while yelling, "Eat your heart out! You'll never win this year!," and other comments along those lines. Dressen was the ringleader of the incident, which is to pastime sportsmanship what *Girls Gone Wild* is to dignified feminism.

As it turned out, it was unwise for Dressen to enrage New York, that go-getting, ethically flexible ball club. Following the taunting incident, the Giants truly lived up to their name, putting up a huge 38-10 run in August and September. New York had gone 5-13 against Brooklyn prior to the bat knocking but afterward the black-and-orange juggernaut went 6-1 against the Dodgers.

Dressen, having initiated a rampage, responded to it by talking at a 6'5" level while producing at 5'5". In September, for example, Dressen publicly accepted a plaque announcing that the Dodgers were already the "1951 National League Champions," even as the plaque champs trudged through the stretch run with a 27-23 record. It was almost as if the team was deliberately testing out Dressen's .500 prediction.

When asked to explain that strange period, Brooklyn captain Pee Wee Reese later admitted that "we were all afraid of making a mistake." Evidently Dressen's team was fearful and mistake-prone enough to surrender a 13-game lead on the way to a flat-footed tie with their archrivals. This necessitated an official coin toss to decide home field advantage in a three-game playoff series. Fortunately, the Dodgers won the coin toss. Unfortunately, they gave it away.

The exact "reasoning" behind the decision has been lost in the mists of time but it hardly matters. It's always helpful to play on familiar home turf among friends and it's never helpful to play in an unfamiliar field while being ringed by foes. These are the unassailable reasons why no one has ever passed up home field advantage in the playoffs. Well, *with one exception* no one has ever passed up . . .

Still, in the next two postseason games, the Giants and Dodgers traded wins. The Dodgers still had a good shot at redemption in Game Three. Alas, they also had Dressen.

In the ninth inning of the do-or-die game, New York was behind by a score of 4–2 with one out but had runners at second and third. At this point Dressen had the choice to order an intentional base on balls to Bobby Thomson and then confront the next hitter in the Giants lineup, a youngster named Willie Mays.

Putting Thomson on base with the potential winning run would've been an unusual move, but in that spot it would've made a lot of sense. An intentional walk would've set up outs at every base and would've also placed the Dodgers one pitch away from the double play they needed to close out the win.

A Dressen decision to avoid Thomson would've been even more prudent in terms of personnel. In 1951 Thomson was a steely six-year veteran who had slammed 17 home runs over the second half of the season, a months-long power surge not far below the career homer rate of Babe Ruth. In Game Three he had two hits in three previous at-bats, including a double and a run batted in. Thomson later said he came into that fateful ninth inning with a sense of optimism and, with those numbers, anyone would've been optimistic.

Willie Mays was in a whole different place. It may be hard to believe in light of his later greatness, but in 1951 Mays was a 20-year-old rookie with a solitary homer in September, a weeks-long slump comparable to the career rate of not Babe Ruth but Ruth Buzzi. In Game Three Mays had gone hitless in three at-bats while falling into, yes, a double play. In subsequent years Mays conceded that, in the ninth, he was praying, "Please don't let it be me, don't make me come to bat now, God." Those were the exact words that Mays later recounted: "Please don't let it be me, don't make me come to bat now, God."

Dressen's choice could hardly have been more stark: take either a player or a pray-er. He took on the hot, confident veteran rather than the ice-cold, frightened rookie.

Even at that late moment, after the months of bungling and with their opponent's best hitter stepping up to the plate, the Dodgers were still very, very close to a victory. Dressen had only to call in the correct bullpen pitcher.

The manager could've selected Preacher Roe, the fully rested ace who finished among league leaders in categories like ERA and base runners allowed and who had limited Thomson to .333 on-base percentage on the year.* As an alternative, Dressen could've taken Bud Podbielan, who had completely shut down batters in five previous games, including the regular season's heart-stopping finale as well as Game One against the Giants. Podbielan also had success against Thomson in 1951, holding the Giant to two singles in five at-bats.

Dressen didn't go with his best starter or most effective available reliever but with Ralph Branca. On October 3, the tenth month and the third day, he called in a man wearing uniform 13.

Branca was a standout performer in his early career but in August 1951 he suffered a triceps injury that caused a disastrous 5.93 ERA for September. He was too hurt to be effective against anyone, but he was especially weak against Thomson, having allowed him a .500 on-base percentage and .917 slugging over the previous seasons. Allan Roth probably knew that.

Branca was a right-hander with an above-average fastball, to be sure, but Thomson had no great weaknesses against either righties or fastballs. In this light, it wasn't too surprising that Branca gave up a crucial Thomson homer only two days before, in Game One.

Even when overlooking those grave disadvantages, Dressen's pick was open to not second-guessing but first-guessing. Branca was given a single day of rest after tossing eight high-intensity innings. After making exactly one late-inning appearance in the previous two months, he was asked to make a late-inning appearance under the most stressful possible scenario. Branca was also asked

---

*Dressen later explained that he withheld Roe in the ninth because he wanted to allow rest before the World Series. Of course Roe's rest led to a lost inning, which led to a lost game, which rendered the World Series moot. Lesson #1, for all you aspiring managers: make sure your plans for the next few minutes don't ruin your plans for the next few weeks.

to work with a rookie catcher (Rube Walker) and, as to the optimal approach to Thomson, Dressen was, for once, silent.

Because Brooklyn had thrown away home field advantage, Branca labored against more stacked odds. The New Yorkers produced a cauldron of sound and, in the Polo Grounds, he contended with one of the most homer-friendly out- fields in the NL. (Thomson was aiming to pull the ball less than 300 feet from home plate.) With the secret sign-stealing operation in place, it was highly prob- able that Branca's pitch selection and target were known to the batter before the ball was even thrown.

And then the "shot" was fired. For all its game-ending finality, however, that Thomson homer is surrounded by questions. What if Branca had been healthy? What if he had worked with either rest or a familiar role? What if the Dodgers were, by rights, back in their home field? What if the signs weren't being stolen?

We'll never know the answers. We only know that Branca couldn't over- come all of Dressen's disadvantages and, for that, he was blamed. It hardly seemed fair, but it may have yielded a measure of justice in the long run.

Having escaped public discredit for the 1951 Dodgers, Chuck Dressen has been largely forgotten since his 1966 death. Some diehards might recall that, within two years of the skipper's 1953 firing, his successor led Brooklyn's stacked rosters to a long-awaited championship . . . and that's about it. People still laugh at "the Giants is dead" and the Spahn incident but most of those unfamiliar with the Dodger collapse cannot distinguish between a Dressen and a dresser.

It's been Ralph Branca who has been remembered and revisited.

For decades after "the most memorable moment in baseball history" was frozen within enough literature and DVDs to stock a medium-size library, the man behind the moment lived to fight expectations. Those who would've depicted Branca as an unlucky young man could also acknowledge his later blessings in terms of family, business, and philanthropy. Those who might've expected to find a bitter individual instead encountered an upbeat chatterbox. Despite the occasional jeer, he never left his home in greater New York.

Branca once lost, but he wasn't a loser. In time, he even won a bittersweet peace with Thomson.

For several decades Ralph and Bobby joined together for conventions, banquets, memorabilia shows, ceremonial events, and on-air interviews. They bantered over the days when New York Giants still roamed the earth. The duo weren't the closest of friends—old-time Giants and Dodgers didn't become the closest of friends—but at the reunions they joked around and discussed their grandkids.

By the time Bobby Thomson passed away in 2010, Ralph Branca was long past blame and bitterness. "I'll miss Bobby," he said.

MYTH #93

When Brooklyn Left the Dodgers

Many people hated Walter O'Malley at first sight, just to save the time and effort in getting to know him.

Dr. Seuss would've written that O'Malley's heart was two sizes too small. As a Brooklyn Dodgers owner he was small-minded enough to push out his early investors. In a reverse-Oprah move, he fiercely resisted a mass gift give-away involving cars. He sued people. For all we know, O'Malley left small tips, illegally parked in handicapped spaces, and re-gifted on Christmas.

And yet, for all his insensitivity, O'Malley could be quite sensible.

By the mid-1950s, O'Malley was, in many ways, the sharpest operator in baseball. The Dodgers were the class of the National League, earning four pennants in the seven seasons between 1950 and 1957, and a winning franchise was also an innovating franchise: it brought New York City its first-ever deals in postwar radio and television broadcasting and, in the person of Jackie Robinson, introduced the first black Major Leaguer of the 20th century. O'Malley was well on his way to the kind of successes that would eventually establish him as a Hall of Fame executive.

For all his club's positives, however, O'Malley could also see ever-worsening negatives built into his team's home. At less than 32,000 in seating capacity, Ebbets Field was the most undersized venue in the NL and by 1957 the 45-year-old ballpark, complete with urinal troughs, obstructed views, and narrow aisles, was held together by little more than peeling paint, rotting wood, and rusting metal. As recounted in Michael D'Antonio's *Forever Blue*, the almost nonexistent parking on Bedford Avenue and Sullivan Place literally turned away commuters.

Even as the Dodgers plowed to their first-ever championship in the mid-1950s, their outdated home could hold barely half the number of spectators welcomed by the league-leading Milwaukee Braves. It wasn't hard to predict how Dodgers would fare if they presented anything less than championship-level contenders.

With desperate ballpark needs O'Malley responded with desperate measures. He handpicked a site on Brooklyn's Atlantic Avenue, a location that traded traffic congestion for a public transportation line. He commissioned architects to design a spacious new venue and offered to pay for the real estate out of his own pocket. Of the New York City government, O'Malley only asked for a few public domain actions within the Flatbush neighborhood.

Fair-minded folks would've acknowledged the owner's need for a ballpark upgrade. Self-interested politicians would've ensured a flagship's long term future in the community. Clear-eyed planners would've seen the sparkling "Dodgertown" training facility in Vero Beach, Florida. Any of them would've worked out a Dodger deal, but an unelected bureaucrat named Robert Moses saw no such thing.

As author Robert A. Caro recounted in *The Power Broker*, Moses reigned as New York City's construction king from the 1930s to the 1960s, effectively overruling Mayor Fiorello La Guardia and Governor Nelson Rockefeller, among others, in connection to industrial-scale projects like highways and subway stations. He was the de facto decision maker for Brooklyn's ballpark, too, and in that role Moses did everything in his power to sabotage the club.

Moses strung along the franchise's negotiations for months and years, only to reject the Atlantic Avenue proposal in favor of parking garages. He offered no alternative means for the Dodgers to expand beyond their single city block, wouldn't cooperate on the eminent domain issue, and gave no useful input on infrastructure. Moses did attempt to push the Dodgers into a former garbage dump in a Queens neighborhood but shrugged when O'Malley rejected the "Flushing Meadow Dodgers" concept. Finally, Moses ignored the way that O'Malley was being courted in a possible Los Angeles relocation. Moses never went so far as to put up a flashing neon sign spelling out the words "D-R-O-P D-E-A-D," this is true, but the intended message came through clearly enough.

O'Malley could only recognize the status quo and, in 1958, turned the Brooklyn Dodgers into the Los Angeles Dodgers.

It was unsurprising that the unlikable Walter O'Malley would be lambasted for the 1958 franchise relocation, but did the charge make sense? If one of the smartest owners in baseball was given a real choice, there's every likelihood that he would've chosen Brooklyn.

Apart from the ballpark issue the Dodgers were mostly happy at home. Kings County presented a decades-old team tradition, a dedicated fan base, a cross-town rivalry with the Giants, and the prospect of another subway World Series versus the Yankees. The borough at the NL's center and, not least, the O'Malley family home was in Amityville. New York presented certainties.

Los Angeles presented risks. In Southern California the Dodgers were faced with startup costs, an unfamiliar fan base, a thousand or more miles of separation from most other NL clubs, and a terra incognita. (Apart from Don Drysdale and Duke Snider, who grew up in the area, most team players and officials were lost among the highways and byways of L.A.) Plans for a new Dodger Stadium faced all kinds of political and financial hurdles. Even the franchise name, based on inner-city "trolley dodgers," was senseless in the wide-open west. The one overriding positive for L.A. was in the way that its civic leaders provided support rather than stonewalling and that, almost alone, proved to be the deciding factor.

Walter O'Malley did move the Brooklyn Dodgers to California but not under conditions of his own making. The Dodgers didn't truly abandon Brooklyn; it was Robert Moses, Brooklyn's unwanted proxy, who abandoned the Dodgers.

MYTH #94

Waiting for Pete Rose

Millions waited on Pete Rose in the late 1970s and early 1980s.

Rose coveted Ty Cobb's record for career base hits, and slowly but surely, the Cincinnati Red found ways to come ever closer to the mark. With a hit here and couple of hits there, Rose climbed closer and closer to the summit, spurring fans to anticipate more and more.

Finally, on the night of September 11, 1985, Rose reached past Cobb with a single to Riverfront Stadium's left field. It's still hard to believe that once, more than 25 years ago, a player accumulated 4,192 career hits.

Of course, no fan had to wait until 1985 to evaluate Rose's playing career. Long before he became the hit king, anyone who knew baseball knew that Peter Edward Rose was one of the best hitters ever to step between the white lines.

Rose had a career full of career years. He averaged nearly 200 hits per season for two decades, a steady excellence that reached its apotheosis in a 44-game hitting streak that represented the most serious challenge to Joe DiMaggio's 56-game hitting streak in over 70 years.

Much of Rose's impact came on his everyday durability. Despite a career full of head-first slides and home plate collisions, no one has ever accumulated more seasons with 600 at-bats and 150 or more games played. No other position player has ever played through 24 straight years, either, but Rose endured to face off against pitchers who hadn't been born when he took the 1963 Rookie of the Year award.

Rose reached many accomplishments well before he took the all-time hit record, yet none of that seems to matter much anymore. Almost no one talks much about the on-field triumphs of Pete Rose the player but the off-field failures of Pete Rose the man. They look past a Hall of Fame–caliber career to focus on a Hall of Fame exclusion.

Most everyone knows the story by now. When Rose served as Cincinnati's manager from 1985 to 1987, he violated Major League rules by gambling on his team's contests. Confronted with accusations in 1989, Rose did his best to lie, deny, and alibi his way out of trouble but eventually agreed to a settlement placing him on the "permanently ineligible" list. The guy who broke a lot of important records ended up breaking a lot of important rules, too, so the "Charlie Hustle" nickname gained a whole new currency.

It has been unfortunate but perhaps inevitable that so much was overshadowed by the scandal, but there's been no need for misperceptions about the Rose ban from the Hall of Fame.

PETE ROSE VOLUNTARILY SIGNED AWAY HIS ELIGIBILITY

While the Rose lawyers conceded that Commissioner Bart Giamatti had "a factual basis" for placing Rose on the ineligible list, they also insisted on language stating that "nothing in this agreement shall be deemed either an admission or a denial of the allegations."

Rose also gained the right to apply for reinstatement within a year, a concession that would've been nonsensical if he was waiving any and all hopes for a return. Both Rose and the commissioner anticipated a day when he would be allowed into the Hall.

GIAMATTI WANTED A PERMANENT BAN

The commissioner initially suggested a 12-year exile, negotiated down to six years, and finally settled for an indeterminate term; at no time did Giamatti ever propose a lifetime ban for Rose. After extensive discussions with Giamatti, Rose came to believe that the commissioner would keep an open mind about reinstatement.

ROSE NOW WANTS TO CHANGE THE TERMS OF HIS AGREEMENT

Those who believe that Rose is his own worst enemy don't know much about Fay Vincent.

When Rose was placed on the permanently ineligible list he was still on track for a Cooperstown induction. No one on the list had ever been enshrined, but there was no strict rule preventing a Rose vote on the merits.

All that changed upon Giamatti's sudden death. Through backroom lobbying, Vincent, the incoming commissioner, maneuvered to ensure that the ineligible list would became a formal ban from the Hall of Fame. Vincent tore up the Rose-Giamatti agreement, in effect, along with any assurance that deals reached with one commissioner will be honored by his successors.

Bad enough that Vincent denied due process to Rose, whom he openly detested; there's no need to elaborate on how Vincent also overrode the wishes of his late predecessor.

ROSE WAS CORRUPT

Pete Rose never bet on his team to lose, never passed along inside information, never encouraged anyone else to bet, and did not improperly influence a contest. He was miles apart from the banned Black Sox of 1919, who committed every one of those sins.

Rose did break an important rule but never inflicted any substantive damages as a result. Has any fan ever suspected the game outcomes from the Pete Rose era? Has anyone ever gambled because he gambled? The notions were so ludicrous that they've never been alleged. This was a ban based on a victimless crime, on a half-remembered PR debacle.

ROSE WAS A PROFESSIONAL DISGRACE

Pete Alexander, Jimmie Foxx, Eddie Mathews, and at least two dozen other Hall of Famers dealt with alcoholism or serious drug habits during their careers. They impaired themselves to the extent that they couldn't give full efforts to win. Rose was 180 degrees from that status; no one doubted him when he said that he'd run through hell in a gasoline suit just to win.

ROSE WAS A PERSONAL DISGRACE

This one's based on Hall of Fame Rule Five, which states that "voting shall be based upon the player's record, playing ability, integrity, sportsmanship, character and contributions to the team(s) on which the player played."

Pete Rose's rule-breaking and lying flunked a strict morals test and there were other issues. He frequented bookmakers, hung out with petty criminals, and evaded taxes. During the 1980 season Rose left game tickets for his wife . . . and his girlfriend. To the same game. And the *girlfriend* got the better seats.

If character is to be used to exclude Pete from the Hall, however, consistency demands that character should be used to exclude those with more egregious failings. Every Hall of Famer who ever threw a brushback pitch, rushed into a brawl, or went into a spikes-up slide has committed, at minimum, a serious assault. Inductees have also been linked to drunk driving, incitement to riot, hard-drug possession, civil rights violation, obstruction of justice, terrorism, public intoxication, manslaughter, domestic violence, child abandonment, prostitution, larceny, and other offenses depicted in the unrated version of *Mad Max Beyond Thunderdome*. Cobb—our familiar Cobb—told a biographer that in 1912 he had beaten a man to death in Detroit, back when murder was still illegal in Detroit. Surely all those miscreants should be denied a Hall pass, too, so that a truly character-based institution can rename itself "The Hall of Stan Musial, Christy Mathewson, and Almost No One Else."

This will never happen, of course. Most everyone knows that it's possible to condemn a man's personal character while simultaneously commending his professional career. In the spirit of proportion, most everyone can also conclude that mistakes made over two or three years don't necessarily negate accomplishments spanning 23 years.

The Rose candidacy isn't being decided by most everyone. It's within an American pastime, not an American democracy.

ROSE IS UNRECONSTRUCTED

Rose has never been a saint. He still hangs out at casinos, but there's no evidence that he has bet on baseball in more than two decades. At well past age 70 Rose is probably too tired to be anything but reconstructed.

ROSE IS BEING PUNISHED

This may be the worst punch line in a long string of not-so-funny jokes.

Rose has been punished by the Hall ban in that he's probably lost some sleep, but he's been the subject of such popular fascination that he's also gained any number of post-retirement autograph fees and appearances. There are dozens of living Hall of Famers but only one former player with a cachet as . . . what? A man whose sentence outweighs his crime. A blue-collar anti-hero, a prodigal son without a return. Someone the establishment can't break. Someone ready and willing to offer more to the game he loves.

The Hall of Fame exile has almost certainly lent Rose a greater spotlight than that coming from an ordinary induction. It hasn't been a "punishment" worthy of the name.

THERE'S NO COMPROMISING ON THE BAN

For all the wringing of hands and gnashing of teeth, there's still an obvious means to break the Rose impasse: the commissioner can open up Hall of Fame induction for Pete-Rose-the-former-player while continuing a ban on Pete-Rose-the-present-day-coach.

Like most compromises, such a deal would have something to set off both sides. The Rose antagonists would be enraged by Pete's big day in Cooperstown;

they might hold on to the thought that "he's gotten away with it." The pro-Rose crowd would find a satisfaction in Rose's official return to the town and the team he helped define, even if the uniform might be limited to ceremonial occasions. A framework could be built sometime in an uncertain future, whenever serious people decide it's time, once and for all, to close a painful chapter in pastime history.

We're still waiting. For one last time, for one last prize, Pete Rose is still counting down.

Extra Extras

A Baseball/English Translator

There's a cottage industry devoted to making a simple game sound complicated but it isn't too difficult to make out hidden meanings. Here's what they are really saying when they talk.

HITTING PROSPECTS

He puts together quality at-bats . . . will not give away an at-bat.
"He walks every so often . . . fouls off pitches."

Battling . . . a beautiful swing.
"Strike One/Strike Two/Strike Three."

Handles the bat . . . moves the runners over . . . puts the ball in play.
"Don't expect too much. He can hit singles, though."

Something of a free swinger . . . not up there to walk.
"A strike zone the size of the Eastern Time Zone."

A defensive specialist . . . calling a great game . . . a speed merchant.
"Cannot defend, call, or speed his way into a lot of offense."

Being paid to hit.
"With that kind of fielding, a piece of scrap metal would work as well as a glove."

PITCHING PROSPECTS

He has electric stuff . . . a live arm.
"His curveball? Ernie Banks can handle it, despite the fact that Mr. Cub is now 81 years old."

More than a thrower—a pitcher . . . a finesse pitcher . . . can really paint the corners . . . shrewd . . . wily.
"Hawk Harrelson can talk faster than that fastball and with more deception, too."

Keeping you close . . . eating up a lot of innings . . . pitching to the score.
"So-so but somewhat durable and backed by a good offense."

A will to be great.
"Plays hard but has no muscles to speak of, so I guess he doesn't have a will to be great, actually, not when it comes to lifting weights."

A good hitter, for a pitcher.
"The job description is 'pitcher,' not 'pitcher/hitter,' but, man, it's amazing that a professional athlete can be so terrible with the bat. My friend Chris, over in Section 222, Row H, Seat 11, can hit better than this guy."

YOUNGSTERS

Doesn't bring a classic athletic body . . . some conditioning issues.
"When he walks into any fast-food restaurant within the city limits they greet him by name and prepare his favorite burger without his having to ask."

May be spreading himself too thin.
"On a first-name basis with half the hookers in town."

Talented but still unpolished.
"I hope he likes the restaurants back in Scranton because he'll be back there next week."

Finally coming into his own.
"Just turned 25 years old."

Hoping to regain his rookie form.
"The league caught up to him."

MENTALITIES/PERSONALITIES

Brings a football mentality.
For players: "Often crashes into things, isn't too bright."
For managers: "Gives rah-rah speeches, isn't too bright."

He's zany . . . colorful . . . a character . . . keeping everybody loose . . . marching to a different drummer.
"Crazy (in a good way)."

Erratic . . . an enigma . . . unapproachable.
"Crazy (in a bad way)."

A bit prickly . . . fiery . . . irascible . . . outspoken . . . brash . . . mercurial . . . not the flashiest guy in town.
"In order: a prick . . . hotheaded . . . temperamental . . . refuses to shut up . . . loudmouthed . . . moody . . . boring."

Better tone down his act.
"When he was hitting .325 we cut him some slack. At .235, not so much."

OUR COMPLIMENTS

Knows how to win . . . has the heart of a champion . . . got the rings . . . a born winner.
"Drafted or signed by a good team."

Without him, the team misses the playoffs . . . getting the job done.
"Taking up playing time without killing the club."

Impossible to understate his impact on the clubhouse . . . whether he's hitting or not, he can influence the game . . . an overachiever.
"He cannot play baseball very well but the roster is so stacked that it can carry him. The good players seem to get along with him on a personal level."

Adds consummate confidence . . . never-say-die attitude . . . panache.
"When the guys go out for lunch, he buys."

Always brings determination . . . game intelligence . . . spark . . . a certain throwback quality.
"Once, back in spring training, the two of us went out to a bar and he bought my drink, bless his heart."

SAY SOMETHING NICE (PT. 1)

There goes a good clubhouse guy . . . overlooked . . . a diamond in the rough . . . taking a selfless approach.
"A fine player who makes friends with people."

Always coming to play . . . flying under the radar . . . getting dirty . . . handling the swingman role.
"A bench guy who doesn't complain."

A role player . . . a super-sub . . . resourceful.
"A spare part."

SAY SOMETHING NICE (PT. 2)

Known as a catalyst . . . firebrand . . . pest . . . table-setter.
"He cannot play very well."

A fighter . . . a grinder . . . blue collar . . . feisty.
"Cannot play very well, is short."

A scrapper . . . student of the game . . . no smarter player in the game.
"Cannot play very well, is short and white."

A hard worker . . . overachiever . . . lunch-pail guy . . . really cares.
"Cannot play very well, is short and white, and currently sporting a two-week stubble-beard."

VETERANS DAY

This guy is a drawing card . . . got all kinds of star power.
"He was really good. Four years ago."

Once great.
"Nearly finished."

Taking players under his wing . . . an established pro . . . a mentor . . . a teacher.
"Washed up . . . the only coach in the world making $3 million per year."

SLUMPS

Looking uncertain at the plate.
"He's currently seeking batting tips from his coach, manager, teammates, wife, friends, instruction manuals, and a veterinarian who claims that in 1996 he hits .320 for the Boston College varsity."

Scuffling . . . battling . . . needs to get started.
"Sucking."

Needs to step away for a bit . . . needs to take some time off.
"Needs to stop sucking as of yesterday."

Being rested.
"Being benched."

Dealing with the lessons of last season.
"He better run faster because he's on thin ice."

There are some professionalism issues . . . a change of scenery might do some good.
"In the last week he picked up a bat and attacked the general manager, manager, #1 starter, bat boy, and Father Flanagan. Fortunately they're all okay because right now he's missing everything."

STATISTICAL VALIDITY

I'm not a stats guy.
"I don't understand stats."

His numbers aren't going to jump out at you.
"Not a very good player."

Everybody gets all caught up in numbers . . . forget the stats . . . about more than numbers.
"Not a very good player but so what?"

RESULTS DRIVEN
Flat . . . lethargic . . . found a way to lose.
"They lost a close one."

Found a way.
"Won a close one."

This might be a good time for the reserves to get some work in.
"Game over."

Going about as far as their pitching takes them.
"This is just like every team ever—if their pitchers do better than their opposing pitchers they'll win."

Just didn't get the big hits . . . didn't execute.
"This is just like every loss ever. If they actually executed with enough big hits then they wouldn't have lost, obviously."

Won by outscoring the other side.
"This is just like every win ever. If you outscore the other guys then, by definition, you win."

This team never got any respect . . . no one gave them a chance . . . they shocked the world.
"This is any team not named 'the New York Yankees.'"

SIGN THIS
We're going to make a splash in the free agency arena.
"We're desperate."

This free agent signing sends a message to the fans . . . brings instant credibility . . . legitimacy.
"We're impatient, too."

There are signability issues . . . the move doesn't make sense from a business standpoint.

"The move doesn't make sense from a team profits standpoint. Our owner is down to his last couple of mansions so belt-tightening must rule the day, you see."

TRADE ROUTES

We're open to the possibility of a trade.

"If anyone's willing to take this mistake off my hands then I'll do the trade and, as sweeteners, I'll toss in one prospect, two suspects, a gently used pitching machine, my nephew, and a *Homeland* Season One DVD box set."

It was a challenge trade.

"Traded our problem for their problem."

Currently dealing with financial realities.

"Dumping salaries."

RELEASES

There isn't enough room on the roster.

"There isn't enough room on the roster for him, specifically. Because he's not good at playing baseball."

Going in a different direction.

"Going in a better direction, because the direction doesn't include him."

Designated for Assignment.

"Rest in Peace."

JUST MANAGING

Created a winning atmosphere . . . culture . . . belief system.

"Has good players who aren't currently at war with each other."

Got them believing they can win.

"They win. It's all there in the league standings. They believe that they can win because they can believe in the league standings."

A touch of class . . . a people person . . . brilliance mixed with a common touch.
"Gets along with reporters . . . calls me by my first name . . . is Joe Maddon."

An old-school manager.
"Screams quite often."

An attitude problem . . . classless.
"Hates reporters . . . refused to give my kid an autograph."

THE FIRE DEPARTMENT

Embattled manager John Smith
"Soon-to-be-fired manager John Smith . . ."

Might be losing control of the club.
"Will be fired next week."

Has been reassigned within the organization.
"Has been fired."

Leaving to pursue other opportunities.
"Leaving to pursue other opportunities, because he has been fired."

MEDIA SPOKESMEN

I'm happy to be here.
(Yawn)

Frankly . . . to be honest with you.
"I'm about to lie."

In the best shape of my life . . . put on "x" pounds of muscle in the off-season.
"Prepare for disappointment."

I want to concentrate on baseball . . . not here to talk about the past.
"My lawyer's number is 1-2-1-2 . . ."

That quote was taken out of context.
"I said something honest and now people are angry at me."

A little banged-up . . . day-to-day.
"This is excruciating pain. Ex. Cru. Ci. At. Ing. Pain."

I injured myself washing a truck . . . moving boxes in my parents' house . . . delivering a care package to the needy.
"I can now confirm that high-velocity dirt-biking is just as dangerous as you might expect, but don't tell the general manager how I found out because there are insurance clauses involved."

In an emotional retirement conference, Mike Superstar announced . . .
"In the sole occasion when it's still socially acceptable for a grown man to cry like a little girl, Mike Superstar announced . . ."

MIND GAMES

Stay within yourself.
"The self must stay within / The within must stay in self."

It is what it is.
"It is what it is / It is not what it is not."

The best thing about this team is that it's a team . . . that's just Joe Smith being Joe Smith.
"The best thing about this grapefruit is that it's a grapefruit . . . that's just a grapefruit being a grapefruit."

TEAM ORIENTATIONS

They're clinging to modest hopes.
"Not to ruin the surprise or anything, but this club is going to be terrible."

A sleeper.
"A third-place team."

Never quits.
"Never ahead."

There are reasons for optimism.
"My boss says that I have to say *something* nice, so here goes . . ."

Doing it with pitching and defense . . . with complementary players.
"Cannot hit much. Looking for a lot of help from their 4-5 starters and part-timers."

Manufacturing runs . . . playing small ball.
"Cannot hit for power . . . praying for some breaks."

Going with a bullpen by committee.
"Going with a bad bullpen."

ALL ABOUT CHEMISTRY (PT. 1)

They check their egos at the door . . . don't put too much pressure on themselves . . . pick each other up . . . expect to win.
"They have good players."

A confident ball club . . . fun to watch . . . all kinds of chemistry.
"Just had a five-game winning streak."

A togetherness . . . having fun out there.
"They're happy about their five-game winning streak."

ALL ABOUT CHEMISTRY (PT. 2)

Holding their own.
"I don't mean that they're literally holding their own. Or that of anyone else."

They played their hearts out.
"They lost. Winners, for some reason, never play their hearts out."

Lacking a certain mental edge . . . missing an aura and mystique.
"Losing . . . some of them are hurt and others are having bad years."

OFF TO THE PLAYOFF RACES

This is gonna be their year.
"Last year was not their year."

Hoping to keep their momentum . . . figuring out how to win the big game.
"Hoping to avoid good pitchers."

Choked . . . collapsed . . . imploded.
"An experienced team that lost."

A lack of killer instinct . . . a building year.
"An inexperienced team that lost."

Hoping to exorcise their demons . . . get payback . . . prove themselves.
"They lost before."

Championship material.
"They won before."

Tested . . . tough.
"A relatively experienced team that'll probably win."

A team of destiny . . . an upstart.
"A relatively inexperienced team that'll probably win."

The postseason is a crapshoot.
"They lost in the postseason."

May be a dynasty in the making . . . a dynasty in progress.
"They recently won in the playoffs. . . they also won a couple of years ago."

IN THE HALL

He deserves consideration for Cooperstown . . . you could make a case for the Hall of Fame . . . a borderline Hall of Famer.
"Not a Hall of Famer."

When you close your eyes when you hear the player's name and you say "yes" or "no" on the Hall of Fame, there's the answer.
"Thinking makes my head hurt."

How many of his SportsCenter *highlights/late-game homers/walk-off hits can you remember?*
"I dislike him."

GRUMPY OLD MEN

Back in my day, pitchers had a complete-game mentality . . . forget the pitch counts.

"Back in my day management rode us like rented mules and there was nothing we could do about it."

My teammate was an intellectual . . . a genius.

"He read books. . . read books without pictures."

An exercise fanatic.

"He exercised from time to time."

A blithe spirit . . . carefree.

"A drunk."

Fun-lovin' . . . high-livin.'

"Hard drinkin'."

Out with flu-like symptoms . . . fined for failure to stay in condition.

"Hung over . . . drunk at this very moment."

A carouser . . . a lady's man . . . a womanizer.

"Never let him anywhere near your sister . . . or your wife . . . or your mother, for that matter."

Players nowadays cannot grasp the fine points of the game . . . no respect for the game . . . noun verb adjective.

"Nobody's as good as I was. Also, get off my lawn."

Back then we didn't play for money.

"Back then we didn't have money."

We played for a love of the game.

"We loved the game and we had no objection to the fame and the girls, either."

MYTH #96

"The Handsome One," "The Killer," "The Monster," and Other Beneficiaries of False Advertising

Pastime nomenclature is almost always colorful, often informative, and sometimes inaccurate. Here are some of the pastime's most egregiously misnamed nicknames:

Joaquin "One Tough Dominican" Andujar: A teammate once put fake snakes in Andujar's locker on three successive days and on the fourth day, just when Andujar thought he had the gag figured out, he found a live snake. The "tough" guy was so shaken that he missed a scheduled start.

Frank "Home Run" Baker: Just how dead was the "deadball" era of the 1910s? Well, its version of a power hitter, Baker, never had more than 12 homers per year and finished with a grand total of 96. That dead.

Roger "The Duke of Tralee" Bresnahan: Bresnahan was born and raised in Ohio; "The Duke of Toledo" was more like it.

"Downtown" Darrell Brown: A Minors-phenom-turned-Majors-flop had enough pop for only one homer in 591 career at-bats. Billy Gardner once said, "That must be an awfully small town."

Ron "The Penguin" Cey: Cey was so bow-legged that he didn't run so much as waddle, but it would be impossible for a flightless little bird to make six All-Star teams while smacking 316 career home runs.

"Prince Hal" Chase: Far from being noble, The "Prince" was a cheating, gambling lout who probably bribed fellow players to throw games. Chase was among the worst human beings ever to walk onto a diamond, which brings us to Ty Cobb.

Ty "The Georgia Peach" Cobb: The Georgia-born Cobb was a bad-guy character straight out of Central Casting, one who battered teammates, service workers, women, even a crippled fan. In no way was Cobb a "peachy guy" or "a peach of a fellow."

HIS MOM CALLED HIM CLARENCE

"Sugar Bear" (Larvell) Blanks
"Rough" (Bill) Carrigan
"Choo Choo" (Clarence) Coleman
"Dizzy" (Jay) Dean
"Rabbit" (Walter) Maranville
"Pepper" (Johnny) Martin
"Ducky" (Joe) Medwick
"Bobo" (Louis) Newsom
"Schoolboy" (Lynwood) Rowe
"Muddy" (Herold) Ruel

Vince "Vincent Van Go" Coleman: The speedy but none-too-swift Coleman once said he had never heard of a baseball pioneer named Jackie Robinson, so it was unlikely that he ever brushed up on a 19th-century artist named Vincent Van Gogh, either.

Brian "The Hulk" Downing: Back in the 1970s Downing was among the first ballplayers to commit to a real conditioning routine, but nowadays, at 5'10" and 170 pounds, he would probably be known as "The Guy with the Ordinary Physique."

"Stunning Steve" Dunning: Dunning started off as a highly touted, highly drafted Stanford grad and then slowly trailed off into obscurity. He once gave up three straight lead-

MULTICULTURALISM
(Richard) "Turk" Farrell—Irish
(Olaf) "Swede" Henriksen—Danish ancestry
Keith "Mex" Hernandez—Spanish American, also Scots/Irish
"Black" Jack McDowell—white
(Emil) "Irish" Meusel—born to a German immigrant family
Honus "The Flying Dutchman" Wagner—German American
Kevin "Greek God of Walks" Youkilis— parents hailed from Romania.

off homers in three straight starts, which *was* stunning, but not in a good way.

(Dave) "Boo" Ferriss: The nickname originally came from a toddler's attempt to pronounce "brother," but "Boo" was one of the most popular (and cheered) Red Sox of the late 1940s.

Frankie "Fordham Flash" Frisch: Frisch had an interest in book learning, but a rival once pointed out that he "majored in baseball, football, and soccer."

Rich "El Guapo" Garces: A Red Sox teammate came up with this one, from a character in *The Three Amigos* movie; it translates to "The Handsome One," a less-than-obvious nickname for a man with a bodily resemblance to a Venezuelan potato.

(Jim) "Mudcat" Grant: When he came up as a rookie in 1958 scouts believed Grant was from Mississippi, the Mudcat State. If they had known he was actually born and raised in Florida, they might have called him "Sunshine Grant."

Bud "Shorty" Harrelson: Harrelson was "Shorty" to Yogi Berra in the mid-1970s, despite the fact that Bud was four inches taller than his Mets manager and, at 5'11", one inch taller than the average adult male.

Burt "Happy" Hooton: Hooton was called "Happy" for the same reason fat guys are called "Tiny."

"Shoeless" Joe Jackson: As far as we know Jackson played without shoes for only one (very brief) time in a unique career, so referring to him as "Shoeless Joe" is like introducing "Barack Obama, who was once an Illinois state senator."

"Sad Sam" Jones: Jones had one of those faces that looked downcast no matter what, but "Sad Sam" cracked jokes and hung out at parties, the usual things. He wasn't sad about winning the 1923 World Series as a member of the Yankees, surely.

"Hot Rod" Kanehl: Hot Rod was only fast enough to compile 17 career stolen bases but he inspired almost as many stories of early 1960s derring-do. After Casey Stengel offered a small bonus to any Mets batter to get hit by a pitch, Kanehl took one for the team and then used a magic marker to ink "$50" on the bruise.

Harmon "Killer" Killebrew: "Killer" was nothing more than an easy pun on the surname, as the kindly Killebrew never murdered anything but fastballs and curveballs.

"Sinister" Dick Kinsella: Kinsella was a stage villain to all appearances, what with a tall frame, thick black hair, bushy eyebrows, dark suits, and "an ominously quiet manner." His friends said he was a nice enough guy, though.

Bill "The Spaceman" Lee: Lee, a dedicated baseball man who dabbled in Eastern mysticism, described himself as "equal parts Yogi Berra and Maharishi Mahesh Yogi." An outspoken environmentalist, "The Spaceman" preferred to be called "The Earthman."

Jeffrey "Penitentiary Face" Leonard: Leonard's game face was fierce but one of his managers described him as "one of the sweetest guys I ever knew."

Jim "The King" Leyritz: Yankee veterans came up with this sarcastic nickname when the swaggering rookie first came up in the early 1990s. They also called him "Jumbo Jimmy," only that one wasn't sarcastic.

Gary "Sarge" Matthews: When Wrigley Field's "bleacher bums" cheered his every appearance during the 1984 playoff run Matthews gave them a drill sergeant salute in return, but he only served in baseball flannels, not military khakis.

Willie "The Say Hey Kid" Mays: When he came up to the big leagues, Mays had trouble remembering names, so his "say hey" greetings basically translated into "hey you, whatever your name is." His memory eventually improved.

Austin "Fireman" McHenry: As a young Cardinal living near the St. Louis ballpark, McHenry smelled smoke one night, alerted the fire department, and proceeded to join in dousing the flames. He was a position player, however, and never pitched an inning as a "fireman" (reliever).

Stu "The Bullet" Miller: Miller was a changeup specialist, so the nickname was sarcastic. Ron Luciano once said Miller pitched at four speeds, those being "slow, slower, slowest, and stopped."

Roger "Wrong Way" Moret: Moret was effective when healthy and focused but that was a relatively rare combination. A Red Sox teammate said his pal "was usually headed the right way but had a habit of falling asleep while going there."

Buck "Nancy" O'Neil: As the story goes, Satchel Paige once had one of his part-time girlfriends set up in a hotel room just down the hall from where he was staying with his steady girl, snuck out in the middle of the night, tapped on the unofficial girl's door and whispered "Nancy? Nancy?" When Paige's steady girl woke up and angrily asked, "Who's Nancy?!," O'Neil opened the door of an adjoining room, quickly sized up the situation, and said, "Yeah, Satch, what is it?"

(Ernest) "The Blimp" Phelps: Phelps was one of the fattest catchers of his day, which was saying something; at one point he refused to travel by air, leading some to call him "The Grounded Blimp."

"Sweet Lou" Piniella: Once, in the Minors, the temperamental Piniella kicked an outfield fence so hard that he brought a 15-foot section crashing down and in another tantrum he smashed a Mr. Coffee machine that Joe DiMaggio had personally donated to the Yankee clubhouse. Andy Messersmith surmised that the "Sweet Lou" nickname "didn't describe his personality—it described his swing."

> **TRUTH IN ADVERTISING**
>
> *Ángel Berroa:* In 2008 Angel played for the Angels in Los Angeles.
>
> *José Cardenal.* Cardenal wore Cardinal uniforms in 1970 and 1971.
>
> *Red Barrett:* The Cincinnati Reds fielded Red from 1937 to 1940.
>
> *Steve Garvey:* Garvey was playing for the San Diego Padres in the 1980s when, in the space of a few years, he divorced the mother of his two daughters, fathered two children out of wedlock, and then married a second wife, with whom he would have another three children. T-shirts throughout San Diego read "Steve Garvey Is Not My Padre."
>
> *Dave Philley:* Played for the Phillies (1958 to 1960).
>
> *B. J. Ryan:* On the Blue Jays, sometimes known to the locals as the "B.J.s."
>
> *Mark Teixeira:* Teixeira's name is properly abbreviated as "Teix" and is pronounced "tay-SHERR-ah," but he was nicknamed "Tex" while playing for Texas. This was, admittedly, easier than changing the entire state's abbreviation to "Teix" or beginning to pronounce the state as "tay-SHERR-as."
>
> *Marvin Eugene Throneberry:* M. E. T. was a Met during the franchise's first two seasons.

Dick "The Monster" Radatz: Mickey Mantle, who couldn't touch the fire-balling Red Sox reliever in the 1960s, once exclaimed, "He's a monster!" Radatz disliked the nickname because it scared children.

Branch "The Mahatma" Rickey: The longtime general manager was once described as "an incredible combination of Jesus, Tammany Hall, and your father" but, in one of life's little ironies, the Bible-thumping Rickey was tagged with the Hindu term for a holy man.

Mickey "Mick the Quick" Rivers: The "quick" reference was to his feet, not his head. Once, in the late 1970s, Rivers tried to duck creditors by using a "Miguel Rivera" alias.

"Tom Terrific" Seaver: When he first came up in 1967 Seaver was expected to win a Cy Young Award, carry the Mets to a championship, make the Hall of Fame, and deliver world peace; he didn't deliver world peace.

"Stormin'" Gorman Thomas: As Brewer fans knew, the rhyme didn't apply to on-field hustle and didn't even work as a rhyme. "Storman' Gorman" might've made sense but spelling, even baseball spelling, can only stretch so far.

"Hard-Hittin'" Mark Whiten: He once hit four homers in a game, but based on a career .415 slugging, it would've been more accurate to make reference to "Alright-Hittin'" Mark Whiten.

Earl "Big Money" Williams: Williams knocked 61 home runs in his first two full years but a lack of effort soon caught up to him. After he posted a .237 batting average for the 1973 Orioles, some started calling him "Small Change."

Ted "The Kid" Williams: People started calling Williams "Kid" when he was a teenager and never stopped, even as he reached an exalted status as a senior states-man. In 1993 *Sports Illustrated* printed a story entitled "The Kid at 75."

Carl "Yaz" Yastrzemski: The family name is pronounced Ya-strem-ski, with a "s" sound rather than a "z" sound, but Bostonians took to calling him "Yaz" anyway; the balloting for the 1967 Most Valuable Player award included votes for "Yaztremski," "Yastremski," "Yastrezemski," "Yastreszski," "Yastremzminski," "Yastrstrenski," "Yazstremenski," "Y'str'mski," and in one exasperated instance, "Yaz-Boston."

MYTH #97

Player Rules That Aren't in the Rulebook

HITTERS

- On a borderline pitch with three balls, a batter who doesn't swing must immediately toss his bat back to the dugout in ultra-casual fashion, as if there's no doubt as to the umpire's correct call. Bonus points if the batter goes so far as to unstrap his little shin pad.
- If the umpire calls a strike anyway, the batter must act completely astounded.
- If the umpire call is a *third* strike, the performance must include arm waving.
- Batting gloves are to be treated with the delicacy of Faberge eggs and the precision of F-22 fighters, which call for *a lot* of delicacy and precision; jewels and jets aren't checked after every pitch.

PITCHERS (PT. 1)

- Pitchers aren't allowed to catch infield pop-ups. Those belong to position players.
- With eye black, same thing.
- When pitchers aren't on the field, they must wear jackets on the bench. Pitchers on the bench are treated like grade-schoolers on a chilly night.
- In sum: pop-ups, eye black, and short sleeves are for big boys only.

PITCHERS (PT. 2)

- On everything except an out-of-the-ballpark bomb, the outfielder has to range backward at least a few steps on home runs, as if to reassure the pitcher that he hasn't given up on an object that has just entered into a low-earth orbit.
- When a third out is recorded on a strikeout, the catcher has to roll the ball back to the pitcher's mound, especially if he's somehow nurtured an uncanny ability to place it just at the very lip of the mound.

- While walking off at the end of the inning, infielders must move to either the right or left of the pitcher's mound. Stepping directly onto the pitcher's mound would be like sitting in someone's recliner chair without permission.

PITCHERS (PT. 3)

- When a manager wants to pull a struggling pitcher from a game, he sometimes sends the pitching coach up to the mound to do the dirty work. It's like Mom having Dad go in to tell their child about a punishment.
- A pitcher is allowed to argue a case for staying in the ball game—up to a certain point. One time a struggling pitcher kept explaining that he wasn't tired, only to have his skipper explain that the outfielders were exhausted.
- When a pitcher's being pulled, he has to hand the ball over to his manager, as if symbolically passing a baton. He must never toss it. A departing pitcher once tossed the ball to Frank Robinson, so Robinson grabbed him by the jersey and got in his face, right there on the infield grass.
- Once the manager gets the ball from his pulled pitcher, the skipper should, in turn, pat him on the butt. In nine times out of ten, it's the hand-off, butt-pat sequence.

FIELDERS

- It's okay if a middle infielder doesn't tag second base at the beginning of a double play, just as long as he's within the same zip code as the bag.
- Even though it's against the official rules, it's okay for a catcher to block the plate.
- It's also fine for an incoming runner to commit anything short of manslaughter while sliding into home plate on a close play.

COACHES

- The rules say that the coaches at first and third bases are required to stand within the lines of the coaching boxes. Reality says that they never stand in there.
- To make up for their peripheral status, most first base coaches have to act as on-field clubhouse attendants; they take the elbow guards of base runners, hand pitchers their warm-up jackets, and straighten the runners's caps. They don't shine shoes.

- First base coaches are expected to shout "Get Back!" when a pitcher is making a throw back to the base, as if a warning could possibly save a base runner who wasn't already in the process of diving back to the bag.

THE RULEBOOK

- As they stride up to the plate, batters can kick the dirt around in order to erase the white-chalk lines of the batter's box. The ump won't say anything.
- According to Section 8.04 of the official rulebook, pitchers must throw a pitch within 12 seconds of their taking the ball. Unofficially? "Ready when you are."
- The rulebook says all players must wear stirrup socks, and some players do wear them almost to their knees, but if someone else wants to wear his pants all the way down, all right, to each his own. The word uniform means "one form" but it's time we started talking about "multiforms."
- In addition, players are allowed to put all sorts of pine tar atop their helmets. For several years there was an unofficial contest over who can most thoroughly obscure his team's helmet logo with gunk that may have been found on a swamp bottom. Craig Biggio probably won the gunk helmet contest.

RETALIATION

- A pitcher may not intentionally plunk a batter. Unless he isn't too blatant about it and the plunk-ee really had it coming.
- When a pitcher unintentionally plunks a guy, he shouldn't feel very bad about it . . .
- . . . He shouldn't feel too good about it, either.
- Teammates should be discreet about post-plunk high-fives, congratulations, and such; it's about retaliation, not celebration.
- If hit by a ball, a batter doesn't need to rub the bruise unless he also needs a stretcher. It's more than okay to hop around, grimace, yell, and curse out the opposition, though.
- When a player hits the dirt on an obvious brushback pitch he should start swearing. The theatrically inclined are free to wave the bat around. Every so often, the batter should also walk toward the pitcher at a pace fast enough to show he means business yet slow enough for someone to "hold him back."

- It's the job of the catcher to hold back an opposing batter, just in case he gets ideas about charging the mound. In this way, the catcher is to the pitcher what the Secret Service is to the president.

CORDIALITY

- Opposing players are allowed to chat and clown around with each other during pre-game batting practices. Somebody once said that the chumminess comes from the fact that the modern-day guys are all related through their business managers.
- When tagging out a dead-duck opponent in a rundown, there's no need for the fielder to humiliate the base runner with a hard tag. He gets a token tap.
- The opposing infielder is allowed to help the opposing base runner brush dirt off his uniform after a successful slide.
- It'd be wise for the infielder to stay out of his pitcher's line of sight with the dirt brushing.
- A close play at second base may call for that same infielder and base runner to collide into each other with the approximate force of two barreling Mack trucks, fine, but until then, no need to be less than cordial.

DON'T HAVE FUN OUT THERE / HAVE FUN OUT THERE

- If they're behind or tied in the game, the players have to comport themselves as if their favorite aunt recently died. It's supposed to be serious out there.
- If they're ahead or tied, they can laugh. It's supposed to be fun out there.

EJECTIONS

- When arguing with an umpire, a manager cannot say anything that ends in the word "you," such as "screw you," et cetera. Usually the manager wants to say something more pungent than "screw you."
- If a manager is tossed anyway, he might as well get his money's worth and start mentioning the umpire's ancestry, mental capabilities, and relationship with his mom.
- Even after he's tossed, a skipper can still set up an informal signal system to keep calling the shots from just inside the dugout tunnel, just as long as

he isn't too blatant about it. True story: an Orioles manager once called
plays while sitting in box seats.

- It's no big deal if someone intentionally gets himself ejected in order to rile
up the home crowd or his own team. It's all right for them to draw an
ejection just so they can catch a rest in the clubhouse, even.
- Umpires don't have to play along, though. One umpire caught on to his
debate partner's act, waved toward the field, and said, "If I have to watch
this then you do, too."

DISCIPLINE

- If someone breaks a team rule, he must be fined $2,000 or so, the rough
equivalent of docking a $50,000-a-year man about three cents.
- When a player shows up a manager through an obvious failure to hustle, a
manager can pull him from the game during the middle of an inning. It's
like a mom dragging a naughty little kid by his ear.

SEX

- It's acceptable to describe baseball in regard to sex: "getting to first base,"
"getting to second base," and so on.
- It's acceptable to think of baseball during sex.
- It's *not* acceptable to think of sex during baseball, however. No one has
enough concentration for two pastimes at the same time.

Fan Rules That Aren't in the Rulebook

CHILDHOOD

- You spent time wondering about your future uniform number.
- As a child, on at least one occasion, you insisted on repeatedly sliding in
the dirt just to see what it would look like if you got three steals in a
game.

- You learned the lyrics to "The Star-Spangled Banner" mostly because they played it before the first pitches.
- You learned the lyrics to "O Canada" from Toronto's road games.
- In your heart of hearts, you wish you had suffered a semi-serious sports injury at some point in your life, preferably one that left a smallish but visible scar that you could lie about during parties. "What's this mark, you ask? Well, you've heard of game-saving diving catches, surely . . ."
- You secretly yearn for your friends to sometimes call you by a distinctive nickname, something like "Pistol" or "Big Seven."

LOYALTY
- A fan who roots for any team other than the local club is to be considered suspicious. At minimum, he owes an explanation.
- If a fan talks about "we" during win streaks but switches to "them" references in bad times, he is to be considered a bad apple; he might be the kind of guy who'll hit on your girlfriend while you're away for vacation.
- It's acceptable to (quietly) root for your fantasy players when they are up against your hometown team . . .
- . . . Just so long as it's late in the season and you really need the points.

FAN(ATICISM) AT HOME
- You've gotten into at least one semi-serious fight in which you've defended the honor of your favorite ball club.
- You've either won or lost a bet involving more than a token sum.
- You've concocted fantastical trade scenarios in which your favorite team acquires a Cy Young winner in exchange for $9,000, two utility infielders, a broken bat, and a previously owned resin bag.
- You've imagined scenarios where your team wins a championship, even if it involves three other teams in the division suffering from E. coli outbreaks from late August into October.

FAN(ATICISM) AT THE PARK
- You emphatically agree with Chris Jaffe, who once wrote that "no one in the world has ever found a convenience fee to be in any way convenient."

- You forgo any concept of a diet once you pass through the ballpark turnstiles. Nachos, ice cream, deep-fried lard balls . . . these are to be taken as culinary challenges, not heart attack precursors.
- You boo when an opposing pitcher throws over to first base too often. And by "too often," you mean even once.
- You never leave a game before the seventh inning, not even if it's 11-0, the starters have been pulled, the batter is Joe Shlabotnik, and you parked on top of a fire hydrant.

YOUR ADORABLE LITTLE CHILD AT THE PARK

- You bring a fielding glove to the game in order to catch a foul ball for your adorable little child, even if you haven't caught anything but a fever in the last five years.
- You feel a small pang of regret over the fact that you've never actually caught a foul ball.
- You feel a larger pang of regret that, if it came down to it, you'd be willing to vault over a family of five in order to catch your first-ever foul ball.
- When a fielder catches a ball anywhere nearby, you expect him to toss the ball to your adorable little child even if he's seated in the mezzanine.
- You form real, if unspoken, opinions as to the video games played on the ballpark Jumbotrons. At Citi Field, for example, you may have noticed that the blue subway car has a real edge over the red and yellow cars in the race to the station.

MEDIA RELATIONS

- You flip to the sports section before the front page.
- If there's a headline reading "World to End Tomorrow," you take some small consolation in the knowledge that you'll die with a first-place ranking in fantasy league.
- You can apply a sports analogy to nearly anything, even if you don't use it. For example, you won't tell your girlfriend that you see her "really coming on as a five-tool player," not unless you have recently seen her hit for power, hit for average, field, throw, and run the bases.

- Given a choice between your cousin's wedding and free tickets to Game Seven, you give the matter some thought and then, with reluctance, do the right thing—and go to Game Seven.

YOUR BRILLIANT CAREER

- When told that your memory is fading, you deny it by conveying precise, pitch-by-pitch accounts of all seven of your sophomore-year hits.
- You custom-tailored your uniform and matched up the pinstripes from your pants and jersey so they were unbroken vertical lines.
- You mention that you once hit back-to-back homers, neglecting to mention that you meant back-to-back seasons, not games.

TERMINOLOGY

- Ballplayers work for ball clubs as they go about playing ball and winning ball games within ballparks. The hitters always hit balls but must take care not to swing at balls outside the strike zone: those are balls.
- Among the permissible terms for baseball fights: "donnybrooks," "melees," "dustups," "fisticuffs," "kerfuffles." Baseball fights are so rare and tame that their slang predates the Civil War.

TRADITIONALISM

- You insist on using time-honored terms like "through the box," "on the black," "bullpens," "horsehides," and "foul poles."
- You use these terms with the full knowledge that there is no box, the strike zone does not contain black (or any other color), neither bulls nor pens are anywhere in sight, ball coverings are donated by cows, and the poles are located in fair territory.

FAN CLASSIFICATIONS

- *Loves baseball*:
  —Can provide a vague definition of the balk rule.
  —Can name at least three Major League umpires.
  —Knows that the Bobby Thomson home run ball was never found.

- *Loves baseball too much*:
  —Can provide a complete and accurate definition of the balk rule.
  —Can name at least six umpires.
  —Knows where the Bobby Thomson home run ball can be found.
- *Should really consider some other outlets*:
  —Can give a complete and accurate definition of the balk rule, along with its legislative history, canons of construction, and applied precedents.
  —Can name at least nine umpires and their home addresses.
  —Is holding the Bobby Thomson home run ball at this very moment.

MYTH #99

"What a Pity that Baseball's So Out of Touch"

Baseball is waaaaay out of touch with modern life and thank goodness for that.

THE SPORT
The Job
Life: working
Baseball: playing

Starting Off
Life: alarm clock/opening bell/morning meeting
Baseball: "Play ball!"

Promotional Criteria
Life: inside connections, flattery, office politics
Baseball: hitting, pitching, fielding

Leader Titles
Life: "Mr. President," "Madame Secretary," "Ms. Winfrey"
Baseball: "Skipper," "Skip," "Joe"

Opportunities

Life: Per Alec Baldwin, "The first prize is a Cadillac Eldorado. Second prize is a set of steak knives. Third prize is you're fired."

Baseball: "Even if you fail in 70 percent of your at-bats, you'll become very, very rich."

Hair Situations

Life: male-pattern baldness

Baseball: caps

Clothes (Pt. 1)

Life: suit and tie, dress smart, the latest fashion

Baseball: home whites, road grays

Clothes (Pt. 2)

Life: Per every fashion consultant since the beginning of time, "The clothes make the man. Or the woman, as the case may be."

Baseball: "Wear this jersey with pride. Just remember that the name on the front is a heck of a lot more important than the name on the back."

Dirty Uniforms

Life: bad news (laziness)

Baseball: good news (grittiness)

Crotch Grabs

Life: highly discouraged, probably illegal

Baseball: "By all means, make yourself comfortable."

Wild Hand Waving

Life (Pt. 1): From gang members, wild hand waving indicates a demand to get out of the neighborhood.

Life (Pt. 2): From Greek grandmothers, they are demands to bring out the baklava.

Baseball: From third base coaches, wild hand waving is an instruction to go for the score or hold up at second base.

Stress Breakers
Life: liquor, cigarettes, hard drugs
Baseball: Gatorade, bubblegum, sunflower seeds

Moral Imperatives
Life: "Leave your sister-in-law alone."
Baseball: "Don't make the first out at third base."

Broken Windows
Life: bad news
Baseball: good news (batters only)

Brawls
Life: always painful, often destructive, sometimes deadly
Baseball: shove-apalooza

Ejection Reactions
Life: humiliation to be followed by degradation
Baseball: a shower, then a day off

Vacations
Life: the finest two weeks of the year
Baseball: Buzzie Bavasi: "I never had a summer vacation. I had a summer vocation."

Ten Children
Life: a dangerously overburdened household
Baseball: a full lineup plus one relief pitcher

Aging
Life: "Oh, grow up."
Baseball: Per Casey Stengel, "The trick is to grow up without growing old."

THE SPIRIT
Can't We All Get Along?

Life: No. Different races, different religions, different regions, different
                 other words that begin with the letter *r*.

Baseball: Yes. Per Hubert Humphrey, "We should take a national view of
               the American League and an American view of the National
               League."

Temporal Attitudes

Life: "Hurry, hurry, hurryhurryhurry."

Baseball: "Did Nomar just take seven minutes to adjust his batting glove?"

Gratitude

Life: Kids never seem to give the proper thanks to their hard-working,
                 ever-suffering parents.

Baseball: Sacrifices are really appreciated, especially when they come in
               the late innings of tie games.

Emotional Engagements (Pt. 1)

Life: "I don't vote, I don't know, I don't care."

Baseball: Per Tug McGraw: "Ya gotta believe."

Emotional Engagements (Pt. 2)

Life: This cannot end soon enough.

Baseball: Per Jack Norworth, "I don't care if I ever get back."

Sense of Possibility

Life: As Hippocrates said, "Life is short, opportunity fleeting."

Baseball: As Ernie Banks said, "Let's play two!"

Failures (Pt. 1)

Life: "There's no tomorrow."

Baseball: "We'll get 'em tomorrow."

Lovable Losers?

Life: losers

Baseball: lovable

Familiarity

Life: "Let me shoot you a quick e-mail."

Baseball: "Let me tell you a 15-minute story about playing catch with my dad."

Historical Memories

Life: may go as far back as 1976

Baseball: may go as far back as 1876

THE MYSTERY

Unanswerable Questions (Pt. 1)

Life: Per François Villon: "Where are the snows of yesteryear?"

Baseball: Per Abbott and Costello: "Who's on first?"

Unanswerable Questions (Pt. 2)

Life: "How did it come to this?"

Baseball: "Why do they sing 'Take Me Out to the Ball Game' when they're already there?"

Angst (Pt. 1)

Life: "Who am I?"

Baseball: "I'm the second baseman of the Philadelphia Phillies."

Angst (Pt. 2)

Life: "What am I supposed to be doing in life?"

Baseball: "I'm supposed to show up on time, play hard, and turn double plays."

Angst (Pt. 3)

Life: "When will it end?"

Baseball: "The regular season will end after a day game in St. Louis on September 29."

PARTING WORDS

Life: Your boss says, "These security guards will now be escorting you
              out the door."

Baseball: Vin Scully says, "And that'll do it, folks."

Addenda

In writing this manuscript there was more will than way. Certain passages were drafted that didn't quite harmonize with chapter sequences, narrative lines, and such. The work was good—as good as the other stuff, anyway!—but didn't quite fit.

Even mis-fits can be worthwhile, though. In the following pages are some alternate versions, outtakes, and supplements. Intrepid readers are hereby invited to press on.

FROM "THE FANS"
The Disparity between Baseball and Football Attendance Is Bigger Than the Disparity In . . .

- the gross domestic box office of *Star Wars* versus *Paul Blart, Mall Cop* ($461 million to $146 million).
- the fastest Daytona 500 race ever versus the HOV lane of I-95 (178 miles per hour vs. 40 mph).
- the population of San Francisco, California, versus Fayetteville, North Carolina (about 817,000 to 204,000).
- the height of Shaquille O'Neal (7'1") versus a junior Hobbit (less than 2', according to J. R. R. Tolkien).
- the weight of an adult grizzly bear versus anyone walking down the nearest sidewalk (more than 700 pounds versus 160 or so).
- Brad Pitt versus a peach pit.

The Poll-ish Crisis

Ask the typical sports fan to name the most popular sport in America and the most typical answer is "football." Polls going back to the 1960s have had the NFL way ahead of baseball, with the gap only widening as the years have gone by; a contemporary Harris poll might have the NFL finishing ahead of MLB by a margin of more than two and a half to one.

This only means that baseball polls, like other kinds of polls, can be very wrong. For years the Flat Earth Society had popular opinion on its side and, more recently, widely cited polls indicated a widespread belief in Elvis Presley's life after death and the existence of UFOs. And yet, for all that, we now know that Christopher Columbus was right, the King had left the building, and, as yet, E.T. has not shown up.

Polls only measure perceptions, not realities, and today's perceptions owe a lot to mainstream media prejudices on league operations.

Take any major sports issue and the NFL's style is assumed to be ideal. Its revenue-sharing racket is taken to be a paragon of equity. Centralized decision making among the owners is called efficient. The piteously weak players union—a players union so piteously weak that it cannot enforce pension rules within one of the most dangerous jobs in America—is constantly praised as it kneels for the sake of labor peace.

The NFL's public relations siege has been so successful that baseball's drastically different methods are assumed to be dysfunctional. The game's reliance on free markets is in need of a perpetual repair through ever more revenue sharing. It is believed to be a cartel rather than an island of sports entrepreneurship. An assertive, competition-minded union is called selfish and so on.

The NFL's public relations image is so strong as to be virtually impervious to reality, even reality-based, overwhelming measures like attendance. Many more unfavorable comparisons are never referenced. Sometimes facts don't have much of a chance against fancies; that's why the polls loved the Flat Earth Society.

Let's Talk about Me(dia)

Take away the Super Bowl's fortunate timing, unfortunate gambling, and trash culture, and what remains is not much. Media outlets never tire of nattering on about the "new national holiday," however, because for them, the Super Bowl really is a be-all and end-all.

It all starts off in the middle of the winter as the media insiders flee from coverage of varsity high school in snowy Jersey or Milwaukee in favor of sunny, glitzy locales like Miami and New Orleans. These are called work trips, but precious little work goes into them. The various talking heads and columnists are herded into interview days with active players, "radio rows" with retirees, and sponsor power-displays, all of them layered by stacks of bite-size, prewritten press releases.

Freed from the need to report, reporters have free time to luxuriate; the NFL spends months setting up four-star accommodations serving the best of the best in food and booze, often for free. The troops are also given invitations to see-and-be-seen parties featuring celebrities and some of the 10,000 strippers who work Super Bowl week.

All of it is interesting but not football interesting. They're bribes and they work for their intended purpose—to get the media to describe the Super Bowl as the most important gathering since the Constitutional Convention. Among the insiders, it is.

To repeat: not 100 strippers, not 1,000 strippers, but 10,000 strippers.

Midsummer Classic Fall Classic

Aside from the fact that it actually counts in the standings, the World Series has much in common with the All-Star Game:

1) The regular season's broadcasting shortages gave the old-time games an overinflated importance but we now have
2) a proliferation in media choices that led to
3) declining ratings but
4) still-solid attendance and ratings relative to today's glut of sports and entertainment options.

For both the All-Star Game and World Series, the fans were once so deprived for full access that they hungered for showcase events. Now, thankfully, no one's deprived.

FROM "THE FANS/THE YOUTH MOVEMENT"
Demographics and Destiny
If you were trying to build the most promising sports audience for the 21st century, you would build appeal among one of the most important demographic groups in the nation. You would build baseball.

It so happens that the game is a passion among Latinos, who now represent the youngest and fastest-growing segment of the American population. In addition, youth-level baseball is growing fastest in sun belt states like Florida and Arizona, which happen to be among the fastest-growing regions in the United States.

Though it's rarely noticed, the pastime is blessed with very promising demographic numbers.

After Midnight
Since baseball is the sport constantly implored to recruit new fans through its playoff scheduling, you would think the sport has uniquely terrible timing. Not so. Here are the average sign-offs for the three major team sports in the 2000s:

MLB playoffs: 11:23 p.m. EST
NFL on Monday night: 12:04 a.m.
NBA playoffs: 12:10 a.m.

Baseball, featuring the most kid-friendly, bedtime-accommodating schedule in American sports, has the most roundly criticized schedule in American sports.

FROM "INTO THE TALENT POOL"
Anybody's Ball Game
According to data recently compiled by the University of Central Florida and the U.S. Census Bureau, here's the racial composition of Major League rosters as compared to the American population as a whole:

	MLB	USA
Whites	62%	68%
Latinos	28%	14%
African Americans	8%	12%
Asian Americans	2%	5%

In recent years, the Institute for Diversity and Ethics in Sport gave baseball an "A+" grade for on-field rosters, an "A" for managers and coaches, and an "A+" for its executive ranks. The institute didn't measure the player popularity, but the *Sports Business Journal* did, and in one recent year the magazine found that the game's ten most marketable figures included three white ballplayers, three Latinos, one player of Asian descent, and three players of mixed ancestry.

In its player representation, managerial diversity, and fan acceptance the national pastime is exemplary. It probably represents the most thorough, successful integration program this side of the U.S. military.

The Best of Everything

Baseball's foreign-born athletes transformed team rosters even as they've bolstered quality of play. There's a message in their presence, too.

In an age when some express skepticism over our nation's willingness to accept immigrants, baseball embraces the aspirations of "a shining city on a hill." While many retreat into the divisions of politics or culture, one sport unites. In a time when American intentions can be doubted, an American pastime is respected as a meritocracy.

Of the game's sense of acceptance Bill James once said:

It's a good thing for baseball. We live in a society which searches out the best in everything and embraces it without disfavor. We go all over the world looking for baseball players and say, "We don't care how weird you are. We don't care what color you are. We don't care what habits you have. If you can play baseball, we want you." And that's very American.

Hear, hear.

FROM "STATE OF PLAY/FUNDAMENTALISM"
Fast Times?

While living in fast times, it's not hard to believe that front offices are rushing along as well, but the claim is empirically unsound. It is, in other words, wrong.

Columnist Joe Posnanski recently did a survey of all pitchers who were 22 years old or younger in the seasons when they first threw at least 150 innings in the Majors. Here are the Posnanski numbers as broken down by decade:

DECADE	DEBUTS
1960s	42 different pitchers
1970s	41
1980s	27
1990s	22
2000s	23

Baseball execs have grown more careful with pitching prospects. It was the old-timers who saw too much, too soon.

FROM "CLUTCHED"
Series of Unfortunate Events

Strange game, baseball. In the short term, the terrific can look terrible and the terrible can look terrific. This is true even when the short term includes playoff series.

Consider the on-base plus slugging (OPS) of the following players in terms of both career and postseason numbers:

	CAREER OPS	POSTSEASON OPS
C: M. Cochrane	.897	.719
1B: S. Musial	.976	.742
2B: J. Morgan	.819	.348
SS: J. Sewell	.804	.619
3B: M. Schmidt	.908	.690
OF: J. DiMaggio	.977	.760
OF: T. Cobb	.945	.668
OF: W. Mays	.941	.660

The players demonstrated common characteristics: they dropped off by at least 185 points from their career numbers through at least two postseason series but waltzed into the Hall of Fame anyway.

Joe DiMaggio was not the worst of the group, though his usual OPS dropped by more than 200 points in October. DiMag's playoff numbers were lower than the career numbers of Eddie Taubensee.

At the other extreme, a lineup can include:

	CAREER OPS	POSTSEASON OPS
C: R. Dempsey	.666	.885
1B: D. Clendenon	.771	1.509
2B: B. Martin	.669	.937
SS: J. Offerman	.732	1.024
3B: B. Brown	.742	1.207
OF: M. Hatcher	.690	.889
OF: B. Hatcher	.676	1.119
OF: W. Aikens	.809	1.215

The common characteristics of this bunch: they hit 150 or more points above their career regular season OPS through at least two October series (with the exception of Clendenon) but couldn't get into the Hall without paying admission.

Again, for the sake of context, Billy Hatcher's playoff games displayed greater productivity than the typical career games of Ted Williams.

Then again, maybe Joe DiMaggio was no Eddie Taubensee, just as Billy Hatcher was no Ted Williams. Severe flukes can happen over a cherry-picked few games, so randomness can render "clutch" numbers meaningless.

"Moments So Absorbing, So Touching, that Children Danced and Adults Wept"

Derek Jeter is large, he contains multitudes. Surely Walt Whitman's poem was written with our D J in mind.

Jeter's career has been defined by hustling overachievement, not the raw talent of a number 6 overall draft pick. He sincerely loves the Yankees, without regard to the fact that they overpay him by several million dollars per year. Jeet maintains a closely guarded sense of privacy except for all the nightclub sightings. He's embarrassed by praise yet finds the time to endorse luxury handbags, shoes, banks, peanut butter, trucks, and sports clothes brandishing his own little silhouette. He's indifferent to money yet lives in an oversize Florida mansion that neighbors call "St. Jetersburg."

The Jeterian multitudes never cease, their limits are never approached. For instance, try to guess which of the following are genuine quotations and which are phony exaggerations:

If you had a daughter, you'd want her to marry Derek Jeter.

—BRIAN CASHMAN, Yankees general manager

An apostle . . . a patron saint . . . as big as any American lion who has traveled up the Canyon of Heroes.

—IAN O'CONNOR, author of *The Captain: The Journey of Derek Jeter*

Dynasty's Child . . . Jimmy Stewart in pinstripes.

—BUSTER OLNEY, *ESPN The Magazine*

Not often does the universe hold true to its promise and grant us the perfect day. Not often does a baseball game on a sparkling Saturday afternoon feel as if it's stitched together humanity.

—*The Sporting News*, on Jeter's 3,000th career base hit

Here were moments so absorbing, so touching, that children danced and adults wept.

—*The Sporting News*, on the 3,000th hit

Jeet belongs to you, the way DiMag belonged to the paisans, the way Mays belonged to the brothers, the way Mantle belonged to the redneck whicker-bill country boys, the way Greenberg belonged to the Jews, the way Clemente belonged to the Puerto Ricans.

—RALPH WILEY, ESPN.com

He might go down, when it's all over, as the all-time Yankee.

—DON ZIMMER

Aha! It was a trick question. *All* of the above quotations, and many dozens of others, were issued by individuals who insisted that they were quite sane and serious, even as they brushed aside questions regarding their homoerotic attraction to a certain shortstop. As of press time we've had no response from Brian Cashman's daughter, American lions, the late Mr. Stewart, redneck whicker-bill country boys, and every other Yankee who has ever lived.

FROM "THE OCTOBER REVOLUTION"
Let the 'Dogs Out

It doesn't get any great notice among the commentariat, but the playoff teams of the wild card era have proved themselves to be some of the most tenacious underdogs of all time.

One-quarter of the postseason teams of the 1995–2009 period made it into October immediately after a losing season. Teams like the 1999 Diamondbacks and 2003 Cubs were only the second and third teams to make the playoffs after losing 95 or more games in the previous season. In addition, many of the qualifiers were incredible finishers, with teams like the 2006 Twins among the dozen teams to ever make the postseason after falling behind by eight games or more in the second half of the regular season. In the way that the wild cards overcame previous struggles, they belonged in the same conversation with 1969's Miracle Mets.

The playoff teams of the wild card era proved just as tenacious within the postseason itself. From 1995 to 2004, for instance, no less than five teams stormed back from two-game series deficits with at least three straight do-or-die wins. The most celebrated team was the 2004 Red Sox, which took an unprecedented four straight elimination games from the Yankees in the American League Championship Series.

By producing so many astounding comebacks, the wild cards lived up to the name.

FROM "THE DRUG PROBLEM/BAD CHEMISTRY"
What Deion Sanders, Dave DeBusschere, and Jan Zelezny Have in Common

We know that some of the greatest baseball players of all time established themselves not through overwhelming physical size and strength but impeccable coordination. Most fans also know that the pastime has humbled paragons like

Deion Sanders or Dave DeBusschere, NFL and NBA Hall of Famers who had unremarkable careers in the Majors.

It's worth remembering that countless other dynamos never made anywhere near the Majors in the first place. Take Jan Zelezny, for instance.

The Czech won acclaim as "the world's strongest arm" by turning in a series of record performances in javelin events, winning a total of six Olympic and world championships from 1992 to 2001. In the middle of his run, in 1996, the Atlanta Braves attempted to give Zelezny instruction in pitching but promptly gave up because his fastballs didn't reach past the mid-70s on the radar gun.

It was yet another affirmation that physical strength doesn't necessarily mean much on a diamond. By relying on skill, a Pedro Martinez physique can qualify for the Hall of Fame in Cooperstown, New York. By relying on muscle, a Jan Zelezny arm cannot qualify for the Rookie League in Danville, Virginia.

The Enablers

There are multiple unknowns in the steroids controversies, but just about everyone can agree on a couple of points:

1) More ballplayers were experimenting in the 1990s and
2) The health consequences were catastrophic.

Between 1992 and 2001 the number of total days spent on disabled lists rose 56 percent (from just under 18,000 to about 28,000). Despite employing some of the best sports doctors and trainers in the world, the game saw soaring injury rates.

While the media never tired of denouncing steroids as a moral pox, they rarely denounced the apparent toll from the drug use. To the contrary, the media worked to enable further abuse.

Without the benefit of a single day of medical practice, most commentators treated the connection between steroids and performance as so obvious as to be above question, then took to treating the word "steroids" as shorthand for potency ("the Grand Canyon is a pothole on steroids," for example). Worse, their constant drumbeat of evidence-free accusation conveyed the impression that anabolic usage was all but universal. Worst of all, they most often associated the drug use with the sport's outstanding athletes.

How was that for a mixed message? "Kids, 'the juice' is wrong but it's all-powerful, all over the place, and the best players are probably doing it." It was kind of like saying, "Boys and girls, cocaine is morally questionable but then again it's an amazing happiness enhancer and a whole bunch of people are doing it, including the most popular kids in school."

What happens afterward? The message makers stand back, astounded, as young people develop a skyrocketing interest in steroids.

FROM "THE DRUG PROBLEM/MORAL DILEMMAS"
Popeye Was Just a Cartoon

Whenever confronted with a tight situation, the animated Popeye character could eat a can of spinach, instantaneously pump up his muscles, and then proceed to beat up the bad guys in a rapid rat-tat-tat flurry. Many commentators seem to believe that steroids are morally wrong because they allow wicked athletes to gain the same cartoonish edge. Like Popeye, the jocks supposedly find success without sacrifice.

This is incorrect. Proteins within muscle tissue tend to break down from high-intensity workouts and anabolic steroids are widely credited for promoting the physical recovery necessary for athletes to continue lifting weights. There's nothing instantaneous or easy about the process; those taking steroids are only preparing themselves to do even more hard work. Even more hard work. If that's a "shortcut," then we need a new dictionary.

FROM "THE DRUG PROBLEM/THE BONDS ISSUE"
"First the Sentence, Verdict Afterward . . ."

Thus said the grinning Queen of Hearts of *Alice in Wonderland*. This approach has been a significant inspiration for the media covering Barry Bonds:

A truly evil man.

—JEFF PEARLMAN, ESPN.com

A bastard prince without a true claim to the throne.

—TOM VERDUCCI, *Sports Illustrated*

A scourge . . . an ailment.

—**Wallace Matthews, *Newsday***

Something sinister, disgusting.

—**Bruce Jenkins, *San Francisco Chronicle***

A thief.

—**Rick Reilly, *Sports Illustrated***

*An asshat whom no one, other than a few deluded
San Franciscans, wishes well.*

—**Neal Pollack, Slate.com**

I can only speculate what these people would've said if Bonds was actually convicted of steroid use but I know that surely, somewhere, a Queen was smiling.

FROM "TAKE YOUR TICKETS"
Up and Down

In recent years baseball executives differentiated their seating prices. They did this for the usual reason—to make money—but the changes were novel in the way that they moved prices both upward and downward.

On the one hand, business analysts discovered that certain home games drew significantly more demand than previously believed, so teams increased prices for weekend games, Yankees visits, and playoff-contention games in September. At the same time, clubs realized that low-demand games involving weekday nights, Royals visits, or meaningless late-season contests should be marked for discounts.

In short, the clubs found ways to respond to demand changes in both directions. Did they raise or lower prices? Yes.

Playing to Win

> *He knew that "you are lucky to play a game for a living,"*
> *writes NPR's Scott Simon.*

—MARK MEMMOTT, "The Cubs's Ron Santo, an Inspiring Figure, Has Died,"
National Public Radio, December 3, 2010, quoting former player Ron Santo

> *It's crazy to think you can make this kind of money playing a game.*

—TOM HAUDRICOURT, "A Hefty Raise," *Milwaukee Journal Sentinel*,
January 17, 2007, quoting player Chris Capuano

Rick Blaine was not the kind of man to be easily moved.

The proprietor of Rick's Café Américain was Casablanca's resident skeptic. He stuck his neck out for nobody. Rick couldn't remember last night and didn't plan for tonight. His bar wasn't for sale at any price.

He also refused all offers to drink with customers, at least he did until a freedom fighter named Victor Laszlo walked through the door. "He's succeeded in impressing half the world," thought Rick as he strode to Laszlo's freshly set table.

"Congratulations," said Rick as he took a seat.

Laszlo placidly replied, "For what?"

"Your work."

Laszlo softened. "Thank you. I try."

The plainspoken owner responded, "We all try. You succeed."

Rick Blaine was just the kind of man who could appreciate the qualitative difference between Major League watchers and Major League players.

For almost all of us game-play never went beyond the backyard or the schoolyard. It could represent exercise, a bonding experience, or a family tradition and, in all those things, it could be dear. Still, we eventually came to the realization that we would never succeed at the very highest level. No one was particularly interested in seeing us try, even, so for us baseball came down to fun and games.

For a very, very select few, though, baseball is something far more. Their playgrounds were treated as proving grounds, the place where they could train for their life's work. From their grade school days, they devoted thousands of hours to mastering baseball's mental demands and overcoming its physical rigors. They cared about little else; they readied themselves for little else.

Finally, after they surpassed ordinary people in the way that U.S. Navy SEAL commandos surpass Boy Scouts, they made it up to the Majors. Their dreams transformed into realities, their passions became their professions.

Back in Casablanca Rick would have said: "We all try. They succeed."

As I'd say: "We all play the game. They win."

Why Is Salary Inflation Such a Bad Thing?

Athletes don't get paid from a giant credit card in the sky but from fans who love to see players play, not to see owners own or to see managers manage. It only stands to reason that the players should cash in.

The anti-prosperity carping can only be explained by:

1) the belief that higher salaries drive higher prices or
2) irrationality and
3) envy.

However:

1) we know that rising salaries can only come through higher demand and
2) it's rational for the best players in the nation to be among the best-paid athletes in the nation and
3) envy is a sin.

Further salary inflation would probably present a net positive to the national pastime, in truth. Larger payrolls would only give management additional incentives to recoup their investments through additional improvements. Goodness knows how they might come about—through better hot dog toppings, greener grass, sharper scorecard pencils—but in whatever their vectors, improvements are improvements. "Excelsior" and all that.

It's possible that one day the bolstered bottom lines won't be enough to make up for the rising payrolls, but the day's never been seen. Since at least the 1970s influential people were saying—in all apparent sincerity—that fair-market salaries would destroy baseball, and the carping kept up even as the game reaffirmed its capacity for growth as the decades rolled on and the billions flew by. The multitudes who discounted the game's power to innovate have always been proven wrong while those who believed in the game's financial future have always been proven right.

At its core the fretting over player salaries seems to be based on little more than an anti-baseball bias. Many cultural elitists simply believe that athletes—no matter how gifted—aren't as inherently worthy as, let's say, opera singers, mimes, other whatever other exotics are embraced by high society. If overwhelming, daily crowds streamed into their beloved opera halls and theaters instead of ballparks, there's no doubt that the elitists would be overjoyed by the affirmation of their tastes. That such a thing has never happened has bred an exceptionally ridiculous (and resilient) sense of resentment for the one cultural force that does carry such an appeal.

FROM "MAJOR SALARIES"
Past Imperfect

On recent occasions Alfonso Soriano didn't give 100 percent on a grounder and Robbie Cano didn't turn on the burners in going for an extra-base hit.

The examples didn't mean that new-millennium players don't hustle. It just meant that they aren't perfect, any more than the players of the past were perfect.

Our generation will always look worse than its predecessors, if only because of its increased technological scrutiny. While contemporary mistakes are available for broadcast on a 24/7/365 basis there will never be any YouTube clips exposing the foibles and failures of past generations. When old-time players are remembered at all they're exceptional enough to be canonized in reverential, Ken Burns–style documentaries featuring baritone narrators, twinkling background music, and sepia-toned pictures. Selective nostalgia is so tempting; the view is always better through the rearview mirror.

FROM "AGENCY"
Report: Jones to Leave C&N Auto Body

Anytown, USA. Inside sources report that transmissions star Bill Jones has opted to leave C&N Auto Body for a 30 percent salary increase at Jimmy's Garage.

Many C&N fans were distraught by the development:

Fan #1: "I would've ignored the richer contract. It bears mentioning that I am a monk and have taken a vow of lifelong poverty, so my perspective may differ from others."

Fan #2: "Jones should've waited around until he was fired."

Fan #3: "This will only teach my little boy, Timmy, that it's possible for workers to snag more attractive work opportunities within their chosen profession. This'll, uh, break his heart."

Alex Rodriguez: "Best wishes to Mr. Jones in his new opportunity."

Pennybags Plays Ball

FADE IN:

INTERIOR SCENE—A MAYORAL OFFICE IN MAJOR LEAGUE TOWN, USA, DAYTIME

HIZZONER, a mild-mannered public servant, is at his desk, reading through important papers and doing the people's business. POINDEXTER, his assistant, is wearing an accountant's green eyeshade as he busily punches an old-fashioned calculator machine, the kind with a comically long roll of ticker tape trailing out behind it.

Suddenly, RICH UNCLE PENNYBAGS storms through the office door. Pennybags is a short, rotund older man with a bushy silver mustache. With his top hat and tails, bow tie, and walking stick, he bears an uncanny resemblance to an iconic character from the Monopoly board game.

Poindexter jumps up in surprise, but Hizzoner is nonplussed by the tycoon's sudden entrance. He rises and extends his hand.

HIZZONER. Why Mr. Pennybags, this is an unexpected pleasure.

Pennybags is too animated to notice Hizzoner's gesture, however. He immediately starts pacing to and fro, wildly waving his stick all the while.

PENNYBAGS. No time for small talk, sir! I've important business to discuss!

Hizzoner lowers his outstretched hand, sighs, sits down, and shoots Poindexter a knowing glance.

HIZZONER. Regarding the ballpark issue, I take it?

PENNYBAGS. I've said it before and I'll say it right now! I demand a free ballpark for my franchise, and with all the trimmings! I'm talking about La-Z-Boy recliners in the bleachers! Mahogany benches in the dugouts! And gold-plated bat racks! And . . .

HIZZONER. Pennybags, you've asked before and I've answered before: no.

Pennybags stomps his little black loafers.

PENNYBAGS. Now, you see here—

HIZZONER (CONT.). We can work out a reasonable price, without a doubt, one that's in line with all the other Major League ballparks, but we don't need any sweetheart deals or boondoggles. I have an election coming up, and I'm not willing to become one of the first big-city mayors to be voted out of office over a bad deal.

PENNYBAGS. Why, you! If you don't pay up I have half a mind to move the team all the way to East Palookaville! As a matter of fact, they've already given me a very generous offer, a very generous offer indeed! I have half a mind to take it and be rid of this two-bit 'burg, once and for all!

Hizzoner arches his eyebrow and winks at Poindexter, who meekly reveals a large ledger titled "MLB Finances."

POINDEXTER. We don't believe you will do that, sir.

PENNYBAGS. Harrumph!

Poindexter nervously adjusts his eyeglasses but proceeds.

POINDEXTER. We don't believe you will move. Because you can't, sir. Our research shows that East Palookaville has a substantially smaller population and per capita income than we have right here in Major League Town. Where would they find the money for a better offer?

HIZZONER. How would *our town* find the money for an unreasonable offer?

PENNYBAGS. Anyone can afford a few million here and there! All you would have to do is cut public schools and safe streets and fire protection and . . .

HIZZONER. I'll be sure to keep that suggestion in mind if I ever contemplate political suicide! As it is, I'm willing to sell the electorate on a modest new bond issue or a few cents in taxes on every cigarette pack, something along those lines.

PENNYBAGS. Oh, you! NFL and NBA teams move all the time! I'll follow their lead!

POINDEXTER. But they have completely different situations.

The other leagues require smaller seasonal attendance than baseball teams—up to seven times smaller—and their leagues have drastic revenue-sharing systems to prop up smaller markets. Those are the major reasons why NFL teams can exist in places like Jacksonville, Florida, and Indianapolis, Indiana, while NBA franchises can play in Memphis, Tennessee, and Salt Lake City, Utah.

Major League teams have to rely on broadly based support from their hometowns, in contrast. You need us because we can provide you with a huge turnstile support and, with it, an independent financial base. Surely a successful businessman like yourself can see this clearly enough.

Rich Uncle Pennybags points his cane at Hizzoner.

PENNYBAGS. My fellow team owners love me.

HIZZONER. Your fellow team owners love money. They know that the game can make more money by keeping a franchise right here in Major League Town, so they'll block a franchise relocation.

If you don't share that opinion then you're free to sell out to one of the dozens of rich folks ready and willing to buy into the national pastime.

PENNYBAGS. Plenty of baseball teams have relocated, you know. Why the Dodgers once moved from Brooklyn! It broke their hearts! I loved it!

HIZZONER. Yes, true, but that was over 50 years ago. Several teams moved from the early 1950s through the 1960s because the Majors had to shift into the growing cities of the west and south but the new markets were snapped up a long time ago. Today's teams are already camped out in all the biggest, richest metro areas.

Poindexter whips out a book titled MLB History.

POINDEXTER. That's right, Your Honor. Ever since then, plenty of teams have huffed and puffed—the Twins said they wanted to move to North Carolina, the Yankees said they wanted to move to New Jersey, the Marlins said Las Vegas. They all backed down. Evidently they didn't want to move after all.

Hizzoner gives a knowing glance to Pennybags, who responds by angrily crossing his arms.

PENNYBAGS. All the sportswriters know that I'm on the edge of leaving!

Hizzoner resists the temptation to laugh out loud. Even the meek Poindexter can barely stifle a giggle.

HIZZONER. Far be it from me to question the kids' section of the news business. However, I don't win elections by buying every bluff that's come down the pike.

Lucky for you, though, I love baseball and my town loves baseball. We're interested in a ballpark deal. A *reasonable* deal that incorporates benefits for the building's surrounding neighborhood, mass transportation lines, civic morale, and so forth.

Pennybags sputters.

PENNYBAGS. But, but—

His shoulders slump.

PENNYBAGS. What about my *blackmail?*

Hizzoner smiles, walks over, then puts a hand on the chagrined Pennybags' shoulder.

HIZZONER. Better luck next time.

The three chuckle. HIZZONER gives a wink, takes the ceremonial baseball from his desktop and then tosses it to POINDEXTER.

POINDEXTER. Now, about your soon-to-be-extended home stand . . .

CURTAIN

FROM "AND IN CONCLUSION"
The Last Ones

Fans constantly slight the pastime's present in favor of its past. This is partially owing to the fact that retrospective perspectives can bring clarity to unfolding story lines.

Baseball is unmatched in American sports partly because of its overflowing past, with appreciations growing richer as fans delve into a seemingly endless inventory of past landmarks, personalities, anecdotes, and all the rest. In a "here today/gone later today" culture, it represents a lasting legacy.

Unfortunately, all that pastime history has a way of piling up like an overflowing memorabilia collection. There always seem to be more players, more games, and more stories. To make matters more coherent, many prefer to simplify matters into a Now and a Then:

- *Now*, situations are uncertain and disjointed. Disaster never seems too far around the corner. Even the glee club is sometimes listless.
- *Then*, situations were certain and whole, at least through the lens of hindsight. Our worst fears never did come to pass. There are those who'll always laud "a more innocent time," "a lost time," or some similar phrase, even in reference to the 1950s or 1960s, when all kinds of beatniks and commies were running around.

Inevitably, the baseball world of the present can appear less appealing than the past. With its loose ends and risks, the present doesn't make a lot of sense. It can be counterintuitive to believe that the present actually features vast improvement in areas ranging from international outreach to racial diversity and scheduling. The past does make sense, though, because one can pick and choose among memories and color them in whatever cheery hues one would wish.

The drift toward nostalgia might explain why such a timeless game is dotted with quasi obituaries. Think about some of the titles on its bookshelf: *Baseball's Last Golden Age*, *The Last Best League*, *The Last Real Season*. The "lasts" never seem to end.

FROM "EXTRAS"
The Brooklyn Dodgers, Stickball, and Doo-Wop

New York chronicler Pete Hamill once said the Dodgers' move to Los Angeles represented a change of consciousness in the city. After the relocation many conversations included the words "before the Dodgers moved. . . ."

The point had some validity. The Brooklyn Dodgers did play in a fondly remembered period when kids played stickball, teenagers sang doo-wop on street corners, vendors sold 25-cent hot dogs, gentlemen wore fedora hats, and *The Honeymooners* depicted Bensonhurst. The first baseman named Gil Hodges organized charity drives and sandlot games in and around his home on Bedford Avenue. "Before the Dodgers moved," there were good times.

"After the Dodgers moved," however, many of the picturesque scenes vanished. The Brooklyn of the 1960s and 1970s saw spiraling crime rates, urban blight, and shuttered shops. Bed-Stuy streets that were once diverse or rough-hewn became splintered or gang-ridden. Mr. Hodges passed away. Like the team they once followed, many fans were eventually pushed out of the borough.

The Dodgers' departure closely coincided with downward trends, but the correlation wasn't causation. The times changed, that was all. No ball club could've stopped them.

Walter and Horace

If Walter O'Malley's relocation to Los Angeles was forced on the Dodgers, Horace Stoneham's relocation to San Francisco was an unforced error for the Giants.

In contrast to their National League rivals, the Giants enjoyed an expansive, 55,000-capacity ballpark that held the potential for league-leading attendance during winning seasons. The Polo Grounds was one of the older facilities in the Majors but it was in significantly better shape than Brooklyn's crumbling field.

Stoneham's advantage was only bolstered by the Dodgers' departure in 1957. For the first time in a franchise history dating back to the 1880s, the Giants could enjoy a monopoly over all NL fans in greater New York. Heck, they could expect the loyalty of most every Yankee-hating baseball fan in greater New York.

If the Giants were dissatisfied nonetheless, they still had ripe options in New York. With city leadership reeling from the loss of the beloved Dodgers, the Giants had the political leverage necessary to either negotiate serious ballpark upgrades or, if needed, construct a new facility in Queens. At minimum, the ball club could've pursued further negotiations with New York, San Francisco, or any market in between.

None of this ever happened, of course, because Horace Stoneham immediately followed the Dodgers out to California. The owner claimed the move was justified by two seasons of low attendance, as if a slightly disappointing past mattered more than a very bright future.

Bibliography

BOOKS AND FILM

Aaron, Hank. *I Had a Hammer: The Hank Aaron Story*. Harper Perennial, 2007.

Abrahams, Peter, and Phoef Sutton. *The Fan*. Sony Pictures, 1996.

Adair, Robert Kemp. *The Physics of Baseball*. Harper & Row, 1990.

Allen, Dick. *Crash: The Life and Times of Dick Allen*. Ticknor & Fields, 1989.

Allen, Maury, and Bo Belinsky. *Bo: Pitching and Wooing*. Bantam Books, 1974.

Asinof, Eliot. *Eight Men Out: The Black Sox and the 1919 World Series*. Holt, 2000.

Barra, Allen. *Brushbacks and Knockdowns: The Greatest Baseball Debates of Two Centuries*. Thomas Dunne Books, 2004.

Belth, Alex. *Stepping Up: The Story of All-Star Curt Flood and His Fight for Baseball Players' Rights*. Persea, 2006.

Benedict, Jeff. *Out of Bounds: Inside the NBA's Culture of Rape, Violence, and Crime*. IT Books, 2005.

Benedict, Jeff, and Don Yaeger. *Pros and Cons: The Criminals Who Play in the NFL*. Grand Central Publishing, 1998.

Berkow, Ira. *The Corporal Was a Pitcher: The Courage of Lou Brissie*. Triumph Books, 2009.

Bissinger, Buzz. *Three Nights in August: Strategy, Heartbreak, and Joy Inside the Mind of a Manager*. Mariner Books, 2006.

Blewett, William. *The Science of the Fastball*. McFarland, 2013.

Bouton, Jim. *Ball Four*. Collier Books/Macmillan, 1990.

Bryant, Howard. *Juicing the Game: Drugs, Power, and the Fight for the Soul of Major League Baseball*. Plume, 2006.

Burns, Ken. *Baseball: A Film by Ken Burns*. PBS, 2011.

Canseco, Jose. *Juiced: Wild Times, Rampant 'Roids, Smash Hits, and How Baseball Got Big*. HarperCollins, 2005.

Caro, Robert A. *The Power Broker: Robert Moses and the Fall of New York*. Vintage, 1975.

Costas, Bob. *Fair Ball: A Fan's Case for Baseball*. Broadway Books, 2000.

Cramer, Richard Ben. *Joe DiMaggio: The Hero's Life*. Simon & Schuster, 2001.

Creamer, Robert. *Babe: The Legend Comes to Life*. Simon & Schuster, 1992.

———. *Stengel: His Life and Times*. University of Nebraska Press, 1996.

D'Antonio, Michael. *Forever Blue: The True Story of Walter O'Malley, Baseball's Most Controversial Owner, and the Dodgers of Brooklyn and Los Angeles*. Riverhead Trade, 2010.

deMause, Neil. *Field of Schemes: How the Great Stadium Swindle Turns Public Money into Private Profit*. Bison Books, 2008.

Diagnostic and Statistical Manual of Mental Disorders, 4th ed. American Psychiatric Association, 2000.

Durocher, Leo. *Nice Guys Finish Last*. University of Chicago Press, 2009.

Eig, Jonathan. *Luckiest Man: The Life and Death of Lou Gehrig*. Simon & Schuster, 2006.

Epstein, Julius J., Philip G. Epstein, and Howard Koch. *Casablanca*. Warner Home Video, 2012.

Fainaru-Wada, Mark, and Lance Williams. *Game of Shadows: Barry Bonds, BALCO, and the Steroids Scandal That Rocked Professional Sports*. Gotham Books, 2006.

Felber, Bill. *The Book on the Book: A Landmark Inquiry into Which Strategies in the Modern Game Actually Work*. Thomas Dunne Books, 2005.

Fusco, John. *The Babe*. Universal Studios, 2003.

Gennaro, Vince. *Diamond Dollars: The Economics of Winning in Baseball*. Maple Street Press, 2007.

Golenbock, Peter. *Bums: An Oral History of the Brooklyn Dodgers*. Dover Baseball, 2010.

———. *Wrigleyville: A Magical History Tour of the Chicago Cubs*. St. Martin's Griffin, 1999.

Halberstam, David. *The Summer of '49*. William Morrow, 2006.

Hamill, Pete. *Piecework: Writings on Men and Women, Fools and Heroes, Lost Cities, Vanished Friends, Small Pleasures, Large Calamities, and How the Weather Was*. Back Bay Books, 1997.

Hawking, Stephen. *A Briefer History of Time*. With Leonard Mlodinow. Bantam, 2008.

Hayhurst, Dirk. *The Bullpen Gospels: The Major League Dreams of a Minor League Veteran*. Citadel Press, 2010.

Helyar, John. *The Lords of the Realm: The Real History of Baseball*. Ballantine Books, 1995.

Hirsch, James S. *Willie Mays: The Life, the Legend*. Scribner, 2011.

House, Tom. *Arm Action, Arm Path, and the Perfect Pitch: Building a Million-Dollar Arm*. With Doug Thorburn. Coaches Choice, 2009.

James, Bill. *The New Bill James Historical Baseball Abstract*. Free Press, 2001.

James, Bill, and Jim Henzler. *Win Shares*. STATS Publishing, 2002.

Jenkinson, Bill. *The Year Babe Ruth Hit 104 Home Runs: Recrowning Baseball's Greatest Slugger*. Carroll & Graf, 2007.

Kaufman, King, and Cecilia Tan, eds. *Baseball Prospectus*. Wiley, 2012.

Keri, Jonah. *The Extra 2%: How Wall Street Strategies Took a Major League Baseball Team from Worst to First*. ESPN Books, 2011.

Kiner, Ralph. *Baseball Forever: Reflections on 60 Years in the Game*. With Danny Peary. Triumph Books, 2004.

Leavy, Jane. *The Last Boy: Mickey Mantle and the End of America's Childhood*. Harper, 2010.

―――. *Sandy Koufax: A Lefty's Legacy*. Harper Perennial, 2010.

Lewis, Michael. *Moneyball: The Art of Winning an Unfair Game*. W. W. Norton, 2003.

Mandel, Babaloo, and others. *A League of Their Own*. Sony Pictures, 1992.

Miller, James Andrew, and Tom Shales. *Those Guys Have All the Fun: Inside the World of ESPN*. Back Bay Books, 2011.

Miller, Marvin. *A Whole Different Ball Game: The Inside Story of the Baseball Revolution*. Ivan R. Dee, 2004.

Montville, Leigh. *The Big Bam: The Life and Times of Babe Ruth*. Anchor, 2007.

Mullen, Maureen. *Yogi Was Up with a Guy on Third . . . : Hall of Famers Recall Their Favorite Baseball Games Ever*. Triumph Books, 2009.

O'Connor, Ian. *The Captain: The Journey of Derek Jeter*. Houghton Mifflin Harcourt, 2011.

Olney, Buster. *The Last Night of the Yankee Dynasty: The Game, the Team, and the Cost of Greatness*. Harper Perennial, 2008.

Pearlman, Jeff. *Love Me, Hate Me: Barry Bonds and the Making of an Antihero*. HarperCollins, 2006.

Pietrusza, David. *Judge and Jury: The Life and Times of Judge Kenesaw Mountain Landis*. Taylor Trade Publishing, 1998.

Prager, Joshua. *The Echoing Green: The Untold Story of Bobby Thomson, Ralph Branca, and the Shot Heard 'Round the World*. Vintage, 2008.

Putnam, Robert D. *Bowling Alone: The Collapse and Revival of American Community*. Simon & Schuster, 2001.

Rose, Pete. *My Prison without Bars*. With Rick Hill. St. Martin's Press, 2004.

Rosentraub, Mark S. *Major League Losers: The Real Cost of Sports and Who's Paying for It*. Basic Books, 1999.

Schwarz, Alan. *The Numbers Game: Baseball's Lifelong Fascination with Statistics*. St. Martin's Griffin, 2005.

Shaughnessy, Dan. *The Curse of the Bambino*. Penguin Books, 2004.

Sokolove, Michael. *Hustle: The Myth, Life, and Lies of Pete Rose*. Simon & Schuster, 2005.

Stanton, Tom. *The Final Season: Fathers, Sons, and One Last Season in a Classic American Ballpark*. St. Martin's Griffin, 2002.

Stump, Al. *Cobb: A Biography*. Algonquin Books, 1996.

Surowiecki, James. *The Wisdom of Crowds*. Anchor, 2005.

Tafoya, Dale. *Bash Brothers: A Legacy Subpoenaed*. Potomac Books, 2008.

The 2010 United States Census, United States Census Bureau, 2010.

Tygiel, Jules. *Baseball's Great Experiment: Jackie Robinson and His Legacy*. Oxford University Press, 2008.

———. *Past Time: Baseball as History*. Oxford University Press, 2001.

Vincent, Fay. *The Last Commissioner: A Baseball Valentine*. Simon & Schuster, 2002.

Walker, Sam. *Fantasyland: A Sportswriter's Obsessive Bid to Win the World's Most Ruthless Fantasy Baseball League*. Penguin Books, 2007.

Watts, Robert G. *Keep Your Eye on the Ball: Curve Balls, Knuckleballs, and Fallacies of Baseball*. W. H. Freeman, 2000.

Weaver, Earl. *Weaver on Strategy: The Classic Work on the Art of Managing a Baseball Team*. With Terry Pluto. Potomac Books, 2002.

Weber, Bruce. *As They See 'Em: A Fan's Travels in the Land of Umpires*. Scribner, 2010.

Will, George. *Men at Work: The Craft of Baseball*. Harper Paperbacks, 1991.

Williams, Peter. *When the Giants Were Giants: Bill Terry and the Golden Age of New York Baseball*. Algonquin Books, 1994.

Williams, Ted. *The Science of Hitting*. With John Underwood. Simon & Schuster, 1986.

"Yankeeography: Derek Jeter." A&E Video, 2009.

Zall, Paul M. *Abe Lincoln Laughing: Humorous Anecdotes by and about Abraham Lincoln*. University of California Press, 1982.

Zimbalist, Andrew. *Circling the Bases: Essays on the Challenges and Prospects of the Sports Industry*. Temple University Press, 2010.

———. *In the Best Interests of Baseball?: Governing the National Pastime*. University of Nebraska Press, 2013.

Zirin, Dave. *Bad Sports: How Owners Are Ruining the Games We Love*. New Press, 2012.

Zumsteg, Derek. *A Cheater's Guide to Baseball*. Mariner Books, 2007.

ARTICLES

American Enterprise. "The Bill James Interview." April/May 2004.

Anderson, Dave. "A Respectful Aftermath to the Zimmer-Martinez Bout." *New York Times*, June 30, 2004.

Antonen, Mel. "Teams Go Back to Basics without Reliance on Home Runs." *USA Today*, March 29, 2006.

Araton, Harvey. "Free-Agent Shoppers Dwindling." *New York Times*, December 4, 2001.

Associated Press. "Marlins Want $60 Million in State Money." January 20, 2005.

Barra, Allen. "In Antitrust We Trust." *Salon*, May 19, 2000.

Bendix, Peter. "The History of Baseball's Antitrust Exemption." *Beyond the Box Score*, December 3, 2008.

Bissinger, Buzz. "All Stars and Layoffs." *New York Times*, July 26, 2008.

Bodley, Hal. "Ichiro's Run Rivals Wee Willie's." MLB.com, September 11, 2009.

———. "Teamwork, Fundamentals Dear to Rice." MLB.com, July 24, 2009.

Botte, Peter. "Most Hall of Famers Say No to Cooperstown for Barry Bonds." *New York Daily News*, December 16, 2011.

Brookings Institution. "New Book Examines the Troubled Business of Major League Baseball." 2003.

Brown, C. L. "Hall of Famer Jenkins Is in Bonds' Corner." *Louisville Courier-Journal*, May 13, 2007.

Bryant, Howard. "Out at Home." *ESPN The Magazine*, June 19, 2012.

Buckley, Steve. "Giant Cheater Shouldn't Prosper." *Boston Herald*, March 9, 2006.

Cannella, Stephen, Albert Chen, Daniel G. Habib, and Tom Verducci. "And While We're At It . . ." *Sports Illustrated*, August 5, 2002.

Caple, Jim. "Continued Losing Main Reason for Empty Parks." ESPN.com, May 20, 2003.

Caputo, Pat. "Why I Won't Vote for Bonds for the Hall of Fame." *Michigan News-Herald*, January 15, 2012.

Carter, Bob. "Bonds Lets His Numbers Do the Talking." ESPN.com, n.d.

CBC News. "Trust, Loyalty among Teammates a Thing of the Past." February 19, 2008.

Celizic, Mike. "How Did the Super Bowl Get to Be Like This?" MSNBC.com, February 5, 2010.

Chad, Norman. "Cash Cow Gets New Barn." *Washington Post*, July 7, 2008.

———. "Time after Time, Yankees/Red Sox Game Drags On." *Cleveland Plain Dealer*, April 26, 2010.

Chass, Murray. "A Man of Many Means." MurrayChass.com, March 14, 2010.

———. "Pampered Pitchers and Their Enablers." MurrayChass.com, March 6, 2011.

———. "When Moneyball No Longer Pays Off." *New York Times*, February 7, 2006.

Chen, Albert. "Nolan Ryan's Crusade." *Sports Illustrated*, May 24, 2010.

Costas, Bob. "Every NFL Playoff Game Is a Seventh Game." *USA Today*, December 23, 2010.

Cramer, Richard D. "Do Clutch Hitters Exist?" *Baseball Research Journal*, 1977.

Dahlberg, Tim. "Baseball Salaries Should Outrage, But Don't." Associated Press, December 13, 2008.

De Vany, Arthur S. "Steroids and Home Runs." *Journal of Economic Inquiry*, March 17, 2011.

Deford, Frank. "Baseball's Sure Thing: Big Money Wins Big." National Public Radio, April 7, 2010.

Deveney, Sean. "Steal This Base." *Sporting News*, May 14, 2001.

Dodd, Mike. "Wild Card Turns Ten." *USA Today*, October 5, 2004.

Donaldson, Jim. "Football, Not Baseball, Is the True National Pastime." *Providence Journal*, November 3, 2009.

ESPN.com. "Boxing's Knockout Punch." 2004.

Fine, Larry. "Mitchell Steroid Report Spreads Baseball Guilt." Reuters, December 13, 2007.

Fordyce, Tom. "Jan the Man." BBC Sports, August 12, 2001.

Fortune. "America's Largest Corporations." May 3, 2010.

Frenkil, David. "Send a Strong Message to Baseball's Cheaters." *Baltimore Sun*, December 28, 2007.

Gallo, Jon. "Canseco Deserves the Hall." *Baltimore Examiner*, December 18, 2007.

Gammons, Peter. "Apolitical Blues." ESPN.com, October 7.

Goldblatt, David. "The Decline of Baseball." *Prospect*, August 25, 2010.

Goshay, Charita M. "Baseball Goes Down Looking on Steroid Issue." Copley News Service, March 29, 2005.

Grann, David. "Baseball without Metaphor." *New York Times Magazine*, September 1, 2002.

Gray, Gary Norris. "The MLB Fraud." BlackAthlete.net, February 7, 2012.

Greenstein, Teddy. "Another Profile Slams into Bonds." *Chicago Tribune*, March 16, 2006.

Hamill, Dennis. "Ballparks Strike Out with Families." *New York Daily News*, May 5, 2009.

Hartman, Sid. "Blyleven Thinks Little of Drugs, Pitch Counts." *Minneapolis Star Tribune*, January 28, 2011.

Haudricourt, Tom. "A Hefty Raise." *Milwaukee Journal Sentinel*, January 17, 2007.

Herrmann, Mark. "A Hitter's Game." *Baseball Digest*, July 2003.

———. "Jeter: A Yankee Doodle Dandy." *Long Island Newsday*, June 13, 2011.

Hoffman, Benjamin. "Complete Games Are Dwindling." *New York Times*, April 9, 2006.

Hyman, Mark. "On Sandlot Day, Children Call Their Own Shots." *New York Times*, March 28, 2010.

Jenkins, Bruce. "So What's the Deal?" *San Francisco Chronicle*, August 3, 2005.

Jenkins, Sally. "Time for Bonds to Go First Class." *Washington Post*, July 16, 2007.

Justice, Richard. "Real Hype Shouldn't Be about Bonds." *Houston Chronicle*, May 15, 2006.

Kaufman, King. "Are Steroids Harmful?" *Salon*, November 5, 2003.

Kelly, Susan. "How Do You Solve a Problem Like Jeff Bagwell?" All-Baseball.com, January 27, 2006.

Kepner, Tyler. "Pitcher Spurns $12 Million, to Keep Self-Respect." *New York Times*, January 26, 2011.

Kettmann, Steve. "The Players Are Loaded." *New Republic Online*, June 7, 2002.

Kovacevic, Dejan. "Selig: Pirates Not Putting Profits over Winning." *Pittsburgh Post-Gazette*, September 29, 2009.

Kroichick, Ron. "Giant in Many Ways." *San Francisco Chronicle*, July 22, 2007.

Kurkjian, Tim. "Mental Mistakes a Real Drag on the Game." *ESPN The Magazine*, April 30, 2010.

Lapchick, Richard, and others. *2012 Racial and Gender Report Card: Major League Baseball*. Institute for Diversity and Ethics in Sport, 2012.

Lemire, Joe. "Amid Debate on Pace of the Game, One Group Is Unconcerned: Players." SportsIllustrated.com, May 7, 2010.

Lennon, David. "Rice Blames Boss, Yanks on Never Winning a Series." *Newsday*, January 18, 2009.

Lorenz, Bob, and Tom Verducci. "Mr. Clutch." *Sports Illustrated*, October 18, 2001.

Madden, Bill. "Derek Jeter a Hit with Don Zimmer Going Back to the Very Start of Yankee Career." *New York Daily News*, September 14, 2009.

Maese, Rick. "Since Talent Is Watered Down, Don't Blame Juice." *Baltimore Sun*, June 13, 2006.

Mahler, Jonathan. "Smaller Markets and Smarter Thinking." *New York Times*, October 14, 2011.

McDonald, Anna. "Jack Clark: Clutch Hitter for Life." *Hardball Times*, August 10, 2010.

McNeal, Stan. "Has Free Agency Damaged Baseball?" *Sporting News*, January 22, 2009.

———. "Memo to Selig's Special Committee: Speed Up the Game." *Sporting News*, December 18, 2009.

Meehan, Brian. "Ramirez Worth the Antics." Newhouse News Service, May 29, 2008.

Memmott, Mark. "The Cubs' Ron Santo, an Inspiring Figure, Has Died." National Public Radio, December 3, 2010.

Miller, J. "Competitive Balance." *Baseball Digest*, August 17, 2010.

Morgan, Joe. "Chat with Joe Morgan." ESPN.com, June 27, 2006.

Morris, Steven. "Baseball Injuries: Mystery Solved." *New York Times*, July 12, 2009.

Neel, Eric. "Fantasyland Author Q&A." ESPN.com, April 6, 2006.

Nelson, Michael Patrick. "Two for the Books." *Long Island Press*, March 9, 2006.

Neumann, Thomas. "Q&A: Hall of Fame Shortstop Ozzie Smith." ESPN.com, May, 10, 2012.

New York Times. "Baseball Could Use Costas as Commissioner." October 5, 2003.

Nightengale, Bob. "Format Blurs the Picture." *USA Today*, October 7, 2009.

Nye, Doug. "Poor TV Ratings Reflect MLB's Popularity Slide." *South Carolina State*, November 3, 2006.

O'Hehir, Andrew. "Football's Death Spiral." *Salon*, February 3, 2013.

Olney, Buster. "Dynasty's Child." *ESPN The Magazine*, August 23, 2004.

Olson, Lisa. "Jeter's Perfect Day Proves Once More That Sports Can Transcend." *Sporting News*, July 9, 2011.

Passan, Jeff. "Passan's All-Overpaid and All-Underpaid Teams." Yahoo Sports, 2008.

Pearlman, Jeff. "Barry, It's Time to Tell the Truth." ESPN.com, August 24, 2006.

———. "Despite Verdict, Clemens Doesn't Belong in Player Development." SportsIllustrated.com, June 21, 2012.

———. "Politics, Athletes Don't Mix." ESPN.com, November 7, 2006.

Pearlstein, Steven. "Next on Baseball Agenda: Fix the Nats' TV Problem." *Washington Post*, May 5, 2006.

Perry, Dayn. "Pumped-Up Hysteria." Reason.com, January 2003.

Pogash, Carol. "New Questions Raised in Bonds Investigation." *New York Times*, January 18, 2007.

Reilly, Rick. "Giving Barry His Due." *Sports Illustrated*, July 23, 2007.

———. "Gutless Wonders." *Sports Illustrated*, August 15, 2005.

Ruck, Rob. "Where Have African American Baseball Players Gone?" *Slate*, March 5, 2011.

San Diego Union-Tribune. "No Joy in Mudville." August 9, 2007.

Schmidt, Martin B. "When It Comes to the World Series, Luck Conquers All." *New York Times*, November 5, 2006.

Scully, Gerald. "Pay and Performance in Major League Baseball." *American Economic Review*, December 1974.

Silver, Nate, and Will Carroll. "Prospectus Q&A: Rickey Henderson." *Baseball Prospectus*, August 26, 2003.

Silverman, Mike. "Commissioner Happy with the 'Golden Era.'" *Boston Herald*, July 12, 2006.

Simmons, Bill. "Slicing up the Red Sox's Boring Pie." ESPN.com, July 29, 2010.

Smith, Jay Scott. "Is Quintin Berry Baseball's Next Great Black Hope?" TheGrio.com, July 25, 2012.

Smizik, Bob. "Parity Is a Dream, Not a Reality." *Pittsburgh Post-Gazette*, October 22, 2006.

Snel, Alan. "Forbes List Compares Baseball's Apples to Oranges." *Tampa Tribune*, April 21, 2006.

Snider, Rick. "It's Always about the Money." *Washington Examiner*, November 21, 2006.

Solomon, Jerome. "Mr. Crane, You Get What You Pay For." *Houston Chronicle*, June 26, 2011.

Sporting News. "Van Slyke Believes Bonds Took 'Roids." March 4, 2004.

Sports Illustrated. "The Baseball Boom." August 11, 1975.

Steffy, Loren. "Free Agency Has Become a Way of Life." *Houston Chronicle*, October 25, 2005.

Street, Jim. "Henry Reveals He Was Fined." MLB.com, March 1, 2011.

Taibbi, Matt. "How I'd Save Baseball." *Men's Journal*, April 1, 2010.

Thorne, Gary. "Baseball's Regular Season Becoming Less and Less Significant." *USA Today*, September 7, 2006.

———. "Corporate Greed Often Wrapped in Ballpark Packaging." *USA Today*, September 22, 2006.

Todd, Jack. "Selig Is a Total Disaster." *Montreal Gazette*, July 19, 2002.

Treder, Steve. "THT Interview: Jim Bouton." *Hardball Times*, January 10, 2006.

Updike, John. "Hub Fans Bid Kid Adieu." *New Yorker*, October 22, 1960.

USA Today. "High Prices Driving away Fans at Baseball Games." March 27, 2009.

Verducci, Tom. "The Consequences." *Sports Illustrated*, March 13, 2006.

———. "Does Clutch Hitting Truly Exist?" *Sports Illustrated*, April 5, 2004.

———. "From Games to Gaming, Schilling On, Well, Pretty Much Everything." SportsIllustrated.com, January 31, 2012.

———. "The People's King." *Sports Illustrated*, July 17, 2007.

———. "When Bigger Gets Smaller, Small Gets Big." *Sports Illustrated*, May 30, 2005.

Wahl, Grant. "The Chosen One." *Sports Illustrated*, February 18, 2002.

WasWatching.com. "Questions with Lee Sinins." April 2, 2012.

Welch, Matt. "If You Build It, They Will Leave." Reason.com, January 2004.

Wiley, Ralph. "It's Jeet's World; We Just Live in It." ESPN.com, 2001.

Wilmington News Journal. "With Bonds and Clemens, Steroids Era on Trial." February 25, 2011.

Wittenstein, Barry. "Q&A with Baseball Legend Joe Garagiola." SNY.tv, March 17, 2007.

Wojciechowski, Gene. "Bonds Dared Feds to Indict Him." ESPN.com, November 16, 2007.

———. "Latest Revelations Seal the Deal for Bonds' Legacy." ESPN.com, March 8, 2006.

Woodward, Tim. "Vern Law's 'Golden Days of Baseball.'" *Idaho Statesman*, January 16, 2011.

Woolsey, Garth. "Is Baseball Really This Dangerous?" *Toronto Star*, April 14, 2008.

Zuckerman, Mark. "A Major Downside to Parity." *Washington Times*, September 1, 2008.

Index: What Was Where

Acknowledgments: To the End

I'm not sure how this should end because I'm not sure how it began.

Early in life I met a very nice man who introduced me to baseball's world by buying my first fielding glove, bubblegum cards, Don Mattingly/"Hit Man" poster, and other treasures. He showed up for Little League games, provided postgame ice creams at Stew Leonard's dairy store, and lived countless other acts of generosity through the years. Dad, you have my love and abiding thanks.

Among the Little Leaguers in Cranbury Field, I came across dedicated coaches who gave both tutorials and introductions to the game's lessons: "hard work pays off," "enjoy yourself but be serious," "be ready." I can still remember the time when they praised my "sweet swing" without mentioning that it rarely hit more than thin air. For your valued words, Coach Bob Corbo and Coach Gary Liberatore, I thank you.

The beginning of this book also came through the support of kin and kind. My sisters, Maria DeVito and Lisa Handrinos, have shined in a constellation that's included the DeVito, Diaconescu, Handrinos, Katsaros, Lathouris, Mitas, Musilli, Nanos, Pappas, Rokanas, and Soutos families. Many thanks to all members of the home team.

It's been said that many writers start off as readers and that was certainly my experience. Lo, years ago, in the libraries of Fairfield County, Connecticut, I began diving into classics by Eliot Asinof, Peter Golenbock, Sparky Lyle, Lawrence Ritter, Mike Sowell, and Bill Veeck, among other luminaries. "I'll never be as good as these guys" was my thought, and the prediction, sadly, turned out to be correct. Even so, I remain thankful for the literary inspiration.

In more recent times I confronted medical issues but found first-rate physicians needed to sustain my health and, not incidentally, my manuscript. Thank you, Dr. Philip H. Gutin, Dr. Andrew B. Lassman, Dr. Hideho Okada, and Dr. Louise Donohue Resor.

With restored health I returned to drafting and, with it, the realization that writing a book is much easier than publishing a book. The dream moved toward reality only when an eminent editor advocated this project within Potomac Books; Dr. Elizabeth Demers, accept my heartfelt thanks.

Finally, this project was honored by the time and attention of dear readers. Here we are, together to the end! I hope all of you found something special within these 88,865 words and, in that hope, you have the last word: "thanks."

About the Author

Peter Handrinos is a graduate of Yale University, a member of the Society for American Baseball Research, and a resident of Norwalk, Connecticut. Of his work, Hall of Fame broadcaster Bob Wolff has said, "I've never seen a young author take on so many sports topics, or approach them with such evident preparation and joy."